Gyan
NBH

D1882427

R
509

Educational Bs
3/1/92

EDUCATION IN AYURVEDA
A Re-constructional Analysis

EDUCATION IN AYURVEDA

A Re-constructional Analysis

BERND PFLUG

GIAN PUBLISHING HOUSE
5, Ansari Road, Darya Ganj
NEW DELHI-110002

GIAN PUBLISHING HOUSE
5, Ansari Road, Daryaganj,
New Delhi - 110002

© Bernd Pflug, 1992

ISBN 1992 81-212- 0399-6

PRINTED IN INDIA

Published by Mrs. Gayatri Garg for Gian Publishing House,
New Delhi - 110002.
Printed at Goyal Offset Printers, Delhi

In memory of

my late parents

Kurt and Paula Pflug

CONTENTS

Preface

I. Introduction

1. Hypothesis and Method 1
2. Health and Health Education in India 7

II. Prevention in Ayurveda

1. Fundamentals of Ayurveda 21
2. Interdisciplinary Approaches 40
3. Worldly and Non-Worldly Outlooks 50
4. Congruence between Content and Form 56
5. The Model of Balance 60
6. An Assessment 68

III. Modern Health Education, Prevention, Ayurveda

1. Modern Health Education 77
2. Levels of Prevention and Strategies of Intervention 87
3. Ayurveda and Lifelong Education 99

IV. Ayurveda Health Education and People's Education

1. Ayurveda Health Education 105
2. Community Health Education 108
3. Ayurveda Health Education and Community Health 115
4. Ayurveda Health Education and People's Education 124

Conclusionary Note 134

Notes 136
Bibliography 189
Index 210

PREFACE

In India, as elsewhere, the definition of health by the World Health Organization (WHO) has been acknowledged. The WHO has defined health as the state of complete physical, mental and social well-being, rather than merely the absence of disease or infirmity. This definition, formulated in the Constitution of the WHO in 1946 for the first time, represents the understanding that health is not only a state of physical well-being but the integrated functioning of the physical, mental and social planes. The understanding of health confined to the physical domain had dominated the health care services of many countries and societies for decades and centuries. With the new understanding counless efforts emerged over the recent past to put the new goal into practice.

In health education, as in the curative areas of medicine, the major challenge was to tackle problems of the mental and social planes of health and disease. To make people feel well all-around implies to develop appropriate means to achieve this. Health education had to be extended to meet the needs of the whole person. One follow-up of the new understanding of health in the industrialized countries was, for example, the intensified research in stress to find out its many relationships with diseases in the cardio-vascular field. Health eduction faced major problems of how to design strategies which included not only the prevention of diseases clearly marked as physical ones but of diseases which originate form particular life-styles. Questions of a balanced diet, of how to relax properly and of how to detect early symptoms of a deviation from normalcy had and have to be answered. This all led to the rivival of the age-old saying that prevention is better than cure.

Large programmes are implemented to detect, check and isolate single risk factors which might be indirectly or directly responsible for a disease or which could announce a potential disease. People are advised to behave in a certain way in order to avoid particular diseases. All the available means of communication at individual, group and mass media level are used to make the complete well-being of man possible. Health eduction is no longer restricted to some more or less simple advice to school children but has developed into a discipline of education with a strong foothold in the behavioural sciences. People are asked to participate in programmes to improve their health behaviour. In the long run a change in attitudes is aimed at. Besides regular health education classes in school, many non-formal activities are offered by the mass media, welfare institutions and the various agencies of adult and continuing education. Health education has become a movement which tries to embrace people from all age groups and from different strata of society.

Despite all these programmeds, at least in the industrialized countries, basic problems have remained, for example, how to enable and stimulate people to live a life conducive to health? Research is conducted in order to answer this important question. Experts in the field discuss whether health education should join socio-political movements in order to participate in the active work to change society if the system of a society is found responsible for the emergence of disseases. Only through a change of socio-economic structures, they argue, would people of the weaker sections be empowered to lead a better, i.e., a healthier life. Other questions are raised in this context. How to coordinate the numerous activities into a strategy with one language and one objective? When to start health education - just after or even before birth or much later?

It soon becomes clear that health education is still lacking basic concepts which are of a theoretical nature and by that of a more universal understanding. The main questions which have to be asked and answered by a philosophy of education are still largely unanswered in health education: What is it? What ought it to accomplish? By what means can this be done? This lack of critical reflection becoms more evident the more we understand health and disease as part and parcel of the emotional and social domains of man.

It is this situation - the broadening of the understanding of health and disease and the lack of critical reflection of it - which has motivated me to work on this study. I am of the opinion that health education can be supported by a philosophy of education to pose a constructive challenge to the mere technocratic solutions which are often preferred today. The latter may be more convenient for daily life, but in the long run it will be of limited help because it does not provide people with a solid knowledge of what one is doing why.

In the following inquiry I shall try to trace aspects of an educational philosophy in Ayurveda, the millenia-old Indian Science of

Life which today is often being mistaken for a system of medicine only. Its concept of prevention will be the main object of the examination. The word Ayurveda is composed of two terms, ayus meaning life and veda meaning science or knowledge. This indicates that Ayurveda was more than a medicine. It dealt with all questions of life, and provided rational means for the treatment of diseases. Health was designated as a fundamental for a useful life. Only a healthy man* was supposed to be able to lead such a life. The classical scriptures of Ayurveda contain many basic principles of a useful life, since Ayurveda was dealing with life and not only with diseases, and ancient Indians had always aimed at studying the basic human nature and situation. That is why we can assume that Ayurveda as a science of life, which was revived in India only in the late 19th and early 20th centuries, may offer fresh ideas for health education in India today.

Education in Ayurveda is first and foremost applied to health. It is either directed towards the health behaviour of the individual which is then health education, or towards the training of physicians which is then vocational education. I shall confine this work to the first aspect, simply because it gives me the opportunity to concentrate on that what I consider to be more essential for the pedagogical process: an individual's endeavour to educate himself rather than the formalized communication between a teacher and a taught, or a group of taught, resulting in learning a vocation. I regard individualized self-education as *the* most important aspect of popular education liberating by this the latter from becoming too rigid. Out of this follows that education in Ayurveda is, here, in fact health education as popular education, i. e., education *by* the people and not for the people. Since health education as any other branch of education contains all the fundamentals of education, I deem it justified to generalize and speak of *education in Ayurveda* as I do in the title of this work.

The examination of the concept of health education in Ayurveda will be introduced through its hypothesis and an overview of the precarious health and health education situation in India respectively. Other background information is given on the fundamentals

---

* Use of the masculine gender in this book does not reflect inadequate awareness, but is purposely used in order to make respective expressions less formal.

of Ayurveda as an indigenous system of medicine, and the interdisciplinary nature of the main source, the Sutra Sthana of the Caraka Samhita. This is then followed by an analysis of the concept of prevention in building up a theory of health education. Thereafter the connections between modern health education and Ayurveda will be studied in order to prepare the ground for a redefinition of Ayurveda Health Education which is done in the final chapter of this analysis.

The examination will not critically trace the evolution of preventive ideas in Ayurveda through the ages, i.e., this study is neither an historical nor a philological one.* Instead, the traditional ideas of Ayurveda from the classical scriptures have been catapulted into our time, they are reconstructed. This can be justified since many ideas and concepts of Ayurveda today seem by and large unchanged compared to their first written elaboration in the texts of Caraka and Sushruta. This may be understood as a limitation but need not be one since an analytical reconstruction has its merits, too, of which a significant one is its dwelling upon a high degree of normative creativity. A more serious limitation is the lack of systematic practical experiences in Ayurveda Health Education in today's India. As far as I know there is no programme of this kind in the country apart form one project near Coimbatore. This means that in the end we have to rely on a theoretical construct only because there is no way of testing the practical relevance of the concept analysis so far.

The major objective of this inquiry is to analyse the hypothesis of congruence between content and form in Ayurvedia's educational thought. This hypothesis conjectures that Ayurveda *aims at the equilibrium* (of health) *while being the equilibrium* (of health). This means that a balanced and healthy life can only be realized through balanced and healthy means of life, including educational, in a society whose socio- economic structure is conducive to this goal. A major finding of this inquiry is the establishment of the concurrence of many a principle of modern health education with many an aspect of Ayurveda's concept of prevention which is governed by the underlying congruence between content and form. These include, for example, the responsiblity for one's own health, the three levels of prevention (primary, secondary, tertiary), self-

---

This is why throughout this study the Sanskrit terms are used in their Latin transcriptions without their diacritical marks which are used in philology. In quotations, however, the original transcriptions, if used, are rendered.

education, and lifelong education. Being appropriate to the health culture of India, Ayurveda Health Education can be defined as an interdisciplinary preventive subject. It can become community health education and through this popular education by modernizing itself and functioning as an entry point to socio- political community development.

I should like to thank Dr. K. Sivadasan Pillai, Director of the Centre for Adult Education and Extension of the University of Kerala, who, some time back, was willing to take over the guidance of this rather unusual study in the field of education as a doctoral thesis for the University of Kerala at Trivandrum, This publication is, however, a revised version.

[illegible] contributions are [illegible] of the [illegible] interdisciplinary [illegible] community [illegible] particularly [illegible] itself and [illegible] community.

[illegible] Professor [illegible] Director of the [illegible] and [illegible] of the [illegible] of [illegible] in the field of education [illegible] is a [illegible] Kerala [illegible] is, however, [illegible].

Chapter 1

INTRODUCTION

1. Hypothesis and Method

Contributing to a theory of education implies also to redefine that what is available. Redefining is part of conceptual analysis. A redefinition does not replace a system but enables us to get clearer about it. It helps to make known what is implicit in a commitment to a topic, but it cannot provide final answers to the ethical issues which it sometimes helps to make explicit. In this process, the suggestion of a hypothesis is an important stage; it is the centre of any inquiry into concept analysis.

Let us start our hypothesising with the basic question how health education is being executed. We are doing it generally by teaching straightforward health messages, for example about the dangers of smoking, viz. that smoking can cause cardio-vascular diseases or cancer, hoping that this knowledge will then prevent people form smoking. Or we are teaching the ideals of a small family, expecting that family planning programmes will be successful. Or we are advocating the integration of handicapped people into normal and professional life, thinking that integration then really takes place. In all these examples we are expecting success because we presume that the knowledge of a problem is enough to change attitudes and behaviour. We are teaching according to the model that if we impart proper knowledge about causes of diseases and problems, those who are taught will immediately grasp the ideas and act accordingly. In our teaching we are consequently trying hard to improve our tools to avoid failure, for example by introducing clearer explanations of the mechanism of cause and effect, or by diversifying our teaching method in order to make the ideas more digestable. But hardly are we more successful then. The reason for this is that we have made a subject of life into an object of an academic process. We have thereby isolated a matter of life form life itself.[1]

One possible way out for health education would be to make others aware of health and diseases as matters of life. This obviously simple strategy is hardly found being practised in health education, because modern health education still puts more emphasis on imparting facts which are generally not closely related to the life of the person being taught but which are part of a syllabus. That is why it ought to be justified to have a look back to a system which did not separate knowledge form life, and vice versa. Ayurveda was such a system which in its original understanding had its supreme duty in the prevention of diseases and maintenance of health, rather than in curing diseases. Ayurveda's approach seemed to be one of complete congruence between content (= teaching, knowledge) and form (= life).[2] Prevention of diseases and maintenance of health were not only incorporated into life, but they were life itself by becoming an integral part of it. Health knowledge was part and parcel of knowing life. It was not a special subject, e.g. health education, but a way of life that enabled people to create conditions for a healthy and happy life. If this was true in ancient India, then we should think of applying it to modern life as well.[3]

For this process of rediscovering and rethinking we need a theoretical framework which could be provided by three levels of prevention. These three levels of prevention are primary prevention which attempts to reduce to a minimum the degree of handicap or impairment.[4] Among them primary prevention is the widest form of prevention. It is life conducive to health, and it is life conducive to health, and it is at the same time health conducive to life. If such a life can be lived (and not only taught), then the outcome is health, happiness, usefulness, productiveness, and praxis. Or the other way round, if one really aims at health, happiness, usefulness, productiveness and praxis, then a life conducive to them is to be lived. In other words, if we want health, we have to 'live' happiness, etc.; if we want life in its fullness, we have to 'live' life in its fullness.[5]

From this we can infer that if life is regarded as form, then health is regarded as content. But if health is regarded as form, then life is regarded as content. This is then complete congruence between content and form which is supposed to be at the centre of Ayurveda's concept of prevention.[6] Modern health education could utilize this concept for the benefit of what is today called 'community health' whose prime objective is to provide the ground for an all around health. A modernized Ayurveda Health Education could make a contribution to this by preparing the ground for, and at the same time being, bhutadaya, i.e., the compassion for the living, and dana dharma, i.e., the duty to give. These two Ayurveda terms have been common household words in India since time immemorial.[7]

This study differs from educational research that is based on a corpus of data collected through questionaires and similar tools. It does not belong to the group of historical studies either though I work with historical sources.[8] Instead I am using the method of philosophizing whose virtue is to enable people to develop a new way of looking at something.[9]

A *first* point which I should like to clarify is my attitude towards that what is known as 'Third-World-Research'. In former years I was convinced of the value of a discipline of education which has become popular in recent decades: comparative education. I thought it was a science of its own and found myself indulging in reasoning and arguing for its promotion. Bereday's approaches of description, interpretation, juxtaposition and comparison[10] became a scientific credo. Questions of cultural bias and comparability occupied a major place in my thinking and so did questions like 'Why are comparisons being made?', questions which are still under discussion.[11] Later on did I understand that international studies are important, simply because the truth is important. A study is then essential when it is inspired by the desire to get nearer to truth regardless of the country and culture which is forming its background. I did well conclude that intellectual wisdom ought to be one and the same for all men at all times. Knowledge separated into national blocks would prevent humankind from finding solutions to questions which are beyond the indiviual or a particular group. Along with this change occurred another one. My former belief in international cooperation was supported by my work in the field of development aid. Continuous and fervent discussions about particiption, ethnocentrism, and transferability of ideas, institutions and concepts were of utmost importance. Though I sympathized with authors who think that developing countries were "not some kind of monument...- to satisfy the exotic romantic needs and yearnings of industiral societies for the past"[12], my feelings were biased by an uncritical desire to justify both: development aid which often exploits openly, and the independence and self-reliance of countries which are often disqualified as 'developing countries'. At the same time, many of us discussed rigorously the concept of 'academic imperialism' - and arrived hardly at any convincing solution for ourselves. Later I had to recognize that even ethnocentrism, which I had blindly condemned over several years, has a second side to which the Polish philosopher L.Kolakowski has referred in a remarkable essay. In it he comes to the conclusion that eurocentrism as a form of ethnocentrism was and is one of the cultural patterns being capable of questioning itself and thereby being open for self-criticism. He also points out that uncritical tolerance towards demands of foreign cultures would lead to the extinction of one's own culture.[13] Understanding another culture, he maintains, is only possible while having firm roots in one's own culture.

In those years I released myself from the obligation to learn from other cultures at any price. This compulsion had partly led to the denial of my own culture. I still continue, for instance, to admire the celebrated indologist Max Müller because of his scholarly work in Sanskrit promotion; I do, however, no longer agree with his view, first published in 1882, that one has to go to India to learn about whatever sphere of the human mind one may select.[14] I do not agree to an attitude either which is en vogue in these years of international tourism and which may be described as'the-West-has-to-learn-from-the-East'. This attitude is obsessed with the desire that the West has to regain the intuitive, the unconscious, and the passive of the East, and that the future of the world would depend on the "marriage" of the "Western mind" with the "Eastern mind".[15]

This is not a study either in which a foreign researcher investigates an Indian topic in order to help solve problems. This is often given as a reason by people form the 'developed world' to justify their 'Third-World-Research'. But I do not want to help through this kind of research; I am sure that Indian intellectual life can do without this patronising attitude. I have only one purpose in mind, viz. to produce ideas which may eventually be of some use in the discussion of a theory of health education as part of popular education wherever this problem is going to be discussed. But I do hope that this study will be in the end not one of the many works on countries in the Southern hemisphere "which are available in various northern institutions, but which are not known in the country where the data was actually collected".[16]

A *second* point which I should like to clarify now is on the technique of philosophizing. L.Elvin represents the view that humane studies are just as important as scientific ones. He calls scientific studies "rigorous", i.e., obliged to emprical methods. But such a study can not include all the criteria of scientific merit likewise; research or study designs will usually select among plausibility, accuracy, systematic importance, intrinisic interest of subject matter, and originality. The majority of these criteria will tend to enforce conformity, while originality and intrinsic interest of subject-matter will encourage dissent.[17] This is confirmed by M.Polanyi who observes that "professional standards of science must impose a framework of discipline and at the same time encourage rebellion against it."[18] I should like to use this last arguement as a justification for a non-empirical study in an academic environment which mainly promotes empirical research in education. But in spite of turning to the philosophical side in this study we should be always aware that all the disciplines of education with their respective research methodologies are equally important because education is concerned with people and therefore with psychology (their behaviour and attitudes), with philosophy (their aims and concepts), and with history (their dimensions in time).[19] Whatever research process we follow, it consists of an inquiry which should lead to more and more substantial meanings. In this science and philosophy are not opposed but different parts of a single continuum of research and inquiry: "Science is concerned with the discovery of knowledge; it can tell what is and why. But this is only a means to an end; philosophy begins where science leaves off, and is concerned with the use of this knowledge." Mouly continues by stressing that philosophy provides the ultimate ends towards which research needs to be directed and the framework "within which a problem can and does exist."[20]

Most educational situations contain many variables "so complexly intertwined that it is next to impossible to isolate each variable and trace out its particular bearing on the total situation". That is why it is often difficult to gain rigid control of each variable and to state its effect on the educational outcome. But there is also a more positive reason for philosophical inquiry, viz. that of not being content with meanings of limited scope and preferring the meaning of the total situation instead. Understanding the total complex of variables, i.e., giving them inclusive meanings and arranging them according to some over-all order, "justly carries the title philosophical research."[21]

It is obvious that this approach attracts disagreement. It is almost inescapable "inasmuch as the philosopher sets himself the formidable task of trying to deal, not with the few variables which can be controlled, but with all the variables, controlled and uncontrolled." This has to raise the suspicion of empirical researchers, maintain Brubacher and Martz, but hasten to add that sacrificing the reliability and objecctivity of the scientist is compensated by "gaining the comprehensiveness of the philosopher."[22]

Philosophy is interested in inquiring into the meaning of facts which it takes from science, history and even tradition and common sense by arranging them into a particular figuration. A philosophical handling of facts is needed when the facts, or at least some of them, arc concerned with values, or when their meanings depend on an analysis of concepts underlying them. But there is also the speculative inquiry which may lead to rich suggestions for future research as happened in the famous example of the concept of evolution "which clearly grew out of a dynamic philosophy of history which was part of the intellectual climate of opinion during the times when Darwin was at work on his Origin of Species."[23] This study, however, though partly of a speculative nature, is inspired less by a particular intellectual climate than by the concern that today's health education has become a technologically-oriented discipline of education which, in the long run, will hardly solve the health problems of the people and the health care systems of countries. Using technologically-oriented research to overcome this would mean to enter a vicious cycle voluntarily and with open eyes accepting the separation of research from critical reflection on education as social function and personal experience. If so separated, research "becomes merely a system of technical skills - a technology whose practitioners have no right to claim, and indeed are only too likely to deny, any personal responsibility for the courses of action their work helps to facilitate."[24]

In philosophy we prefer starting from the integrating capabilities of the human mind, rather than from the observable elements of human behaviour. We like to begin from what is whole rather than fragmented, from what is hidden rather than displayed for the observer to observe.[25] Philosophizing is therefore the handling of concepts which are no clear-cut entities, no precise material things. That is why we have to be careful because the sands inevitably shift while examining the concept of an elusive abstraction.[26]

The vital first step towards an hermeneutic Understanding[27] is to understand the problem situation in which a theory arises.[28] Following Popper's argumentation, our study is not a contribution to historiography, i.e., it is not an interpretation of Ayurveda, but a situational analysis of health education. This analysis is occupied with the problem whether Ayurveda and its ideas related to education would suit the needs of modern health education or not. Popper states that in this process of analysing it is a poor ideal to avoid error for "if we do not dare to tackle problems which are so difficult that error is almost unavoidable, then there will be no growth of knowlege".[29]

2. Health and Health Education in India

The recent history of health care services in India is rich in excellent reports of committees analysing the health situation in the country very critically. Among them, the most famous is the "Report of the Health Survey and Development Committee" of 1946, popularly known as Bhore-Report after the Chairman of the Committee, Sir Joseph Bhore. The original volumes of the Report[30] bring about a feeling of thoroughness and the will to improve the health lot of the people. Set up by the colonial government of India in 1943, the recommendations of the Committee, threeyears later, provided an almost revolutionary alternative to the existing health care system. These recommendations were guided by the principles that (i) no person should fail to secure adequate medical care because of his "*inability to pay* for it", (ii) health problems should, from the beginning, lay special emphasis on *preventive* work,(iii) as much medical care as possible should be provided to the vast *rural* population of the country, and (iv) the doctor of the future should be a *"social physician"* who is guiding the people to a healthier and happier life.[31] Many of the recommendations of the Bhore-Report are also timely today. They have, however, never been put into practive, but considerably diluted in the years thereafter. Though the governments of independent India readily accepted the recommendations of the Committee there was a great delay to put on the ground even those diluted versions of the recommendations. This was due to the political orientation of the leadership which tried to perpetuate the colonial tradition of urban-based curative medicine. And this has resulted in a situation which, about 45 years after the Bhore-Reoport, may well be summarized as follows: (i) Probably more than half of the Indian population is *unable to pay* for adequate medical care,(ii) health care programmes are still *curative-oriented,* i.e., they are programmes fighting diseases rather than promoting health, (iii) medical care is concentrated in *urban* areas, and (iv) the physician's image today resembles very often that of a *businessman.*

Just one example here to compare the Bhore-Report recommendations with today's reality. The Committee spoke of the towns and villages as "factories of diseases" which would continue to be the origins of a number of diseases if not safe drinking water supply, suitable housing, sanitary surroundings, means for the early detection and prevention of epidemic and communicable diseases and improvement in nutritional standards were introduced.[32] It is known, however, that today about one third of India's population are suffering from parasitic infections and soil-transmitted helminths. This is the lowest result from research, whereas the level of infections is generally quoted to be around two third and often as high as 80 per cent. This is mainly due to lack of proper latrines and disposal of sewage. Only 20 percent of the rural population have some sort of access to toilets, in urban areas the figure is about two third when taken all the existing kinds of latrines together.[33] And the Estimates Committee in its 48th Report of 1983 even said that the coverage of sanitation facilities in rural Inda was less than one per cent.[34]

The Bhore-Report was followed by numerous other reports till today, and they all were and are important for the development of the health system of the country, at least in theory. But their fame was the same. Only a tiny fraction of their suggestions have been realized. The health care needs of the mases have always been neglected so that, according to D.Banerji, in all "as many as four-fifth of the population does not have access even to the most elementary health care services"[35], though the Constitution of as early as 1950 is precise about what ought to be done to tackle the problem at its roots.[36]

In the history of independent Inda. there was so far only one successful national programme for the eradication and control of a major disease. In 1977, *smallpox* was declared eradicated from the country. This state has since been successfully maintained.[37] *Cholera* cases have since been brought down to about 2.650 in 1984 from 176.300 in 1950. The death rate was in the same period reduced from about 50 per cent to about 2.5 per cent.[38] *Malaria* still causes a lot of human suffering. In the sixties a national programme was very successful in reducing the incidence from 75 million cases and 750.000 deaths in the post-independence period to less than 100.000 in 1965 with no death being reported. But sincce 1965 the number of cases was continuously increasing till 1976 when about

6.5 million people suffered from the disease. After this climax, again a decrease was observed. In 1984, 2.18 million cases were reported[39], probably due to a change in drug regimen. The reasons for the ups and downs are partly explained by vector mosquitoes having developed resistance to DDT and partly by ineffective supervisory measures, as another official government source analyses.[40] Certain environmental changes would also increase the danger of more cases. It is known that an increase in irrigation in rural areas, for instance, will lead to a greater number of people suffering from malaria. One reason for this is the increase in average humidity through irrigation which makes the survival of mosquitoes possible. In 1984, about 3.1 million *leprosy* patients were recorded. Out of them about 2.9 million were reported under treatment.[41] It was, however, estimated that nearly 400 million of India's 684 million population in 1981 were living under the shadow of getting infected by leprosy, so the report of a working group set up by the Union Health Ministry in 1981.[42] *Tuberculosis* is understood to be the biggest health problem at present in Inda with nearly 500.000 people die of this disease every year. The number of patients at any time is estimated to be over 8 million, one fourth are likely to be infectious.[43] For them, there were the following treatment facilities available in 1984: 17 TB demonstration centres,319 TB clinics, and 360 district TB centres. Altogether only about 45.000 TB beds were provided in 1984 for in-patient treatment.[44] *Filaria* is another mass disease whose expansion has not been curtailed despite a massive national control programme. A comparison reveals the dramatic increase: in 1953 there were 2.6 million people exposed to the risk of filaria, whereas in 1976 the number had increased to 231.6 million which is only partly due to the rise in population. No estimate has been made after 1976.[45] Only about 32.4 million people are reported to be protected in 1984 through various institutions.[46] It is estimated that 10.5 million have manifestations of the disease and 20.1 million have filarial parasites in their blood.47 Besides these programmes, other campaigns for the prevention of *goitre* and of *visual impairment* and control of blindness have been launched, but these diseases are far from being under control. And more and more 'modern' diseases are being diagnosed. In all, nearly 920.000 people suffering from *Sexually Transmitted Diseases* were treated in 1984.[48] This estimation is by no means trustworthy because only a minority of patients will and can consult a special clinic. According to other sources, about 20 million and 30-40 million respectively are supposed to suffer from veneral diseases annually. Hardly 5 per cent of them would visit government hospitals for treatment.[49] For *cancer* patients only 142 hospitals having special treatment faciilities were available in 1984. They had admitted about 41.200 patients in the same year.[50] But it was already estimated about two decades ago that about 500.000 people die of cancer in India every year.[51] Another disease of modern civilization is rapidly increasing. It is supposed that 2 per cent of the total population suffer from ischaemic *heart diseases*. Though no one knows precisely how many suffer or die from heart ailments, a figure of about 4 per cent of the population is cautiously advanced by some experts and a few sample surveys.[52] The overall figure for *mental disorders* shows that the common belief that mental disorders are rare in Eastern countries is wrong. The admission figures for 1983 and 1984 to specialized mental hospitals (46 and 34 respectively) were about 47.200 and 48.500 respectively.[53] But these figures are probably only the tip of the iceberg as an epidemiological study had already indicated in 1974. It was a study of 539 households in Vellore Town (Tamilnadu) with 1.887 members above 12 years of age. The results of the study showed a prevalence rate of neuroses (hystery, anxiety, depression) of 48 per 1000. Of them, 37 per 1000 were in need of active psychiatric treatment. It was found that the prevalence rate was the highest in the age group of 30-40 years and commoner among those who belonged to lower classes and to nuclear families.[54] Other studies have shown that 30-45 million Indians suffer from psychiatric problems, but only about 1000 paychiatrists, 500 clinical psychologists, 300 social workers and 600 nurses who can provide them with expert care are available.[55]

It is well-known that the greatest health menace of poor countries are the *communicable diseases*, with dysentery on the top. For India, in 1981, 10.14 million cases and about 28.800 reported deaths comprised nearly one sixth of the reported diseases (of about 59.5 million) and nearly half of all the reported deaths (of 56.150).[56] This reporting to government agencies was by no means complete because out of then 31 states and union territories there had been no replies received from Assam, Bihar, Jammu and Kashmir, Manipur, Nagaland and West Bengal. And how many diseases and deaths are not reported at all due to no access to medical facilities and thereby registration is anybody's guess in a country of India's vastness. If we take the statement of

D.Banerji seriously that as many as four fifth of the population have no access to even elementary health care, then the statistics quoted above would cover only about 20 per cent of the population. Then it seems not to be too extravagant to take into account about 350 million of the population suffering from various diseases at any time of the year. This is about 40 per cent of India's population today. It may thus not be an exaggeration to speak of India as a biologically decaying country.[57] It appears that though the average Indian may now live longer (today's life span has more than doubled against the 26 years half a century ago) his, and in particular her, morbidity is only marginally less than that of former generations. People continue to be largely prone to the same diseases as they were, and the prevalence of chronic and degenerative diseases is obviously increasing without infectious diseases necessarily diminshing in prevalence.

The extremely low priority of the health sector is documented by getting only about 2 per cent of the national plan actuals and outlays. The health and family welfare financial investements of the national development plans were:

3.30 % for the First Plan (1951-56)
3.00 % for the Second Plan (1956-61)
2.60 % for the Third Plan (1961-66)
2.10 % for the Annual Plans (1966-69)
2.10 % for the Fourth Plan (1969-74)
1.90 % for the Fifth Plan (1974-79)
1.82 % for the Annual Plan (1979-80)
1.86 % for the Sixth Plan (1980-85)
1.88 % for the Seventh Plan (1985-90)[58]

These figures gain more of a practical dimension when viewed under the per capita aspect. On an average the per capita health expenses were Rs 13.18 in 1975-76, Rs 16.12 in 1976-77, Rs 16.56 in 1977-78, Rs 25.67 in 1980-81, Rs 30.63 in 1981-82, and Rs 37.15 in 1982-83. There were great variations among the states, for example in 1982-82 Nagaland spent as much as Rs 322.79 per capita, Sikkim Rs 102.63, but Uttar Pradesh only Rs 22.18, and Bihar a lowest of Rs 18.46.[59]

As to the health planning structure, an investigation of 21 directorates of health services and the Centre conducted in 1979-80 came to the conclusion that planning in health based on the needs of the community is not possible in India because the health planning units are not properly staffed, there is no continuity in leadership, the concept of a mulitdisciplinary team is almost always lacking, no mechanism has ben designed for collection of data, for monitoring, and for quick and ready feedback from the field, officers-in-charge of these nuclei cannot generally execute their expected role nor do they have the training to be effective in the planning process, and the changing political complexion in the country enables decision makers in the states to have their own values prevail in health planning.[60]

In sum, it seems to be justifed to suppose that the respective Indian governments were and are not demonstrating enough political will to improve radically and seriously the miserable health lot of the majority of the population. Extremenly low finances for health purposes do indicate this. Moreover, the governments have so far failed to create a planning infrastructure which could successfully cope with the massive health needs of the people. Though a recent government "Statement on National Health Policy" (1982) expressed, again, a lot of concern about the health situation, and though the former and the present governments have, finally, come to the conclusion that probably a more intensive "Collaboration with Non-Governmental Organizations in Implementing the National Strategy for Health for All" (1985) seems to be necessary[61], it may still be justified to speak of the two republics people in India have to face, viz. the Republic of India and the "Republic of the elite island of India".[62]

Alternatives in the health care system are widely demanded, so for example the primary health care concept.[63] But a most urgent pre-requisite of all alternatives is a change in political will. The former Director-General of the World Health Organization, Halfdan Mahler, one of the strongest advocates of the WHO-slogan and strategy "Health for All by the Year 2000", laments that the stiffest opposition against changes in the health care system still comes from the medical establishment, the scientific community, and the pharmaceutical, the infant foods, the tobacco, and the medical equipment industries.[64] They all would fear to lose their huge profits if primary health care in its fullest sense was widely introduced. All these profit- makers are usually patronized by political leaders who then get their share by the industries to be able to stay in office. Mahler has certainly not excluded India from his criticism.

Along with the traditional understanding of health and health care in India go most of the health education efforts. It is not surprising that representatives of health education do see their work synonymous with educating ignorant, backward, superstitious and usually illiterate people. Their programmes try to impart knowledge while using the one-way communication channel, from the teacher to the student or from the top to the bottom. They try to make communication a perfect instrument which then deserves the label "'top-down' health education".[65] They neglect the fact that health education has to be a continuous process, and they often try to impose certain preconceived values which may not be necessarily in the interest of a particular community other than their own. One of the strong critics of this traditional health education is D.Banerji who demands that it is the "responsibility of the health educators to ensure that the natural science essentials of health practices are inserted into a new 'envelope' or 'coating' that will harmonise better with the social, cultural and economic environment of India."[66]

But precisely this is missing in publications of the Government[67] which fail to provide instruments inviting full participation of groups of people belonging to the weaker sections of society sharing similar social, cultural and economic environments. The underlying assumption in these publications is that people would accept health innovations with enthusiasm only if they were educated; and people were to blame if this did not happen. We cannot but suspect that health agencies publishing such books too often pay lip service to the objectives of participating, living, and being in health and health education.[68] It is true, inviting people to participate or, even better, to create favourable conditions for participation, and by this accepting everyone's right for self-determination and self- reliance, makes the work much more difficult. For example, a programme fighting malnutrition, which is often accompanied by diarrhoea, will not be successful if it is based on a nutritional programme in which food is merely distributed and information about balanced diet is simply handed out. Instead, an integrated development programme is needed because malnutrition is often the result of a combination of factors: poverty, infections, ignorance, lack of motivation of parents, social pressure to spend available resources in other ways (e.g.on weddings, ceremonies), lack of faith and confidence in doctors or health workers, too much effort required to take the child for treatment and losing wages for that day's work.[69] To tackle this, health education has to become part of a community development programme and through this an integral part of the socio-economic development of the people.[70] But this is not all. It is also the 'spiritual' basis of health which is necessary for health education. J.P.Naik thought that in this regard the Indian concept of the four ashramas was superb: first to become a disciplined student, a brahmacharya; second a householder, a grihasta; third a retiring or retired person, a vanaprastha; and fourth a man who renounces the world and contemplates God, a sanyasi. This model can be questioned for today's life, but we have to admit that today we are probably not much aware of the spiritual dimension of health in general and the processes generating health in particular. It may be the most distinguished objective of health education to help create this awareness.

It is no more a technical problem in these days to spread developmental work in India. An infrastructure of mass communication is available and is daily improving. This infrastructure is effectively utilized by government and private agencies, mainly for the sale of goods even in the remotest village or for disseminating political ideas whenever necessary. There are five major agencies in the field of helath education which could exploit this infrastructure: the Central Health Education Bureau (CHEB) and the State Health Education Bureaux, primary and secondary schools, adult and continuing education organizations, hospitals, and village health workers.

The *CHEB* was set up in 1956. Its stock-taking in 1982 gives a somewhat proud picture of conferences and seminars conducted by the Bureau[71], but it is chary of praise about its foremost task for which it was created, viz. to train health education personnel, among them teachers in the formal education system. Though its School Health Division came into being as early as 1958, a first "Workshop on Strengthening Inservice Training in Health Education in States" is mentioned only for 1974. Other divisions of the CHEB are the media division, the audio-visual division, and the research division. There is no national programme of health education designed and inspired by the CHEB or the State Health Education Bureaux. We know that the health attitudes of the people have hardly changed over these past decades despite an enormous input and an impressive administrative set up. This leads to the suspicion that this input has been mainly used for the sake of the administration itself, justifying the harsh comment by K.Deb on development work in India and the role of the government set-up: "... the quality and magnitude of work done by them was anybody's guess."[72] The CHEB information materials are contrary to that for what they are praised by the institution itself. They are *not* highly useful because they are unimaginative in design and informational value; they are *not* holding great potential in putting across health information to the people because they are hardly ever used in practice. They are only objects for distribution of a government agency which has to prove its existence. It is not only bad printing and poor illustrating but obvious lack of commitment to improve the health situation of the public.[73]

The *formal education* network with its millions of schools all over the country is expected to nip health problems in the bud. But so far health education has not become an integral part of general education which means that healthy life-styles of pupils and their proper guidance from the earliest beginning of school education are not a major goal. A Government Report of 1965 referred to the Basic Education of Gandhi as a system containing the essential ingredients of a school health education programme.[74] But this early reference was apparently only a routine remark, for a look at some school programmes reveals that except some medical check-ups not much is being done in health education. The South Kanara Health Report, for example, states that even these medical check-ups were a failure with only 18 per cent of the schools investigated having conducted them.[75] For the practially non-existent school health education programmes, at least neatly designed syllabi for three different age-groups have been available since 1970.[76]

In *non-formal education*, health education elements have already gained a prominent place, at least in the programmes of some movements and institutions, e.g. the Kerala Association for Non-Formal Education and Development (KANFED).[77] How important people regard their health, indicates a review undertaken by the Tamilnadu Adult Education State Resource Centre in which it was found that among six content areas which had evolved from analysing the problems of the community, the health related ones were dominating like the physical self and the mental self including personal hygiene, dietary intake, common ailments, preventive and curative measures, healthy and unhealthy emotions, mental hygiene and health facilities available in the village.[78] On the other hand, non-formal education is, despite its rhetorical openness to need-oriented content, still too much tied up to literacy as its main content area so that it will probably take decades before other topics will find their legitimate places in non-formal education practices.

Another important institution for health education is the *hospital.* It is in this institution that success in health education seems to be surer than elsewhere, because it is in the hospital situation that the social distance between physicians, nurses and patients is narrrower than normal and ensures a better understanding. In-patients and out-patients are generally very keen to learn more about their diseases, how they are caused, how they can be cured, and how they could be avoided. Detailed studies about health education in hospitals are, however, not available. We have to assume that not many hospitals do take up this educational task. One study reports a 100 per cent desire of patients to know more about their disease, 80 per cent of them had no knowledge at all about the factors causing their diseases.[79]

The "Health Information India - 1988" reports, as on the beginning of 1987 and 1988 respectively, a number of about 9.700 hospitals and 27.500 dispensaries with altogether about 600.000 beds.[80] And though this government source is short of information about the number of patients, it was already estimated in the mid-seventies that there were annually about 180 million out-patients and 8.5 million in-patients being treated in hospitals and dispensaries.[81] This big 'reservoir' is providing sufficient opportunities for health education. That it can be introduced very successfully was proved by T. Dharmalingam in his programme study at the Kasturba Hospital at Gandhigram in Tamilnadu in 1977-78.[82] Before starting the intervention, the author studied the morbidity pattern of this rural hospital. The pattern[83] spoke for itself and for the urgency of health education since many of the diseases could have been prevented through proper health behaviour.[84] The intervention consisted of trainning prorammes for physicians, nurses and auxiliary workers and resulted in the following improvement: The target groups after the intervention were able to identify opportunities for the introduction of health education, to use different educational methods and aids, to plan their sessions well and to perform them in a prescribed time limit,and to achieve team work.[85] The attitude level of the involved staff towards educational tasks changed considerably from before the intervention to after the intervention. Before the intervention, 45.5 per cent of the staff had a positive attitude towards educational tasks, but after the intervention this had risen to 81.8 per cent.[86] There is, however, one pedagogic problem involved for those who conduct these supplementary functions[87] not related to cure. In a study of two hospitals attached to medical colleges, one in a metropolitan city and the other in a district headquarter, and their associated health centres, it was found that most of the communication between workers and patients was instructional and directional rather than educational. The conception of health education by the staff was a narrow one, seen as a change in knowledge rather than in attitude and behaviour, too.[88] Instead of taking care of oneself as a prime goal, this kind of health education followed the principle of being taken care of.[89]

In India, personnel in only a few hospitals are well- qualified to take up appropriated health edcuation programmes not only for their patients but also for the *community* in which the hospitals are located. One of them is the Padhar Hospital of the Eveangelical Lutheran Church in Bethul District, Madhya Pradesh. This hospital has set up a community health team among which the health educator, a teacher by training, is an integral part. This team works in a target area of 10 km radius of Padhar Hospital(82 villages with an estimated population of about 36.000) for Gond tribal people. Its tasks are to survey and analyse data collected from the area, to spread health education, to select and train village health workers, to conduct initial and in-service training of traditional birth attendants, to provide immunization, family planning facilities and minor medical care, and to arrange non-formal education "in needy areas such as literacy and agricultural development, health and hygience."[90] The report about the project does not contain evaluation results, but it is hoped that the achievement at the end of a two year period would be a 50 per cent reduction in infant mortality, an increased acceptance of family planning methods, a 10 per cent reduction of diseases of Vitamin A deficiency, a 50 per cent reduction of malnutrition, a 50 per cent reduction in scabies, an increased acceptance of immunization of underfive and women, an increase in the literacy rate, and improved farming methods.[91]

According to the ideas of the Government, the *village health worker* should play a crucial part not only in raising the health status of the rural masses but also to make them health-conscious. The duties of these frontline workers range from giving first aid, treating of minor ailments and of referring of cases to a sub-centre or a primary health centre to helping in antenatal and postnatal care, assisting in systematic disinfection of wells, and health education. A comprehensive health education investigation in the field of the Multipurpose Health Workers Scheme came to the result that modern preventive work in India should concentrate on immunization, maternal and child health, (environmental) sanitation, family planning and nutrition.[92] This is supported by the disease pattern and the social conditions prevailing in the country. At Jamkhed (Maharashtra), for example, the Comprehensive Rural Health Project provides a population of about 80.000, scattered over 30 villages within 16 km of Jamkhed, with primary health care at local level. Each village selects a female village health worker who is a resident of the village. She is given intensive training in care of pre-school children and maternal care as well as health education. Volunteers of the Young Farmers Club take part in organizing mass health activities such as immunization programmes and family planning campaigns. Some of the achievements of the Project are documented by comparison. In 1971, the percentage of those who practised family planning was 2.5 per cent, in 1976 it was 50.5 per cent; in 1971 the birth rate was 40/1000 whereas in 1976 it had been reduced to 23/1000; in 1976, 84 per cent of the children under five had immunization status against less than 1 per cent in 1971; the infant mortality rate could be reduced in these five years from 97/1000 to 39/1000 live births; and the antenatal care of pregnant women was 78 per cent in 1976 over less than 0.5 per cent in 1971.[93] An integrated health services project at Miraj (Maharashtra) specified the health education duties of their basic health workers. The female staff has to visit homes half a day every day. During that time she, amongst other things, has to teach and demonstrate "good health behaviour". The male staff has to do health teaching during house visits once a month. Both, female and male staff, shall use simple visual means in their teaching.[94] But so far we know little about successes and failures of these health workers as to their impact on health education as a mass movement.[95] We may, however, assume that as soon as these village health workers are embedded in an integrated health programme with a basic orientation towards the people their work promises success. These programmes are, however, only useful when health education for the poor and deprived social groups involves from the very beginning participation of the 'target' group. Then, and only then will village health workers emerge from villages themselves. These workers will then have a deep sympathy with the poor, a spirit of humility and the courage to new approaches.[97]

What has been said about for health education activities in general is also valid for *research* in health education. There are no coordinated efforts though there are some remarkable investigations. But many studies have produced results which can be best described as being of common sense.[98]

The situation is slightly better in the field of *training* of health educators though the health education specialist is not widely accepted as a professional in the country. People think that it is sufficient to give rudimentary training in health education to medical and paramedical professionals. They do not see that these additional training strategies, when in existence at all, are class-room bound and too academic. The curricula are conspicuously lacking offers in behavioural sciences which are relevant to the development of skills required in health education. It is harldly recognized either that the health education specialist should not replace the numerous health workers who can help people learn, motivate them and enable them to help themselves. But, instead, he should support them as a member of a health team in which he should help make adequate disgnoses of the educational requirements of a programme, supply others with teaching tools, make many of the community contacts which are outside of the usual sphere of others, and help assess reasons for progress and failures. If every health worker is a health educator, the health education specialitst's role will become more vital.[99] The only professional training courses for health educators as health education specialists are conducted by the CHEB on behalf of the University of Delhi (since 1971), the All India Institute of Hygiene and Public Health on behalf of the University of Calcutta (since 1966), and the Rural Institute of Health and Family Welfare at Gandhigram on behalf of the University of Madurai (since 1964). These institutions offer a one year post-graduate diploma course for health education specialists. Each batch has about 30 students, and the syllabi of the institutions are almost identical. They were revised and standardized at a workshop at Gandhigram and published in 1974. In 1980, the Gandhigram Institute slightly revised the syllabus by stressing the behavioural sciences and health education.[100] But talks with students of the 1981-82 batch at Gandhigram concluded in their assessment that the course was overloaded with theoretical topics, despite having various forms of practicals, which were taught in a bookish way. The multitude of teaching and learning methods which were suggested in the course description were not applied in the course itself, and students were instructed to communicate effectively with others, but their teachers, except a few, were not able to do the same in the course itself. Asked about the chances of former students to put into practice what they have learned, the responsible professor of health education said that most of the students needed the diploma for their promotion in office, and a significant aspect of their work after completing the course was their "under-utilization" as to their qualification.

Chapter 2

Prevention in Ayurveda

1. Fundamentals of Ayurveda

Once, in 1921, M.K. Gandhi wrote that the study of European medicine would deepen India's slavery.[101] On the other hand, he blamed the truly deplorable condition of the indigenous medicine with physicians being engaged in money making only. Because of their greed and mental laziness the science of Ayurveda was at a low ebb.[102] He went even further and said, in 1925, that many of the Ayurveda physicians pretended to know more than they actually did, and that Western physicians and surgeons boasted a brilliant array of discoveries and inventions against not a single one of any importance on the part of Ayurveda physicians.[103] This situation, if it was ever true, has considerably changed as the research progress in Ayurveda in the past decades has shown. There are many quacks working in the medical profession, but they are found among modern, indigenous and folk practitioners, and among trained and untrained people alike.[104]

The data known do not allow us to claim that Ayurveda is the dominating system of medicine in India.[105] On the other hand, they cannot prevent us from asserting that Ayurveda is one among the accepted systems. It seems that the system becomes more and more popular, may be due to some of its unique features, viz. emphasizing the preventive aspects, treating man as a whole in a psychosomatic approach, taking into account the basic constitution of an individual while diagnosing and treating him, having less side effects, and acting in accordance with the customs and traditions of the people.[106] This uniqueness is essentially based on the fact that Ayurveda is not only medicine but a guide to a healthy and happy way of living covering aspects of religion, philosophy, hygiene as well as the treatment of ill-health. The chief objective of Ayurveda is the maintenance of the metabolic equilibrium of man and the restoration of the same if it is disturbed by undesirable factors. The eight branches of Ayurveda to help achieve this were kaya chikitsa (internal medicine), shalya tantra (surgery), shalakya tantra (ear, nose, throat and eye treatment), bala tantra (peadiatrics), agada tantra (toxicology), bhuta vidya (psychiatry) rasayana tantra (geriatrics), and vajikarana tantra (science of aphrodisiacs).[107] An Ayurveda physician had to be well-trained in all these eight branches, but during the course of time and the ups and downs of Ayurveda this standard could not be maintained. Whole branches were neglected or nearly, like surgery, forgotten. Today efforts are being made to revive this branch in particular, and there are already remarkable results being achieved, for example at the Banaras Hindu University.[108]

While reviewing the early history of Ayurveda one cannot but agree with J.Filliozat that "the legend of its origin and the transmission of the Ayurveda is only pseudo-historical with a veneer of the scientific doctrine."[109] The French author continues in his work that has become a classic in the history of Indian medicine: "There is, however, a contrast between the value of the expositions concerning the history of the Ayurveda which is nil and that of the meritorious efforts made to explain rationally health and disease".[110] There is, indeed, a lot of discussion and confusion about the chronology of the earlier stages of Ayurveda which cannot be clarified until more reliable data will be available.[111] Prior to 326 B.C., the invasion of Alexander, or at any rate before the time of Buddha, historians can only draw on the evidence of the literary and religious texts of the Vedas, the Brahmanas, the Puranas, and of lay literature. We should therefore renounce the repetition of the mythology of Ayurveda which says that the healing knowledge had come down as an eternal tradition. Instead, we should concentrate on the 'mundane' history of the science.

For the Vedic period, the Atharvaveda is *the* compendium of medicine. Hundred-and-fourteen of its hymns contain medical themes and the most primitive and the most highly advanced stages of therapy. The following diseases are mentioned: consumption,scrofula, dysentery, boils, swellings, convulsions, ulcers, rheumatism, headache, jaundice, cramps, eye diseases, fractures and wounds, bites of snakes and harmful insects, poisoning in general, lunacy, and leprosy.[112] Various aspects of psychotherapy, naturotherapy and drug therapy were known.[113] The Samhita period, beginning with the 8th century B.C., was the period of systematic and scientific compilation with its highest achievements during the time of Ashoka. It was in this period that the two great books (later known as Sushruta Samhita and Caraka Samhita) were probably compiled proving that a vast amount of empirical research and experimental work must have gone before the conclusions embodied in them.[114] It was J.Filliozat who took a lot of pains to prove that a certain Caraka who might have been a major editor of the Samhita can be placed in the 2nd or 1st century B.C.,[115] whereas Sushruta was not an historical person at all. The Sushruta Samhita was, according to Filliozat, anonymously edited; it was a manual of a school which had probably selected a Sushruta for patron.[116] In its totality the work would go back only to the first centuries B.C.[117] The academic progress of Ayurveda was well maintained during the Buddhist period between 500 B.C. and about 600 A.D. Buddhist literature knew seven branches of tikiccha (this term replaced Ayurveda in their literature); the only branch which was not mentioned was rasayana tantra. Its non-inclusion was very purposeful because the main goal of the life of a Buddhist monk was to attain emancipation during his life time and hence there was no need of prolonging his life span.[118] Then followed the long standstill of Ayurveda in its scientific development and original thinking. It was during this 'medieval' period that India suffered from frequent foreign invasions. Peace in the country had largely vanished. Later, Western civilizations introduced Western institutions, among them the Western system of medicine, Allopathy. Original movements like Ayurveda were discouraged to flourish. Ayurveda lost the patronage of the educated classes because of their attachment to English literature and science.[119] But this total deterioration of Ayurveda standards during the 18th and 19th centuries, brought about by a handful of Englishmen, could only take place because of a long phase of neglect of scientific thinking and cultural consciousness prior to the political, cultural and scientific conquest through the English.[120] In the late 19th and early 20th century, along with a general revival of Indian heritage, Ayurveda got a fresh thinking which was then supported by the national independence movement.[121] Between 1921 and 1963 nine expert committees installed by the state governments and six constituted by the Central Government looked into the problems of Ayurveda and suggested measures to develop the system and the science.[122]

Ayurveda is deeply rooted in Indian philosophy. There was no clear distinction between science and philosophy in the hoary past. Science was not only analytical description, and philosophy was not only synthetic interpretation as it is understood today.[123] The founders of Ayurveda had an integrated view of man and life in the universe. To them, man cannot be split into different entities which would exist by themselves, nor could they be changed or cured without touching other entities of man and the universe. It is mainly the Sankhya school of philosophy from which Ayurveda draws its understanding of the evolution of the universe and of man. Briefly stated, the evolution of the universe and of man is on these lines: First, there is the Unmanifest, the primordial nature of man (prakriti and purusha) from which the understanding, intellect and endowment (mahan), is born. From the intellect arises the ego (ahankar), from which thereafter evolve five proto-elements (mahabhutas): space or ether (akash), the kinetic force or air (vayu), the thermogenetic element or fire (agni), the uniting force or water (jala), and gross material or earth (prithvi). In orderly succession follow the evolvement of mind (sattva or manas), the five cognitive and sensory organs (gyanendriyas), the five cognitive organs (karmendriyas), and the five sense objects (indriyarthas). Thus the whole man consists of 24 elements. For the sake of brevity, man is described as composed of six elements, namely the five proto-elements and one spirit. A further abridgement leads to man composed of three elements, namely mind (sattva), soul (atman), and body (sharira). In all, man appears as a psycho-somato-spiritual complex. His mind and body are considered the seats of diseases, whereas the pure soul is ever defectless.[124]

The Sankhya school has adopted a thoroughly realistic attitude. It is maintained that even a false object, that is a thing in illusion, is existent and has being: "Non-being not only does not exist, but also is never perceived. How can anyone perceive Non-being with his senses? Non-being is only a concept."[125] This understanding is the reason why an Ayurveda scholar cannot escape from the knowledge of natural sciences on the one side and the wisdom of philosophy on the other. Though in history, the philosophical schools of India have neglected Ayurveda because it was an applied science, Ayurveda has always tried to utilize its philosophical roots at its best. It has taken similarly from other branches of knowledge, so from biology, theory of matter, cosmology, and psychology. But this comprehensive view is not found in later works which pay more attention to the topics of medicine. One basic common idea of medicine and philosophy is that whatever one finds in the universe or cosmos is found also in the human body. This means, there is only a difference of degree between the macrocosmos and the microcosmos but none in quality. That is why it is necessary for Ayurveda physicians to study the physical constitution of the universe in order to understand the body properly.[126]

Indian philosophy is a way of life, not merely a way of thought.[127] It is neither mere intellectualism nor simple moralism, it includes and transcends both.[128] Contrary to European tradition, where thinkers came one after the other offering their independent speculations, the principal systems of Indian philosophy had their beginning in times of which there is hardly any record. Later, schools of pupils carried the tradition of a particular system from generation to generation. Though there was much rivalry between the different schools, there were also fundamental points of agreement. The first common idea was the karma theory (which was, however, not accepted by the Carvakas philosophers[129]). This means that whatever action is taken by an individual, it leaves behind some sort of potency which has the power to ordain for him joy or sorrow in future. The second common doctrine is that of mukti. This means that somewhere in the chain of karma there is an end which is to be sought with man himself as the actionless self which neither works nor undergoes rebirths, which neither suffers nor enjoys. Third, the doctrine of soul (except in Buddhism) agreed that the soul is pure in nature and that all impurities of passion and action do not form a real part of it. Though these doctrines appear to lead the individual to passivity, there was (and is) the firm conviction that only moral greatness and true knowledge uproot sorrow once and for all. To achieve emancipation (mukti) does not mean to avoid intercourse with the world. There was never a tendency to shirk from the duties of one's life but to rise above them through right understanding and right performance.[130] This understanding is the nucleus of the six darshanas (insights[131]) mimamsa, vedanta, sankhya, yoga, nyaya, and vaisheshika,. Ayurveda is basically following their principles and understanding, but is departing a little from the line in one major point: "It does not advocate a neglect of the body which is unstable but stresses the need to take care of it to prevent its destruction, to promote its stability, to infuse it with vitality and vigour, in order to prolong existence at the peak of health." But at the same time "it also enjoins one to exercise self-restraint, to cultivate detachment and to make constant efforts for the realization of the self."[132] One common quest of the darshanas and Ayurveda was the elimination of pain. While philosophers have laid more emphasis on the spiritual aspects of the elimination of pain, Ayurveda has put more stress on the means of elimination of physical and mental pains (adhyatmika). Health is a means, not an end. It should be maintained to achieve full living and true salvation which is dharma (righteousness), artha (wealth), kama (pleasure), and moksha (liberation).[133]

Philosophy and Ayurveda are also joint through their common acceptance of the means of knowledge (pramanas). These are experience and observation (pratyaksha), reasoning and inference (anumana), intuition (arthaputti), and testimony (shabda). The different schools of philosophy know different hierarchies of these methods, but the chief method of Indian philosophy is intuition and introspection and insight culminating in the verdict of Vyasa: "Through Yoga must Yoga be known."[134] In Ayurveda, experience and observation are considered to be the best methods of knowledge but they should be based on trustworthy information about methods, techniques, procedures and parameters to ward off fallacies and doubts. They are derived from the authorities who have examined them experimentally before establishing their truth.[135] All the four means of knowledge are, however, used in Ayurveda. They are utilized for practicing yoga and for attainment of emancipation, for the identification of drugs and the verification of their properties and actions, for the investigation of a correct diagnosis, for judging the constitutions and temperaments of persons and standards of health in healthy persons, and for preparation of food and drugs.[136]

Since Ayurveda is rooted in Indian philosophy, it is also closely related to Indian psychology because the latter is an off-shoot of the former. Psychology is the science of consciousness, its subject is the be-all and end-all of life and thought. The existence of a supreme consciousness as the source of all that what constitutes the universe is accepted by Ayurveda. Indian philosophy and psychology have a totality of vision because no aspect of human life and the universe has been left unexamined. Philosophy and psychology stand on strong foundations of deep and everlasting fundamental truths as to the nature of reality, the ultimate goal of human life, and problems that have confused human mind.[137] Ayurveda is embedded in this thinking. Philosophy (and psychology) as they have been developed and practised in India are the sources from which Ayurveda draws its concept of wholeness and its justification as a science of life and not only a mere science of medicine.

For this study, I think, the following conceptual terms of Ayurveda are important and should therefore be explained: the three doshas, the seven dhatus, the three malas, then agni, the seven prakritis, manas, health and disease, and treatment.

Health and disease are governed by the dynamic equilibrium of doshas, dhatus and malas. Any imbalance of them in the body results in disease, decay or death. But a complete metabolic balance does not exist as the psychosomatic and metabolic structure is not fixed and rigid. It fluctuates within the individual himself and from individual to individual. Ayurveda tries to prevent the metabolic activities from falling below a certain minimum. In this, the basic forces of life, the three *doshas*, vayu or vata, pitta and kapha, play a dominant role. The three doshas are composed of the five proto-elements of the universe and govern the physico-chemical and physiological activities of the body. Their balance forms the maintenance of positive health. Their preponderance or lack leads to the diagnosis of a particular disease and its treatment. The three doshas pervade all over the body but are primarily located in some elements or organs. The primary seats of vayu are the urinary bladder, the intestines, the pelvic region, the two thighs, the legs and the bones. Important seats of pitta are the sweat, the lymph, the blood and the stomach. Kapha is primarily found in the thorax, the head, the neck, the joints, the upper portions of the stomach and the fat tissues.[138] The doshas and their equilibrium are influenced by every word, thought, action, experience, occurrence or substance, coming into physical or psychic contact with the living organism, however small they may be. That is why the tridosha complex is also known as the "physico-physio-psychological organismal phenomena-complex".[139]

Vayu or vata is actually the factor of communication in the body. Modern research has found some evidence that vayu indicates the nervous system. Its activity can be measured by estimating acetylcholine both in the cerebral cortex and also in the whole body at the nerve endings of the parasympathetic nerves and the peripheral nerves or voluntary muscles.[140] Vayu is regarded as the prime sustainer of life. In a recent study, 18 functions are assigned to it, from causing speech and hearing to keeping the body as a whole intact.[141] Pitta is the basic factor for transformation, digestion and metabolism. Its activities closely resemble that of the sympathetic nervous system. So its main seat may be the hypothalamus, while its neuro-humour is catecholamine consisting of adrenaline, noradrenaline and dopamine.[142] Kapha gives the body shape and form and has to do with all the material substances in the body which are substrates for all actions of life. It regulates the fluid balance in all the tissues and organs. Histamine may be the substance that stimulates the activities of kapha.[143] A summary of the three doshas may come to the conclusion "that kapha is the principle which provides the substance for pitta, which is the principle of processes or transformations constituting life activities and functions in the body, and vata is the organizing principle of all of that, as well as a link of communication between body and mind (but not the site of the mind)."[144] This overall dominance of the doshas corroborates the interpretation that doshas are principles of perception which form man's relations to himself and his environment.[145]

The *dhatus* are the tissue elements of the body. They are the sustainer of the physical body and are also composed of the five proto-elements. They are seven in number: rasa (the transport-liquid principle/chyle including lymph), majja (bone marrow), rakta (energy-carrier principle/hemoglobin fraction of the blood), mamsa (flesh or muscle principle/tissue), medas (fat principle/tissue), asthi (bone principle/tissue), and shukra (reproductive principle/sperm in the male and ovum in the female). When these dhatus get vitiated, disease starts and one or more of the three doshas become a real dosha or vitiator. The three doshas mentioned above are originally three dhatus when in perfect balance, and become doshas when vitated what normally is always the case because there is virtually no perfect balance possible in life. Then the doshas act on the seven dhatus and bring about disturbances which cause disease.[146]

The three *malas* are stool, urine and sweat and are the waste products of the body. Their proper elimination is also essential for the maintenance of health. Some diseases are manifested by vitiation of their respective circulation channels (bladder and kindneys, colon and rectum, adipose tissue and hair follicles). The pivot of metabolism is *agni* of which there are 13 groups. They are the responsible factors for making heterogenous substances into homogenous ones; food is broken up in the body, absorbed and assimilated. Agnis represent various types of enzymes in the gastro-intestinal tract, in the liver and in the tissue cells themselves. Whenever there is any disturbance of the equilibrium of the doshas, the functions of these agnis are also impaired. The concept of agni which refers to the manifold functions of pitta is at once comprehensive. It not only includes chemical agencies for gastro-intestinal digestion but also metabolic events - energy synthesis and maintenance metabolism. In addition, it comprehends photo- and chemo-synthetic processes. Agnis prevent the channels of circulation from being obstructed by converting or eliminating the waste products.[147]

Another fundamental of Ayurveda is its knowledge and application of seven psychosomatic types of humans -*prakritis.* According to the three doshas they are vata-prakriti, pitta-prakriti and kapha-prakriti and four mixed prakritis. A person belongs to vata-prakriti when he shows characteristic features of vata-prakriti. Accordingly the other prakritis are formed. In relation to one's constitution, a person of vata-prakriti tends to get vata-types of diseases. The other prakritis generate diseases accordingly. It is therefore of utmost importance for Ayurveda treatment to classify the constitution of a patient. The constitution of a person depends upon the following factors: the condition of the sperm and ovum, the nature of the season and the condition prevailing inside the uterus, attributes of food and regimens adopted by the mother during pregnancy, and the nature of the five proto-elements comprising the foetus. It is believed that the constitution is also being determined by caste,family traits,locality, time, and age of parents. Persons of kapha type of constitution are said to be endowed with excellence of strength, wealth, knowledge, energy, peace and longevity. Persons of pitta type of constitution should have got moderate strength, moderate span of life, moderate spiritual and materialistic knowledge and wealth. Persons of vata type of constitution should possess strength, span of life, procession, accessories of life and wealth in lesser quantity.[148]

Another major concept of Ayurveda is *manas* which is generally used to indicate mind. This term refers to the instrument or agency which is primarily responsible for thinking. But there are five other significant Sanskrit terms describing different aspects and attributes of mind - citta, caita, hridaya, svanta and hrit. Various schools of Indian philosophy present three different views of mind: (i) being of atomic size and the link between the soul and the sense organs helping in the production of knowledge (nyaya, vaisheshika, mimamsa); (ii) being of spiritualistic value; and (iii) being plastic and transparent, so that it becomes modified into the shape of the object it perceives (sankhya, yoga, vedanta). Heart and brain are both considered to the be the seats of mind, but Ayurveda texts give more importance to the heart as the seat. Primary function of the mind is to perceive the stimuli communicated by the senses and to transmit them to the intellect. Then the mind communicates the reaction of the perception to the motor organs and reflexion results. There are three types of mental faculties: the sattvika type which is free from defects and endowed wth auspiciousness, concscience and purity, the rajasika type which promotes wrathful disposition, and the tamasika type which suffers from ignorance. But by permutation and combination there are indeed innumerable varieties of mental attitudes.[149]

The prime goal of Ayurveda is the maintenance of *health* and not the cure of diseases. Today's understanding of Ayurveda as a system of medicine is due to modern civilizations which very often uproot life as a result of major external changes and influences. Modern civilization is inclined to subject-wise thinking. This may finally lead to prevention of diseases and maintenance of health as special branches of medicine, or any other science, with particular training programmes which have to be implemented and supervised by (medical) experts. Such a development is a typical process of mystifying a once holistic process-of which medicine has developed so many. So-called traditional or indigenous medicines are going to follow this track as soon as they go commercial as today. They also get mystified as soon as they do not adopt health as the result of 'normal' conduct of life of an individual in his social and physical environment. The classical doctrine of health in Ayurveda is extremely individualized. No two persons are found alike in behaviour, attitude or appearance. This is signified by the term 'swa', which means one's own individual constitution of health (swastha). Since Ayurveda is aiming at the maintenance of the equilibrium of the psychosomatic constitution of a person and at its restoration to normal if the homeostasis is disturbed by undesirable factors, health is defined as (i) a well-balanced metabolism (dhatusamya) and (ii) a happy state of being, the senses and the mind (prasanna-atma-indriya-manah). That is why the two terms sukha and arogya are synonyms, meaning happiness and health respectively.[150] The concept of health is undivided and integrated because it represents the whole of the mental and physiological element (sattva), the spirit or soul (atma), and the physico-chemical component (sharira) comprising the basic elements dosha, dhatu and mala. But there is never a stable equilibrium and a person has to adapt himself to the ever-changing environmental factors. Health is achieved when the prevention of deviation from the maintenance of the norm is succeeded.

The prevention of vitiation of doshas is directed by personal hygiene (swasthavritta) and supplemented by a code of conduct (sadvritta) "which inculcates discipline of the senses and the mind and the regulation of moral and social life so as to accord happiness and good not merely of the individual but also of humanity as a whole."[151] To maintain health means to adhere to certain rules, strictly observing the daily and seasonal routine. The three pillars of life - food (ahara), sleep (nidra) and physical and mental and spiritual self-control (brahmacharya) - should be ruled by this routine in order to live the full span of life (of 100 years). Because of the importance of the responsibility of the individual for his own health, a popular definition says that health is the coordination between mind and body.[152] Besides aiming at a healthy life (sukhayu), Ayurveda is aiming also at a life useful for others and the human society at large (hitayu).[153]

Doshas can be aggravated by every thought or action. These aggravations, when not prevented or cured in time, cause diseases of different nature. Some major responsible factors for aggravation are quoted here to demonstrate the wholeness of the concept of health (and disease):

"Vāta gets aggravated by the suppression of manifested natural uges, taking food before the previous meal is digested, remaining awake for long at night, speaking with a loud voice, physical exercise in excess of one's capacity, exposure to jerks because of travelling a long time, intake of ingredients having pungent, bitter and astringent tastes, intake of dry fruit, excessive worry, sexual indulgence, fear, fasting, cold and grief. It also gets normally aggravated during the onset of (the) rainy season.

Pitta gets aggravated by the excessive intake of pungent and sour things, alcoholic preparations, saline, hot, vidahi (things which cause burning sensation) and sharp things. Other factors which are responsible for the aggravation of pitta are anger, excessive exposure to sun and fire, fear, fatigue, intake of dry vegetables and alkalis. Indigestion and irregularity in taking food also aggravates pitta. Pitta normally gets aggravated during (the) autumn season.

Kapha becomes aggravated by sleep during the day time, by the intake of sweet things, cold things, fish, meat, heavy, sour and slimy things, preparations of sesamum, sugar-cane and milk; unctuous things, intake of food even after satisfaction, and intake of diet and drinks containing salt and water in excess and during the spring season."[154]

The acceptance of all these and many more vitiators of doshas leads consequently to the widest possible definition a science of medicine has ever got: "Nothing exists in the realm of thought or experience that cannot be used as a medicine (therapeutic agent)."[155] This means that all existing phenomena, physical or physiological, psychic or emotional, have a bearing on the chemistry of the body. This includes, for example, anger and tranquillity, joy and sorrow, fear and confidence, love and hate, foods and drinks, drugs, fasts, massages, postures and exercises, desirable and undesirable experiences or situations, social, climatic or geographical conditions, laudatory or adverse comments, abuse and praise, good, bad or indifferent thoughts.[156] All these would affect the body and mind of an individual to a lesser or greater extent, either as factors causing vitiation and thereby diseases, or as means for prevention or healing. Thus, there is nothing that cannot cause disease, and there is nothing that is not medicine. The terms dukha (misery or unhappiness) and vyadhi (disease) are synonymous because any state of discomfort or pain is included under the disease. It does not even exclude thirst and hunger, nor does it exclude jealousy, avarice, passion, etc. The vitation of doshas is caused by indulgence in various improper habits and acts. The number of diseases is uncountable, yet the number of doshas is definitely three. The unity of doshas is acknowledged for it is more important for diagnosis and treatment than the names of the diversity of manifold diseases which were given for popular use only. More emphasis has been laid in Ayurveda on the humoral aspects of diagnosing and treating rather than on emphasizing the names of diseases. The latter would only lead to putting the diseases into watertight compartments and to neglecting the whole of a person.[157]

Diseases are generally classified into four categories[158]: (i) adventitious diseases (agantuka) which are caused by external mechanical injuries or poisons; (ii) physical diseases (sharivaka) consisting of internal ailments, nutritional and metabolic imblances, growths of inflammations, diseases of infection and tissue generation; (iii) mental diseases (manisaka) are represented by states of anger and wrath, pride and vanity, greed and avarice, indiscipline and uncurbed desires, etc.; and (iv) natural diseases (svabhavika) which cover birth, natural old age, death, natural hunger, natural thirst, etc. A unique contribution of Ayurveda to the detection, cure and prevention of diseases is its understanding of the pathogenesis and manifestation of diseases. There are six stages of neuro-humoral abnormalities before a disease produces its full-fledged clinical features. The earlier an Ayurveda physician is able to diagnose these stages the better for a successful treatment which in its early stages is more of the nature of prevention than of actual treatment. The six stages are [159]:

(i) The stage of stagnation of a deranged dosha or deranged doshas and its (their) accumulation in its (their) primary site(s), which is in the abdomen for vayu, in the umbilical region for pitta and in the chest for kapha. In the language of modern physiology it might be an excessive turnover of acetylcholine in the cerebral cortex which usually gives rise to symptoms of too much worry, sleeplessness and nervousness. This stage is called sanchya.

(ii) In the second stage, called prakopa, a dosha becomes provoked or excited at its primary site and develops proneness to spread. In modern physiology it may be the excessive activity of catecholamine in the hypothalamus which leads to increased activity of the nervous system producing symptoms like irritability, palpitation, rapid pulse and other similar symptoms of the circulatory system.

(iii) The third stage, prasara, is the stage of migration. The accumulated excited dosha spreads over the body from its primary site. Modern physiology sees it as an increased level of histamine both in the brain stem area and in the peripheral tissue leading to functional disturbances of all the organs and resulting in lethargy, weakness, and rise in temperature.

(iv) The fourth stage is sthansamsraya or localization. The excited dosha settles in certain tissues or organs. It is the stage of interaction of doshas and dhatus affecting an organ which has remained weak partly due to genetic inheritance and partly due to various environmental factors of a person. In this stage, specific symptoms of a disease appear.

(v) In the fifth stage, vyakti, the disease is completely manifested in the organic disfunction or tissual disorder. Symptoms are now clearly referable to organs and tissues involved.

(vi) The sixth stage and last stage is bheda resolving in the final outcome, which is either recovery, disability, or death. It is a full-fledged lesion. It is believed that only in these late conditions modern science often recognizes the disease process.

Physicians of modern medicine still have the tendency to scoff at any claim by physicians of indigenous medicine of curing a disease considered uncured by the former. It is probably true that many a 'miracle cure' claimed by Ayurveda physicians is nothing but an attempt to draw public's attention. At the same time, there is, however, ample evidence that Ayurveda may have non-toxic remedies at its disposal for quite a number of diseases for which there is only a toxic answer in modern medicine. But Ayurveda is still lacking a complete screening and standardization of its medicines though this process has already begun in many research institutions.[160] But Ayurveda not only comprises drug *treatment.* The four kinds of diseases should be treated surgically (adventitious diseases), or medically (physical diseases), or psychologically (mental diseases), or spiritually (natural diseases). According to this understanding of health and disease, the definition of treatment (upashaya) in Ayurveda is the widest imaginable: "A salubrious use of (a) drugs (Aushada), (b) diets (anna), (c) practices (vihara), prescribed jointly and severally, or (i) contrary to the cause of the disease, (ii) contrary to the disease itself, or (iii) contrary to both the cause and the disease, or (iv) similar to the cause of the disease, or (v) similar to both the cause and the disease, constitutes treatment (Upashaya)."[161] This makes clear that Ayurveda is not using exclusively herbal drugs but is a science which also covers all the principles of Allopathy (treatment of contraries), Homeopathy (treatment by similars) and Naturopathy. An Ayurveda medicine is to counteract the imbalance of the doshas and to set right the derangement of the whole system. Ayurveda medicines are principally classified into three main categories, those which counteract the excess of kapha, the excess of pitta, and the excess of vayu.[162] Here are some examples illustrating the wide scope of remedies:

Aggravated vayu which causes 80 diseases like paraplegia, tachycardia, aphasia and facial paralysis, is alleviated by drinks, diet, regimens and medicines which are unctous, hot, stable, aphrodisiac, strength promoting, saline, sweet, sour, oily; by exposure to sun, by bath, massage, enema, inhalation, sleep, taking rest, and application of hot ointments. Aggravated pitta causing 40 diseases like burning sensation in the chest, cracking pain in the body, jaundice and haemorraghe, is alleviated by drinks, diet, regimens and medicines which are bitter, sweet and astringent; by cold wind, shade, night, water, moon rays, underground residence, fountain, lotus, embracing the body of females, taking ghee, milk, by purgation, sprinkling of water, blood letting, and ointment. Aggravated kapha causing 20 diseases like drowsiness, excessive excretion of excreta, goitre and obesity, is alleviated by drinks, diet, regimens and medicines which are rough, alkaline, astringent, bitter and pungent; by exercise, spitting therapy, sexual indulgence, walking, fighting, remaining awake, aquatic games, putting pressure on different parts of the body, smoking, exposure to heat and sun rays, errhine therapy, emetic therapy, and application of hot ointments.[163]

Drugs like other things in the universe are composed of the five proto-elements. On the basis of the taste of drugs it can be ascertained to which combination of proto-elements a drug belongs and to which disease it can be applied. But other factors have also to be taken into consideration while selecting a drug: its attributes, its potency, its taste which comes out after the material is digested, and its specific action. Drugs are taken from the vegetable, animal and metal kingdoms.[164] Ayurveda attempts to give nature its fullest chance and does not normally force a tired system to work. The famous dhara measures for cure of notably vayu diseases and rejuvenation are very good examples of this principle. Their soft and oily massages whose fat contents and medicinal factors in the unguents are absorbed by the skin acting as food and active medicinal agents, together with a strict regimen to ensure perfect physical and mental rest, give the body the best chance to recoup its strength and functional efficiency.[165]

The main term of treatment in Ayurveda is chikitsa meaning cure of, or relief from, disease. But there are at least eight synonyms of it indicating the vast field Ayurveda treatment covers.[166] To render a satisfactory treatment, an Ayurveda physician has to examine the individual as a whole before prescribing a treatment. To this examination belongs: the vitiated body tissues for which no exact measure exists (thus a physician can only find them by discovering the signs of perfect health in the individual); his habitat, the season, his strength and vitality or resistance, his digestion, his individual constitution, age, psychic constitution, and nutrition. The examination of a patient if followed by an examination of the disease with the help of etiological factors, prodromal symptoms, signs and symptoms, pathogenesis and certain therapeutic tests. For assignment of the effect of the treatment, the following signs and symptoms of cure must be examined from the beginning to the end of the treatment: relief from pain and disease, accession of voice and complexion, increase in body weight, regaining or increase of vitality or strength, desire for food and sleep at proper time, not seeing frightful dreams, timely and proper digestion of food, happy awakening, elimination of flatus, stool, urine and semen, and freedom from impairment of any kind of the mind, intellect and sense organs.[167] The lines of treatment are manifold but there are fourteen major groups which clearly show that there is sometimes no sharp boundary between treatment and prevention[168]:

(i) Purification (shodana) of the body by eliminating morbid doshas through what is called panchakarma therapy (emetics, purgation, enemata, nasal medication and blood letting). This is supported by the subsidence of diseases and symptoms (shamana), for example fasting or light diet, restriction of fluids, exercises including yoga, and sun bathing. (ii) Methods of treatment which are meant for the reduction of body weight, kapha and fat, or for the increase of body weight. These methods are six in number and are called upkrama. (iii) The panchakarma treatment as mentioned above and its preparation with oleation and sudation. (iv) Intake of sufficient and adequate food. (v) Treatment to remove the products of impaired digestion and metabolism; this is mainly done by fasting, light diet or digestive medicines. (vi) Divine therapy. Mental control or psychological treatment restraining oneself from the desire of unwholesome objects. (vii) Internal purification treatment consisting of medicines taken orally or internally. External application of medicines consisting of oil massages, sudation, effusion. Operative treatment. (viii) Antagonistic treatments to provoke doshas. (ix) Treatments which directly act on diseases. (x) Treatments to purify the channels of circulation in order to get normal flow of the flowing material and to make the morbidity subside. (xi) Treatments which increase physical, mental and spiritual strength. (xii) Treatments which control the aging process, prevent diseases, increase vitality and bring a healthy long life (rasayana). (xiii) Diet and other regimens suitable in health and disease. (xiv) Procedures to be followed during states of health and disease.

After this overview of Ayurveda fundamentals, we may now classify Ayurveda as within the realm of those medical systems which are known as 'holistic disciplines' like Acupuncture, Homeopathy or Naturopathy. These disciplines are based on the idea that a whole cannot by analysed without residue into the sum of its parts. They share a set of assumptions about the nature of health and disease:

- Health is defined in a positive way. The harmonious functioning of body, mind and spirit is a state of freedom. It enables people to carry out activities of daily life, to work, to play, to think, and so forth. Anything without man that prevents him from exercising his inherent freedom as thinking and willing organism is disease.
- Disease is the imbalance of the integrated functioning of the organism. Health is achieved by reducing susceptibility to disease producing influences within oneself and from outside.
- There is a tendency in all living things to respond in a self-curative manner towards disease. This healing force is nature.
- Bacteria overgrowth is generally viewed as a product rather than a cure of disease. That means there is an unknowability of underlying processes which cannot be directly perceived with microscopes and the analysis of other instruments. Thus laboratory diagnostic procedures are less important than the physician's observation and the patient's report about how he feels.
- Treatment can begin on the basis of symptoms. It is determined by the picture of the patient as a whole and as an individual rather than by the similarity of his disease to this of other people with whom he may have some symptoms in common.[169]

It is here not my intention to establish Ayurveda as the best possible system of medicine and, consequently, other systems as less valuable, but it seems justified to put emphasis on its positive factors. Though I do not share all his conclusions which were once worked out by Pandit Shiv Sharma, I have yet to find a better analysis of the basic principles of Ayurveda. That is why I like to summarize the nine salient differences between Ayurveda and Allopathy he has given.

(i) The first significant difference between the two sciences lies in the meanings of their names. The term Ayurveda is singularly free from any reference to medicine, cure or therapy. It does not give the remotest hint that it is a system of treatment, but alone is a term that implies an approach to total life and living. Against this the term Allopathy clearly denotes that it is a treatment of diseases with contradictory measures.[170]

(ii) The second major difference lies in the nature of their origins. The development of Ayurveda was based on intuition and relevation in which the ancient seers have leaned heavily on observation and inference. Modern medicine has progressed through observation and experimentation without claiming to be of divine origin as Ayurveda does.[171]

(iii) The third important difference is found in the balance between the twin faculties called knowledge and wisdom: "Ayurveda is the product of an age when the relationship between knowledge and wisdom was well balanced. Allopathy is the product of an age in which knowledge has advanced by leaps and bounds but wisdom has failed to grow."[172]

(iv) The fourth essential difference lies in the belief of Ayurveda in God, Karma and prayer, phenomena which generally find no place in Allopathy. Ayurveda looks at the phenomena of matter and spirit from a triple angle. Moulding of matter by spirit is under one aspect science, under another art, and under a third religion.[173]

(v) The fifth substantial difference lies in the attitude towards the patient and the disease. Ayurveda treats a patient by destroying the disease in a process of reinforcement of the resistance of the patient or the tissues invaded by the disease. Allopathy attacks the disease directly and helps the patient through the destruction of the disease. Ayurveda medicines are probiotics whereas medicines of Allopathy are antibiotics. In sum, Ayurveda is more patient-oriented as against Allopathy which is more disease-oriented.[174]

(vi) The sixth considerable difference can be regarded in the absence of side effects in Ayurveda whereas the strengths of the bactericides or antibiotics in Allopathy have often to be raised to such proportions that side effects are unavoidable.[175]

(vii) The seventh outstanding difference is the psychosomatic concept of Ayurveda inherent in its base of tridosha. Any thought, substance and experience that brings about the smallest change in the body chemistry does not leave the mind unaffected, and vice versa, Allopathy is only reluctantly accepting the intimate connection between physical and mental diseases.[176]

(viii) The eighth salient difference is found in the different concepts of truth adopted by the two systems. Ayurveda accepts different approaches to diseases as parallel truths which do not necessarily contradict each other. In contrast, Allopathy (as well as Homeopathy and Naturopathy) takes a more rigid stand in this matter. Its concept of truth is regarded as one and indivisible. This works admirably in a confined setting of a single approach to disease but may easily fail when it comes to avitally different angle of looking at the same picture.[177] In other words, the aim of Ayurveda is synthetic whereas that of Allopathy is analytic. Ayurveda physicians feel that synthesis helps them formulate a comprehensive plan of treatment.

(ix) The ninth and last difference lies in their different concepts of standardization. The term used in Allopathy is strictly confined to the chemistry of the drug and does not cover the uniformity of action on the patients as Ayurveda does. In Ayurveda the patient is accepted as a non-standard and un- standardizable entity. His reactions to standardized drugs are such like. There are numerous factors responsible for the differences in the metabolic pattern of different individuals, chief among them are the geographic, climatic, seasonal, racial, familial, behavioural, constitutional, and dietetic factors.[178]

2. Interdisciplinary Approaches

The *Sutra Sthana* of the Caraka Samhita is taken as the main source for our analysis. Since it contains the fundamental issues of Ayurveda it is accepted as the nucleus of Ayurveda.[179] The Sutra Sthana is one of the eight sections of the Caraka Samhita and is dealing in thirty chapters with the compostion of the universe, its relationship with the composition of the body, the basic principles of the drug compositon and treatment, and the ideas about the maintenance of health and prevention of diseases. The Sutra Sthana is divided into seven catushkas (quadruples), each consisting of four chapters whose topics (should) belong together; only the chapters 29 and 30 are separate ones.[180] A first understanding of Ayurveda's concept of maintenance of health and prevention of diseases may come from a *structural analysis* of the *sequence of content* of the Sutra Sthana.

The Caraka Samhita was elaborated and, only later, written down for teaching and learning purposes. A student who came to his teacher was orally taught shloka by shloka and had to recite them with due consideration. "After proper understanding, he should repeat his recitation with a view to removing his own deficiencies and testifying to the deficiencies of others. He should continue with his practice in the noon, in the after-noon and night without break."[181] But later, for the procedure of study, the selection of a suitable text was very important. The Caraka Samhita demands twelve didactic qualities from a good medical text. It should be followed by great and wise physicians, be rich of ideas and respected by reputed experts, be conducive to the intellectual growth of disciples of all the three categories (highly intelligent, moderately intelligent and less intelligent), be free from defects of repetition and should have well-knit aphorisms together with commentaries in proper order; it should have elegant ideas to convey, be free from vulgar and difficult expressions and should cover ideas in an orderly manner, deal primarily with the determination of real objects, be free from contradictions, convery ideas quickly, be equipped with definitions of etiology, and it must not confuse.[182] The Caraka Samhita itself is without doubt conducive to these demands though it appears as if the demands for intellectual balance and avoidance of repetitions are, occasionally, not met by the Samhita itself. There are frequent repetitions, most of them are apparently used as didactic reinforcements to make known that certain ideas are really significant. And whether the text is also to understand by the less intelligent student is a matter of definition of intelligence. The advice to maintain one's health through proper conduct is numerously repeated, for example in Sutra Sthana VI:45 (importance of following the regimen for healthy persons) and XXVIII: 34-35 (ideal approach for prevention). These repetitions seem justified since the overall objective of Ayurveda is to make people healthy and happy and through this capable to achieve the four basic objects of life - dharma, artha, kama and moksha - with which the treatise starts.[183] Less convincing, however, seems the demand that medical texts should be conducive to the intellectual growth of disciples. The intellectual standards of the Caraka Samhita as well as the Sushruta Samhita are almost always very high whatever portion we take. It appears as if it was impossible for a moderately intelligent student, leave alone a less intelligent one, to master these texts and to become a good physician. This demand also contradicts other qualities which a good student should have. Among an impressive 25-point programme of what a good disciple should be, it is claimed that he should possess a presence of intellect, a power of reasoning and memory, an inquisitiveness for truth, the ability to understand the real meaning of things, a love for study, a devotion to study, and an uninterrupted taste for the theory and practice of science.[184] These qualities could hardly be acquired by moderately or less intelligent students.

What is the sense behind the sequence of statements within the arrangement of ideas in the Sutra Sthana? This question is provoked by the claim in the Caraka Samhita itself that a good medical text should convey ieas in an orderly manner.

It might be worth to study the system which is behind the sequence. One is certainly surprised at the classification of the chapters of the Sutra Sthana. Their titles, it seems at first view, are selected at random. For example, when interested in the "Duties of a Qualified Physician" as chapter XVI is headed, we are not provided with a detailed description of the general duties of a good physician but 'only' with the special duties of a good administration of emesis and purgation. Duties and qualities of a good physician on a larger scale are in return described in chapter XXIX with its obviously misleading title "The Ten Resorts of Life". The answer to this problem is a formal one. The titles of some chapters are based on the first words or the first paragraph (verse) of these chapters. On the other hand, there are chapters whose titles are truly based on the content discussed therein. The chapter, for example, entitled "Oleation (Therapy)" is wholly dealing with this topic starting with queries about fats and sources of fats, enlisting further complications arising out of this therapy and ending with the preparations of drugs useful for this therapy. Thus, titles of chapters are, indeed, hardly of much help to find a system behind the sequence of the topics. Out of the 120 chapters of the whole Caraka Samhita, 34 chapters belong to the 'first-word-category' and 86 to the 'subject-category'.

What then about the classification of the Sutra Sthana into seven catushkas or quadruples? They elaborate, in this consecutive order, drugs, maintenance of positive health, physicians including medicines, therapeutice measures, diseases, therapeutics, and dietetics, followed by two separate chapters of a summarizing nature. The third quadruple, for example, seems to be totally misplaced and mistitled. It has probably become a quadruple only in order to serve this kind of classification. This quadruple, Nirdesha Catushka, contains the chapters on the four aspects of therapeutics, the three basic desires of life, and vata and its merits and demerits. These chapters can be separated into three parts. First, the two chapters,one minor and one major, on therapeutics (covering the physician, the medicament, the attendant and the patient); second, the three basic desires of life, namely longevity, wealth and happiness (in future life); and third, the merits and demerits of vata. The second and the third parts constitute major philosophical and physiological ideas of Ayurveda whereas the first part occupies topics which, in modern language, would rather belong to a sociological framework of medicine . Neither this quadruple nor the other quadruples can help much in searching for a system of how ideas in the Sutra Sthana are compiled in an orderly manner. Thus, we are left to find a suitable approach to an eventually appropriate answer that may throw some light on the structure of the Sutra Sthana. For this purpose, a simple but perhaps effective table will be used to classify the content of the Sthana in its relation to some (modern) subjects, viz. medicine, philosophy/religion/psychology, and sociology. I strongly assume that Ayurveda as the Science of Life will cover all these subjects which are significant for the physical, mental and social well-being of a human being. By classifying, it is more important and more adequate to refer to the adjectives of the chosen subjects because we certainly cannot find complete modern sciences in Ayurveda texts,nor can we suppose that the textual material would completely fit into the scheme we have of modern sciences. It is thus better to understand the classification as medicinal, philosophical/religious/psychological and social/sociolgical. The names of the subjects are used only for the sake of brevity. Medicinal classification means dealing with physiology, treatments, drugs, diets, diagnosis and health. Philosophical / religious / psychological classification means dealing with the universe, matter, mind, spirit, consciousness, knowledge, learning, perception and behaviour. These three fields are taken together because a detailed distincation is not necessary for the purpose of our analysis. Social/sociological classification means dealing with communication, interrelationship, factor of time and location, social relations, status, and the postion in a community. This procedure may appear simple,and technically it is simple and certainly not valid for exact statistical purpose, but it seems justified as a procedure to indicate *trends*. How important this may be, becomes clear when we examine a modern book on physiology in modern medicine; the one edited by W.A. Sodeman[185] is taken just for illustratration. This textbook contains 31 chapters on nearly 1200 pages. Its index on 47 pages does not even once contain a term which indicates a relation to philosophy. Psychology plays no role either. For example, while dealing with the disturbances of emotions in breathing, the authors come to this seemingly rather helpless conclusion that it is "difficult to evaluate the role of the emotions in disturbances of breathing" and that, indeed, "the origin of the emotional tone evoked is often obscure.[186] The 31 chapters only once mention prevention while dealing with infections. But this hint is restricted to the control of environment by enumerating the "public health measures administered by officials responsible to the community".[187] Against this narrow view of modern medicine which accepts no factor other than from a highly specialized natural science point of view, even the simple procedure adopted for the following tables will yied eye-opening results and will indicate the broad outlook of a system of medicine and life as ancient as Ayurveda.

Table 1: The chapters of the Sutra Sthana in relation to their Medicinal, Philosophical/Religious/Psychological, and Social/Sociological Aspects (x = covering the aspects, o = dominating the aspects)

	Chapter	Med.	Phil.	Soc.
1.	Quest for Longevity	o	o	x
2.	Dehusked Seeds of Achyaranthes Aspera Linn.	o		
3.	Cassia Fistula Linn.	o		
4.	Six Hundred Purgatives	o		
5.	Quantitative Dietetics	x	x	x
6.	Qualitative Dietetics	x	x	x
7.	Non-Suppression of Natural Urges	x	x	x
8.	Description of Sense Organs	o	o	x
9.	Brief Chapter on the Quadruple of Thera peutics	o	x	o
10.	Detailed Chapter on the Quadruple of Therapeutics	x		x
11.	Three Basic Desires of Life	x	x	x
12.	Merits and Demerits of Vāta	x	x	x
13.	Oleation Therapy	o		x
14.	Fomentation Therapy	o		x
15.	Requirements of a Physician	x		x
16.	Duties of a Qualified Physician	x		x
17.	Enumeration of Diseases Relating to Head	o	x	
18.	Three Types of Swelling	o		x
19.	Eight Abdominal Diseases	o	x	
20.	Major Chapter on Diseases	o	x	
21.	Eight Types of Undesirable Constitution	x	x	x
22.	Reducing and Nourishing Therapies	o		x
23.	Refreshing Regimen	o		x
24.	Blood Formation and the Regimen Therefor	o	x	
25.	Origin of Man and His Diseases	x	x	x
26.	Discourse Among Atreya, Badhrakāpya etc.	x	x	x
27.	Properties of Diet and Drinks	o	x	x
28.	Various Types of Food and Drinks	o	x	x
29.	Ten Resorts of Life	x		o
30.	Ten Vessels, Having their Roots in the Heart	x	x	x

Table 2: Chapter VIII of the Sutra Sthana "Descriptions of Sense Organs" in relation to Medicinal, Philosophical/Religious/Psychological, and Social/Sociological Aspects (x =covering the aspects)

Verses		Med.	Phil.	Soc.
3	Enumeration of the topics of the chapter	x	x	
4-7	Mind and its characteristics	x	x	
8	Five sene faculties	x	x	
9	Material constituents of sense organs	x	x	
10	Five sense organs	x	x	
11	Objects of five sense faculties	x	x	
12	Five sense perceptions	x	x	
13	Spiritual elements and their actions	x	x	x
14	Pañcabhūtas in five sense faculties	x	x	
15-16	Principle of Psycho-Pathogenesis	x	x	x
17-18	Provontion of psychic disturbances	x	x	x
19-29	Code of ethics	x	x	x

Table 3: Chapter XI of the Sutra Sthana "Three Basic Desires of Life" in relation to Medicinal, Philosophical/Religious/Psychological, and Social/Sociological Aspects (x = covenng the aspects)

Verses		Med.	Phil.	Soc.
3	Three basic desires		x	x
4	Desire for longevity	x	x	x
5	Desire for wealth	x	x	x
6	Desire for happiness in future life	x	x	x
7-16	Life after death		x	
17-26	Four-fold means of correct knowledge		x	
27-33	Proofs of rebirth		x	
34	Seven triads	x	x	x
35	Three supports of life	x	x	x
36	Three types of strength	x	x	
37-44	Three groups of etiological factors	x	x	x
45-47	Classification of disease	x	x	x
48-49	Three courses of disease	x		
50-53	Three types of physicians	x		x
54-63	Three types of therapies	x	x	x

These three tables indicate that the Sutra Sthana, and consequently the whole Caraka Samhita, is governed by the principle of *interdisciplinary* thinking. Out of 30 chapters only three - II, III and IV - are dominated by medicinal aspects alone. Those chapters are mere lists of drugs; all the other 27 chapters are composed of various combinations of subjects. The combination of medicine, philosophy/religion/psychology, and sociology can be observed fourteen times. In most of these chapters medicinal thoughts predominate over those of the other two groups. But this does not mean that philosophical and sociological thoughts are of minor importance. Since health and happiness are the supreme goals of Ayurveda, medicinal thoughts have to be the prime ones. But , in Ayurveda, they necessarily need the relation to the purpose of life, the origin of life, the desires of life, on the one side, and the relation to one's own behaviour in certain situations, in certain communites and countries and at certain times on the other side. The combination of medicine and the philosophy group alone is mentioned only four times. It has to be admitted that a more exact analysis could probably reveal a higher number of combinations. But for our purpose, it is sufficient to demonstrate their clear occurrence. The combination of medicine and sociology is as high as nine times. This means, nearly one third of the chapters of the Sutra Sthana are concerned with social aspects of medicine and life. Only in seven chapters of the whole Sutra Sthana does social/seciological thinking play no (important) role. This is a surprisingly low rate.It seems to justify the supposition that sociological thinking should be inculcated in discussions of problems of health care and health eduction in modern India, too. Social/sociological thinking (in modern language) was not only known to Ayurveda physicians but extensively applied in day-to-day life as an inherent part of health behaviour.It therefore took a prominent place in the ancient Science of Life.

Table 1 shows a clear structure of the system of conveyance of ideas. The Sutra Sthana is first governed by medicinal and sociological thinking; second are, in more or less regular intervals, comprehensive elucidations of philosophical, religious and psychological issues. They are functioning as a supportive structure containing basic thoughts about life, health, ill-health and death. The medicinal and sociological thoughts are forming the practical frame which is the base for application. The concepts of the philosophical group invite a continuous reflection on the basic questions of life. These concepts are the conscience not only of the Sutra Sthana or one scripture but of the whole Ayurveda.

The Caraka Samhita calls upon a physician to what would be, in modern language, described as continuing or lifelong education.

The physician should always try to enrich his qualities and qualifications.[188] There are 39 qualification of a good physician listed, among them he should be well versed with the three principles of Ayurveda, namely etiology, symptomatology and management of good and bad health, the fundamental principles of life and their elaborations, the three sources of drugs, the factors responsible for the maintenance of positive health including diets, drugs and regimens, the determination of the nature of diseases , the three pursuits of life, the various methods of preparation of drugs and therapies of oleation, fomentation, emesis and purgation, the rule of dietetics food preparations which are wholesome and unwholesome by nature, and the diets and regimens which are foremost in nature among the patient's class.[189] The physician was accepted as a guru. He had to know the whole life, not only its medicinal aspects. He had to be well versed not only in one science but in many as the above list of his qualifications indicates. We have classified Ayurveda into the broad subjects of medicine, philosophy/religion/psychology, and sociology. Accordingly the duties of an Ayurveda physician can be classified. The list above shows that he had to cover not only medicinal questions (e.g.etiology, drugs) but also philosophical (e.g. the three pursuits of life) and sociological (e.g.diets and regimens of different classes). This demonstrates the interdisciplinary nature of Ayurveda again.

There is, however, the opinion by K.L. Bishagratna, furnished in the introduction of the second volume of his translation of the Sushruta Samhita,[190] that Ayurveda textbooks were treatises on "Biology" in its true meaning and by this going beyond what we call today interdisciplinarity. He tries to explain the intermixture of certain parts of the Sushruta Samhita, for example that chapters on midwifery and management of infants follow close on the heels of those on anatomy and physiology, and those again are immediately mixed with chapters on psychology.[191] He holds that this analomy could not be satisfactorily explained unless we looked on Ayurveda "as *general* truths of Biology, elucidated by the introduction of *special* truths exclusively collected form the science of medicine".[192] Ayurveda would distinctly possess every characteristic that make the science of biology in which the "knowledge of the molecular construction of the body is just the thing with which Biology is concerned".[193] The acquaintance with the molecular construction of an organism was quite a sufficeient function as reliable guide to treatment.[194] He concludes that vayu was the force of all the various energies "which under the name of heat, light, electrictiy or consciousness, etc., manifest themselves both in the Physical as well as in the Metaphysical world, and that Prana...is another name of the same force".[195] This is ayus, life."Shortly speaking, this is the Biology of the Hindus. This too is the sum and substance into which (as a department of Biology), Physiology unfolds itself. This too evidently serves as the line of demarcation between sukhāyu, dukhāyu, hitāyu and ahitāyu. From this too Health and Disease, Hygiene and Treatment, Psychology and Sociology have all their origin and start. In fact, Biology forms the basis upon which the great edifice of the Indian Medical Science, as a collateral branch, has been developed. The *general* truths of Biology are all there in Ayurveda; but the *special* truths from medicine have been given so great a prominence that the real character of the book has been over-shadowed and it has been transformed into a Science of Medicine."[196] There is a statement in the Sushruta Samhita which concludes that the "Science of medicine is as incomprehensible as the ocean. It cannot be fully described even in hundred and thousands of verses". Its "occult principles...would ..sprout and grow and bear good fruits only under the congenial heat of a (medical) genius. A learned and experienced (medical) man would therefore try to understand the occult principles herein inculcated with due caution and with reference to other Sciences."[197]

This, of course, is more than interdisciplinarity which is a process of a former segmentation. Ayurveda, on the other hand,starts form a nucleus, the whole life, and ends there. Consequently, it does not accept the separation of life into different sciences: "Though it is customary and convenient to group apart such phenomena as are termed mental and such of them as are exhibited by men in society, under the heads of Psychology and Sociology, yet it must be allowed that there are no absolute demarcations in Nature, corresponding to them, and so in the entire Science of Life psychology and socilogy are inseparably linked with Anatomy and Physiology, nay more with Pathology and Hygiene and above all with Treatment. In short the Biological Sciences must deal with whatever phenomena are manifested by living matter in whatever condition it is placed. Life is health...as well as Life is disease....".[198] The idea behind this concept is certainly deeper than that beind modern interdisciplinarity. It is the primacy of Being which is the foundation of all existence.[199] Ayurveda stresses this origin of all instead. Demonstrated in a picture, it would be a circle from whose centre (life) all the other things 'in life' emanate. But there would be no common zeal to arrive at certain phenomena of life, drawn as a wrapper (see graph A). A model of interdisciplinarity would show a circle from whose wrapper, i.e., the phenomena of life, questions arose about symptoms and 'problems' and sometimes led to the centre (life) itself (see graph B.) In Ayurveda , the centre, life itself, is more important than its environment, whereas modern science originates form the thinking to improve the environment since it forms and dictates the symptoms, problems and phenomena of life. Consequently, these symptoms and phenomena are tackled by research which is spread over numerous subjects and sciences of 'environment'.

Graph A

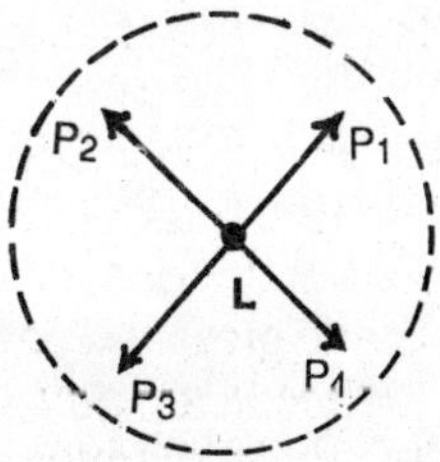

Graph B

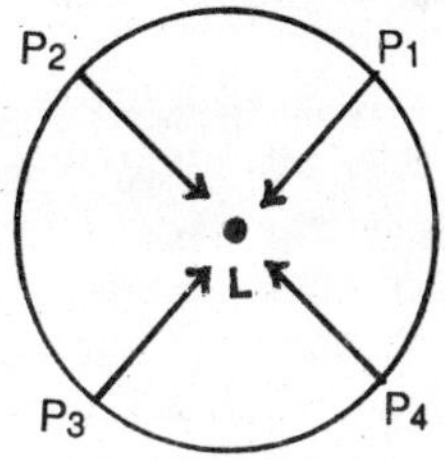

When taking all this into consideration it seems to be evident that the structure of the Sutra Sthana is not one that can fully satisfy rational, analytical and linear thinking of modern science.Yet, it is not an exaggeration to assume that, apart from the chapters 2-4, all the other chapters of the Sutra Sthana deal more, than less, extensively with positive health and the prevention of diseases because health is 'nearer' to life than disease. The interwovenness of positive health in the whole treatise indicates its extra-ordinary significance . It also shows that Ayurveda cannot be regarded as a pure medical science wherein prevention would be only the quick affair of one compartment (as in modern medicine). It further yields evidence that Ayurveda is really a Science of Life in which the treatment of diseases and the maintenance of health are equally handled. It may be regretted that Ayurveda does not contain a similar systemacy as in the subject-wise oriented modern sciences.It cannot, however, be criticised for ingnoring health wihle dealing with diseases. Ayurveda represents a complete system of health promotion and has given this system an outstanding position in its theory of life (and medicine).

3. Worldly and Non-Worldly Outlooks

So far we have been taking maintenance of health and prevention of diseases as equal parts of an overall understanding of prevention. But there is, in fact, a difference between these two concepts with which we shall deal later when I try to explain the concept of health education in Ayurveda. The overall understanding of prevention embraces removal and maintenance, that means maintenance of good health by removing the obstacles in its way, as the Caraka Samhita points it out: "One should regularly take such articles which are conducive to the maintenance of good health and are capable of preventing the attacks of diseases."[200] In the commentary based on Cakrapani Datta, this verse (on wholesome diet) is explained like this: "The maintenance of the flame of a lamp may be cited here in this connection. The flame of the lamp is maintained by providing oil and wick thereto and also by removing its extinguishing factors like insects, wind, etc. The obstacles in the path of good health are of two kinds, viz. those vitiating vāta etc. due to non-observance of the ethical rules, and also those natural forces which are difficult to overcome like the exposure to hemanta or winter season which vitiate kapha."[201]

We may even go one step further by inferring that if there is a "universal therapeutic utility of matter"[202],then there is also a *universal preventive utility of matter.*Before elaborating the basic assumption behind, namely that *Ayurveda is congruence between content and form,* some preliminary remarks on the character of Ayurveda are necessary. Neither the universal therapeutic nor the universal preventive utility of matter is an instrument justifying each act in life. It is not at all allowed to use this assumption for explaining crimes, injuries to human rights, or wars. There is clear and unequivocal evidene in scriptural testimony that Ayurveda does not advocate careless and irresponsible injuries and death. On the contrary, it is the sustainer of life by maintaining or restoring health which is the root cause of the four objects of life - dharma (discharge of duty), artha (acquirement of wealth), kama (gratification of desire) and moksha (emancipation). Longevity is the prime goal, not premature death; so is happiness and not unhappiness. To live is the basic desire of life. It is this desire to which priority should be given . The Caraka Samhita makes it clear that "with the end of life there is the end of everytthing".[203] In both the Samhitas the term "destroyer" is often used as a synonym for disease. This hints at the importance of the sustainer, the consciousness (which is without any beginning and which cannot be created by anything else). It also refers to a more worldly understanding, namely that humankind can enjoy life only through good health . Sinful acts (adharma) as causes of diseases are therefore to be avoided. It is also expressed that "non-violence" stands first and foremost among the promoters of longevity of living beings.[204] An idea, close to nihilism, justifying life of any human being as unimportant or useless, does not get any legitimation from Ayurveda which regards nihilism "the worst of the sinful."[205] A nihilist cannot claim Ayurveda's support for he believes in the accidental creation of the universe whereas Ayurveda believes in the existence of the Absolute and the empirical soul. Ayurveda further considers examination of a thing, of the efficient or material cause of a thing, of the existence of gods and sages, and of the results of actions. A nihilist would not accept the four means of acquiring knowledge, scriptural testimony, perception, inference and reasoning. As to Ayurveda, a nihilist could not become wise and virtuous and thereby leading a happy life. Only well-wishers of all creatures can lead a useful life : "Those who are not afflicted with physical and mental ailments, who are endowed with youth, enthusiasm, strength, virility, reputation, manliness, boldness, knowledge of arts and sciences, senses, objects of the senses, ability of the sense organs, riches and various luxurious articles for enjoyment, who achieve whatever they want and move as they like, lead a happy life; others lead an unhappy life." But this is not enough; in the same verse it is said that only those lead a happy life "who do not aspire for the wealth of others, who are truthful, peace loving, who examine things before acting upon them, who are vigilant, who enjoy the three important desires of life, viz.virtue, wealth and pleasure without the one affecting the other, who respect superiors.....,who serve the elders, who have full control over passion, anger, envy, pride and prestige, who are constantly giving to various types of charity, meditation, acquisition of knowledge and quiet life (solitude),who have full knowledge of the spiritual power and are devoted to it, who make efforts for the existing as well as the next life and are endowed with memory and intelligence."[206]

We may say that Ayurveda was an early advocate of the inclusion of the ethical and practical rule of conduct in the health (life) conception: "Thus, Ayurveda is, in fact, at once all, the Science, Art and philosophy of life."[207] We may further say that Ayurveda, perfectly practised, would make the entire medical science purposeless. In fact, even modern authors have taken up this utopian view. [208] But this seems to be an extravagant-way of thinking. We have only to think of the incredibly low standard of cleanliness ('institutional',less personal) and sanitation in India today in order to return as quickly as possible to realistic and down-to-earth problems. We know from historical eviedence that the standard of sanitation in ancient India was probably higher than today. Principles of hygiene can be inferred form many a rule in the Grihya-sutras. In Kautilya's Arthashatra, the high standard of sanitation in towns, hospitals is being described, resembling much what is said in Ayurveda scriptures.[209] Strong punishments were imposed on those who violated the sanitary or hygienic rules.[210] In ancient times, purity of the body and environment was as much inculcated in life as was the purity of mind : "The Ancient Indians did not cultivate cleanliness as a mere habit. They had developed a passion for it."[211] Perfect cleanliness accompanied strict self-discipline in order to maintin health and to prevent disease.[212] Hygienic paractices "had become part and parcel of the culture of the land", principles of hyiene "were interwoven with religious beliefs and observances".[213] Important rules of hygiene had actually attained "the status of religious customs and were regularly and universally practised."[214] But even in the glorious past epidemics were known indicating that despite strong rules of hygiene and sanitation these measures were not fully effective. [215] Today, it is not the complete eradication of diseases which should be realistically aimed at but a substantial relief from pain, mental, social and physical sufferings . If for many people the financial burden could be lowered, they would be finally able to lead a healthier life. We shall, later, examine whether Ayurveda can contribute to these aims which it has propagated from time immemorial.

The nucleus of the concept of prevention in Ayurveda is its theory of equilibrium or balance. In a world where more and more balance is lost due to the development in modern societies, a mode of health as a model of balance appears to be attractive. It may enable people to regain some of their lost balance . But striving for balance can be also regarded as a traditional, a conservative attitude, for maintenance of balance means often maintenance of the status quo. It can also stand for inactivity which does not change any situation which has obviously to be improved. That is why we have to answer the question whether the maintenance of balance pursued in Ayurveda really implies passiveness and sticking to the old values only.

Health in Ayurveda is defind as the state of the equilibrium of dhatus, the tissue elements , or doshas. The object of Ayurveda is to maintain this equilibrium.[216] But absolute equipoise of the dhatus (doshas) is, in fact, not possible: "For example, kapha invariably gets vitiated in the first part of the day and night, immediately after taking food and during childhood. In similar other circumstances, pitta and vata also invariably remain vitiated."[217] Arogya, which is health, is also defined as happiness. But happiness is also a relative value which varies form individual to individual: "For, no worldly happiness can ever be called in absolute terms."[218] Thus, slight variations in the equilibrium of dhatus (doshas) may be called a state of health and happiness though. On the other hand is disease the cause of misery, but not misery itself. Ayurveda regards absolute misery as possible, but absolute happiness as impossible .[219] Disease is not the disturbance of the equilibrium of the dhatus (doshas) itself but the outcome of this disturbance. So the disturbance itself "is regarded as a causative factor of a disease rather than a disease itself."[220] This is the point where prevention steps in. Maintenance of health and prevention of diseases are achieved while following the right path of wholesome regimen: "In order to prevent the unmanifested diseases and to cure the manifested ones, an individual desirous of happiness, should follow the regimen prescribed...All the psychosomatic activities, of living beings, are directed towards the aim of achieving happiness. A wise man follows the proper path. An ignorant man makes an individual to go astray."[221] Ignorance would lead to disease and misery, to an unhappy life. No one does on purpose anything just to invite misery and unhappiness for himself. "But those who are ignorant of the science of medicine sometimes choose for themselves a wrong way of life, assuming that this will bring about happiness."[222]

The equilibrium of dhatus (doshas), comprising mind, soul and body, can be disturbed by everything in the universe because the individual is regarded as an epitome ot the universe. The identity of universe and man is decisive for health and disease. It provides people with true knwoledge, so that they themselves can be responsible for their state of happiness or misery. Believing in the transmigration of the soul and the absolute goal of salvation (as Ayurveda does), results in the final objective that the prevention of diseases in its fullest sense is to achieve "detachment to happiness".[223] It is here that a serious contradiction comes to light. On the one hand, there is a completely worldly attitude of Ayurveda and its preventive concept which goes into the smallest detail [224], on the other hand is Ayurveda attached to the ultimate goal of Indian philosophy, the liberation from bondage which is explained in numerous places of the texts. One example will suffiçe: "Sānti (Liberation) is synonymous with vipāpa (free form sinful acts), viraja (free from attachments),śānta (serene), para (absolute), aksara (indestructible),avyaya (immutable),amrta (immortal), Brahman (God) and nirvāna (the state of extinction of all miseries)."[225] The difficulty for a discipline like eduction or its branch health education lies in the acceptance of both,everything ends with life (the worldly attitude) and the ultimate goal of health preservation is happiness in future life (the non-worldly attitude). Happiness in this life can be easily accepted by a discipline like education, but happiness in future life is too distant a goal for it. Thus, education has simply to focus on the worldly approach which is happiness in this life, leaving it to the individual to accept it as a road to happines in future life or not. This view is supported by S.P. Gupta in his interpretation of the Caraka Samhita: "Caraka does not preach the ideal of leaving off desires, attachment, feelings and actions of all kinds, nor does he advocate the Gita ideal of the performance of duties without attachment. He no doubt shows a lip sympathy with the ideal of giving up all actions..., but his real sympathies seem to be with the normal scheme of life, involving normal enjoyment and fruition of desires."[226]

The worldly and non-worldly approaches are also reflected in Ayurveda's stand on knowledge. Ayurveda propagates both, the utility of knowledge of the individual as an epitome of the universe as well as the detailed knowledge of the body for one's well-being, that means practical health knowledge: "One who sees equally the entire universe in in his own self, and his own self in the entire universe is in possession of true knowledge. Such a person experiencing the entire universe in his own self believes that none but his own self is responsible for happiness and miseries. The Individual self being subordinate to his own action indulges in various activities only when impelled by hetu (cause) etc. As soon as he realises his indentity with the entire universe, he is in possession of true knowledge which stands him in good stead in getting salavation."[227] And the other side of the coin: "Detailed knowledge of the human body is conducive of the well-being of the individual. Understanding of the factors that constitute the body provides knowledge regarding the factors which are responsible for its well-being. It is because of this that experts extol the knowledge of the details of the body."[228] Ayurveda's worldly approach mainly consists of the three supports of life - observance of brahmacharya, intake of food and regular and good sleep: "Being supported by these three well regulated factors of life, the body is endowed with strength, complexion and growth, and continues uptill the full span of life, provided a person does not indulge in such regimen as are detrimental to health."[229] Sleep and food have got a prominent place in Ayurveda's concept of prevention. Food is described as a "sacrifice": "Playing due consideration to the quantity and time, a self-controlled man should regularly take such useful food and drinks as are conducive to the internal power of digestion including metabolism...who takes diet conducive to the power of digestion being aware of the wholesomeness of food and drinks, who resorts to meditation of 'Brahman' and charity, enjoys bliss without any disease during the present as well as future lives."[230] Food sustains life of all human beings and provides them with complexion, clarity, good voice, longevity, geniusness, happiness, satisfaction, nourishment , strength and intellect.[231]

In sum, it seems justified to speak of a balance of worldly and non-worldly approaches and goals in Ayurveda. The complete Science of Life does not cast any doubt on the supreme goal of Indian philosophy, namely to achieve moksha. It is, however, realistic and flexible to concentrate on its preconditions, health and happiness in this life, by prolonging life to its full span (of 100 years), by attaining enough wealth to enjoy life, and by attempting to maintain one's health as the root cause for enjoying life. Absolute happiness might be achieved only in a future life, but relative happiness of a healthy man ought to be realized in this life.

4. Congruence between Content and Form

The question now arises by which overall principle were people to arrive at this equilibrium. My hypothesis is that Ayurveda achieves this through the practice of the principle of congruence between content and form. Two analogies shall make the principle clearer. An example from the field of health education is the oft-quoted case of a physician who advises a patient to stop smoking in order to prevent further complications of the functioning of blood circulation and the heart. His advice is the content, that what is contained in speech.[232] But the physician cannot stop his own smoking, sometimes not even in the presence of the same patient. The physician's behaviour is the form, that what is visible and what represents his attitude.[233] If the patient sees this behaviour of the physician or is aware of it, he will not be generally willing to accept the physician's advice. Another example of this incongruence between content and form is when a nutritionist suggests a particular balanced diet (= content), say for an infant under five; but if the family of this infant is not being able to afford this diet (= form), his expertise will be useless.

These examples signify two levels of the principle of congruence between content and form. In the first example, it is the attitude of the physician which impedes implementation of the advice. Why should the patient stop smoking when the physician is not doing the same? If smoking is injurious to health, so the patient may rightly think, it is not only harmful for me but for the physician too. Yet he, the physician, continues smoking though he knows it better. This means his advice need not be taken seriously. The form of the advice (made less convincing because of the physician's continuous smoking) governs the content of the advice (to abstain from smoking). In this example it clearly governs in the negative because the form does not correspond with the content. In such a case, even the most plausible ideas, which for example precisely establish the cause and effect of a disease or the nexus between disease and one's behaviour, are hardly ever put into practice. The power of congruence or incongruence between content and form is so strong that it can be decisive for the success or failure of a simple advice as well as a whole health education programme. That is why educationists like to conclude that any "effective communication which seeks to influence the people derives content primarily from the experience of the people themselves. In that sense the very content and the form of it is itself a part of communication."[234] To be more successful than our physician, a congruence between the patient's and healer's concepts is needed. In our example it would be the concept of the functioning of a role model. The second example is different in nature but nevertheless frequently occurring. Here, content (the balanced diet) and form (non-availability of means to buy and to prepare this balanced diet) do not correlate with each other irrespective of the behaviour of the person who gives the advice. Here, it is a socio-economic reason which prevents the advice from being put into practice. It is, above all, poverty that is the root cause of the inefficiency of an advice like this. Only if poverty could be removed (form), an advice regarding balanced diet for a family of the poorer strata of society would be helpful (content).

Besides these two categories of congruence or incongruence between content and form, there is a third one. In an entry on health in a dictionary of philosophy, F. Vonessen states that "all relations have to reconcile themselves to the *one* harmony which imbues the universe."[235] The author uses the picture of the body and its shadow to symbolize the congruence between content and form. He also says that one of the relations of body and soul was health and purity; health would only originate in order and providence.[236] There is a similar philosophical understanding in Ayurveda regarding this third category of congruence between content and form. After describing it in detail in the picture of growth development cycles, S.C. Dhyani comes to the conclusion that this process "stands in conformity with the order or evolution".[237] I think that this indicates that it is justified to speak of *'life'* as a superimposed concept for health or disease. And we may proceed like this: If there is no life, there will be no matter (= content) and form, since matter is the "component of the essence of any thing or being which has bare existence, but which requires the addition of a particular 'form'...to constitute the thing or being as determinately existent".[238] Form is the "particular character, nature, structure or constitution of a thing, the particular mode in which a thing exists or manifests itself".[239]

What does this mean for the hypothesis of congruence between content and form in Ayurveda's concept of prevention? It means if *life* as a micro-organism and as a macro-organism is regarded as the prime *content*, then *Ayurveda* as the Science of Life is its prime *form*. If, thus, Ayurveda did not correspond with life as a micro-organism and a macro-organism, then life would not be successful, that means healthy and happy. Ayurveda itself has to enter a balanced relationship with life in order to be able to develop all its potentialities. On the other side, *Ayurveda* can only develop this when it has been designed on the experiences from life itself. It has to consider the needs of life (as micro-organism and macro-organism) as well as its limitations. A 'balanced life' can then be realized by a 'balanced Science of Life'. This would be a complete state of congruence between content and form, life being the content and science being the form. The theory and practice of Ayurveda is aiming at this congruence or equilibrium while being the equilibrium. The congruence between content and form is, thus, *oneness*. This is more than holism which is restricting itself to the inter- connection of all the parts of the body and mutually affecting each other and to the constant interaction of the body with, and affected by, the physical and social environment.[240] C.R. Bijoy, elsewhere, comes to a broader outlook thereby extending Ayurveda's holistic concept from body and environment to life:

"Ayurveda is the science, whose fundamentals are based on human factors and their intrinsic casual relationship. Its fundamental postulates being...:

1. everything in nature takes places according to the laws inherent in nature,

2. though immutable, these laws are nevertheless knowable, and

3. the knowledge of these laws brings power of nature, which medically speaking, means ensuring long life.

The unity of man and nature (of micro-organism and macro-organism or micro-cosmos and macro-cosmos, BP), which in modern technology would mean the unity of man and his environment, the socio-economic and cultural character, is in essence not just a holistic approach towards health but life itself."[241]

Ayurveda describes what is good and bad in life[242] and thereby inherits a model of balance which heavily depends upon life. Life is understood as a combination of the body, the sense organs, mind and soul, but it is also a continuum since it consists of dhari which prevents the body from decaying, jivita which keeps the body alive, nityaga which serves as a permanent substratum of the body, and anubandha which transmigrates from one body to another.[243] The combination of mind, soul and body (= purusha) is sustaining the world (the macro-cosmos) and the life of the individual (the micro-cosmos). It is the substratum for everything, it is sentient.

This is the subject matter of Ayurveda.[244] Mind is only one, it transcends all and causes the respective sense perceptions. Lastly it is responsible for the causation of balance or imbalance through excessive utilization, non-utilization or wrong utilization of the sense faculties or mental faculties.[245] Deviations from the general code of ethics and from the many specific rules of conduct would lead to diseases, but a "conformity to these rules is sure to crown him with health (and) satisfaction".[246] Life in accordance with the rules and regulations of life guarantees a healthy life, which is a happy life, which is a balanced life. The main supporter and carrier of this is Ayurveda which is a science being in accordance with the basic and advanced needs of life. It is a science of conformity, which is a science of balance.

Ayurveda must be given the credit of providing prevention with the universal principle of congruence between content and form. This is the vantage point from which Ayurveda's concept of prevention and the abundance of rules should be viewed and understood. Ayurveda is convinced of, and propagating for, the inter-relationship of mental and physical powers in human beings. It rests on the faith in the potential of each human being. I have noted above that if there is a universal therapeutic utility of matter, then there must be also a universal preventive utility of matter. All matter is composed of the five proto-elements.[247] This has led to Ayurveda's understanding of the universal therapeutic utility of matter. But this has to be, slightly, restricted since "at the same time everything cannot be used for treatment of every disease" because a drug "is useful in specific conditions and situations" only. This means, "the selection of drugs is to be made in accordance with the propriety of its administration and therapeutic needs."[248] The same restriction has to be attributed to the universal preventive utility of matter. A drug or a regimen is only of preventive value when it is utilized according to its necessity. In the absence of this, there is no universality of preventive measures. There is, however, a latent universality of preventive measures as well as of therapeutic matter. Everything *can* become preventive in nature, if a particular situation or condition claims for it. These situations and conditions are governed by the overall principle of congruence between content and form. If a form demands a certain content, this content will become a preventive one; and if a content demands a certain form , this form will become a preventive one. We may exemplify this by means of the attitude of a physician (in Ayurveda) towards incurable diseases and death. It is frequently stated in Ayurveda texts that a physician after diagnosing a patient who suffers from an incurable disease and is certainly going to die in due course "should feel detached with those who are towards death".[249] If he attempted to treat the patient instead, he would not be proficient in the science of medicine.[250] This attitude and behaviour of a physician could be valued as cruel but, in fact, it is understood to be preventive. The physician is preventing himself from inefficiency, for only an efficient physician is able to attain virtue, wealth and pleasure. But the physician does not give up a patient before he is not sure about the patient's incurable disease. He then does not give up the patient but leaves him in the protection of the family members as it is elsewhere said. Such a physician acts in accordance with the rules of his own ethical conduct. He is the sustainer of life as long as possible but he is not the mourner for the dead. His own equilibrium depends upon being in accordance with the rules of his life, his content and form, or in the meaning of the Bhagavadgita, the science of reality and the art of union with reality.[251]

5. The Model of Balance

There is the oft-quoted statement of Yoga experts that Yoga could be only fully understood while practising it. The same, it seems, applies to Ayurveda. Only while living according to the rules of Ayurveda is one able to understand Ayurveda in all its depth. If this be true, then prevention has also to be practised first before we know its ultimate value and scope. The practice of prevention leads to the understanding of prevention; the practice of balance leads to the understanding of balance. If this be true, it has great consequences for the practice of prevention. Prevention should then not be conducted in isolation, say as a single measure, advice, etc. (as in the above examples of the physician and the nutritionist), but, instead, should be planned and lived in an integrated form, as a whole, "having no part of element wanting", "having its complete or entire extent or magnitude".[252] Its concept (and thereby its overall principle) would be more important than the sum of its rules and regulations. Isolating the rules would mean to break them out of the model of balance.

The following diagram attempts to demonstrate the model of balance of Ayurveda from the preventive point of view. In fact, this model is a cycle which repeats itself without a beginning and without an end. It represents the following fundamentals:

(1) The cycle is of *holistic dependency.* We may begin the cycle where we like. The starting point will be immediately embraced by the adjacent parts like the body by the shadow and vice versa. The starting point is completely interwoven in the whole system. The diagram could therefore be changed, for example: Having on the top 'world' or 'environment' would only mean that the same concepts would end the cycle and begin it anew. It does not matter where to begin the cycle. Out of this follows that it is not possible to eliminate one factor without destroying the whole. This has consequences for practical preventive activities which should not become isolated measures or programmes. Instead, prevention has to be intrinsic and extrinsic, covering at the same time the inner world of the individual and the outer world of the individual, the environment. These two are constituted of the same, namely mind, soul and body.

The model of balance in Ayurveda

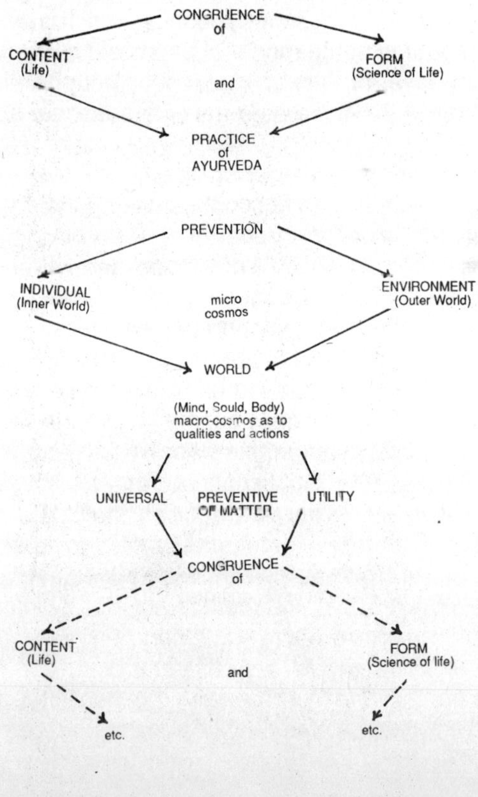

(2) The cycle is a *total integration.* Life is the supreme factor. It is the product of integration of the three constituents, mind, soul and body (= purusha). Life will perish if these constituents disintegrate. Thus, life is not only content but form too. It is the individual and the world, it is preventive utility of matter and congruence. That is why life is the most important factor of prevention. Life integrates the model of balance, at the same time it *is* the model of balance.. The cycle of prevention is imbued with life. Prevention maintains life, and life maintains prevention. The (empirical) soul is caused by something and therefore has a beginning, it is ephemeral. But the (absolute) soul is beginingless like the process of evolution of the various elements. The absolute soul is omnipotent and omnipresent.[253] Though it is located in one body and permanently associated with the mind, it is still present in all other bodies. The entire universe consists of the two categories, sentient and insentient. Both are composed of the five proto-elements. Thus, both have consciousness, but of different level, either latent, sub-latent, or fully manifested.[254] It is the consciousness which is instrumental in the total integration of the model of balance. Consciousness is found on every level of the cycle (except through the absolute elimination of desires which would not only eradicate all miseries but life too).

If we want to see this model of balance in Ayurveda being realized, we have to take into account some important fundamentals of prevention on which it is dependent. According to me, these are the ideal personality of a human being, the self-control of a human being, the strengthening of the positive factors of a human being, and the responsibility of a human being.

The *ideal personality of a human being* is closely related to the goals and methods which have to be followed in order to achieve the ideal personality. But this has become difficult in a world where "we are more engaged to determine what we are, how we behave and why we behave." S.P.Gupta continues that we "may claim that an unparallel advancement has been made in the field of materialistic subject but the human, mental and psychological dilemma is to-day on the same mark, as it was few centuries back. To some extent we have fallen back, and there is not a bit of improvement in this respect. So in spite of our revolutionary progress, psychologically, morally and ethically we are still perturbed..."[255] Ayurveda, however, has not avoided this challenge, but has taken it up in an unprecedented manner. Ayurveda is one among the Indian schools of thought which are throughout purposive in nature. It distinguishes between the three basic desires of a person: he should be able to live, to earn and to perform virtuous acts.[256] The first pursuit is pranaishana and has got the topmost place among the three ideals. It represents the biogenic aspect and is more or less attained through the realization of ideal health. Ideal health is one of the chief components of the concept of the ideal personality in Ayurveda. This biogenic aspect is not simply an instinct but a "dynamic concept of life, through which the ideal and beneficial life can be developed."[257] The second pursuit is dhanaishana. It is the next in importance after pranaishana and is the desire to acquire wealth; it represents the socio-economic and sociological aspect of forming, becoming, and supporting an ideal personality. Ayurveda has always stressed this aspect and given it an important role in man's life. This cannot be said of many other Indian philosophical schools, but Ayurveda is of the opinion that without a minimum of wealth and socio-economic security men are not able to achieve the ideal personality.[258] The third pursuit is paralokaishana and represents the aspect of self-realization, the spiritual aspect, leading to final renunciation. As we have mentioned earlier, Ayurveda has not put the same emphasis on this aspect as it has laid on the first two. Instead, other philosophical schools in India have stressed this third pursuit, and by that, sometimes the worldly affairs had to suffer from neglect. Ayurveda, however, has directed its prime duty towards the more worldly pursuits.[259] Ayurveda's approach towards the ideal personality is, again, a balanced one, "in which all the facts related to realities of life have been included, while formulating the fundamental postulates of ideal human life and of ideal human personality."[260] It is particularly in the first and second pursuit that prevention is given its proper place. We may claim that prevention is *the* path in Ayurveda which leads to the attainment of a happy and beneficial life, of a maximum life span while enjoying life, and ultimately achieving the goal of renunciation. Ayurveda's way is an extremely individualized one. It is apparent that no two human beings have similar personalities because the prakriti is different from one person to the other: "No two persons, normal, or abnormal will describe similar experience in like manner."[261] This requires a concept of prevention which is able to fit in this entire scheme of individualization. It might be possible that the model of balance can guarantee this, but it still has to be asked (later) whether health education or some other discipline could realize this in practice.

The sine qua non of achieving this ideal personality as well as ideal health is the *self-control of the human being.* It is, however, more than an instrumental method; it is an attitude which should pervade one's whole life. Self-control is the ability of the human being to trace the right path and being not too much indulged in any activity. The Caraka Samhita describes it like this: "One should not be in the habit of postponing things nor should one indulge in any activity without proper examination. One should not be a slave to senses nor one should let lose his fickle mind. One should not inflict too much burden over the intellect or the senses. One should avoid over-dilatory practices. One should not do things in a fit of anger or rejoicing. One should not be under continued grief. One should not be conceited over achievements nor be desperate in loss. One should always remember his own nature. One should have faith in the correlation of the cause and effect (that is, good and bad actions and their corresponding results) and should remember his insults."[262] It is, above all, the control of the sensory organs and faculties which are governed by the mind and which are the factors of communication and reaction to the outer world. They are responsible for "sinful acts", "intellectual blasphemy", and the three-fold utilization which causes diseases. The three-fold utilization is excessive, non- and wrong-utilization of time, mental faculties and objects of sense organs.[263] Self-control belongs to the foremost factors among those which prompt longevity, strength, nourishment, delightfulness and happiness.[264] It particularly stands first among the promoters of delightfulness, and is closely related to knowledge and understanding of truth. Self-control is an extra-ordinary means of prevention. It is a fine example representing Ayurveda as an 'as-well-as-science' which gives scope to all and every in a balanced form. Self-control is one of the carriers of this attitude. It implies material and non-material values on whose proper relationship the total well-being of a human being depends.

A third fundamental of Ayurveda is the attitude to *strengthen positive factors in the human being.* Ayurveda lays more emphasis on the 'field' than on the 'seed'. It has recognized and elaborated the existence of organisms and their role in the causation of several infective diseases.[265] But neither for cure nor for prevention, drugs and therapies are aimed at killing these organisms (which does not exclude bacteriostatic effects of some of these medicines): "If the field is barren then the seed howsoever potent it may be will not germinate. Similarly, howsoever potent the germs or the bacteria may be, they will not be able to produce a disease in the human body unless the tissues of the body are fertile enough to accept it and halt it in its growth and multiplication."[266] V.B. Dash concludes that killing these germs by medicine would not solve the problem permanently. It might give instant relief and prevent further attacks because the body resistance would be sufficiently developed as a reaction to the infection, but man "cannot live in an absolutely germ-free atmosphere even though he can minimise it. The only thing that can be done safely is to keep the tissues of the body barren and unreceptive towards these germs. Once the body is afflicted, the tissues should be so conditioned by drugs and diet and other regimens that these germs or bacteria...will find the atmosphere hostile towards their survival, multiplication and growth."[267] That is the reason why rasayana has gained such a dominant place in Ayurveda. Rasayana is the way of treatment which prepares the tissues barren and unreceptive towards germs. It purifies, prunes and strengthens all the vital elements of the body and the mind. It is a way of treatment and prevention "which not only prolongs the span of human life but also refreshes and invigorates the vital organs of man."[268] Rasayana rejuvenates and maintains the healthy metabolism of the cells of the various body tissues in advance, that means before they are going to be degenerated. It is advised to undergo this treatment "early or at least in the middle age of a person" in order to beget "longevity, good memory, intelligence, perfect health, youthfulness, lustrous healthy complexion, good voice, generosity, strength to the body and sense organs, power of expression, increased sexual potency and charm".[269] It not only strengthens the body but its "benefits have a comprehensive nature embracing all the faculties of the mind and the physique simultaneously."[270] It encourages the development of the three-fold strength which is constitutional, temporal and acquired.[271] With C.R. Ramachandran we may summarize that rasayana mainly intends "to add life into years but not years into life. In other words the intention is to improve the quality but not the quantity of life."[272] This strengthening of positive factors in and of a human being is invaluable for the health and well-being of a person. Through it, prevention realizes itself to its fullest potential. Diseases are not allowed to ensue from the negligence of one's mind, soul and body. This is prevention par excellence.

The fourth fundamental of Ayurveda's preventive concept is the *responsibility of every human being for his own health.* The whole Ayurveda is a plea for this responsibility, as for example in the simile on personal vigilance: "A wise person should be vigilant about his duties towards his own body like an officer-in-charge of a city and a charioteer towards the city and the chariot respectively."[273] Then the meaningfulness of both the analogies is explained: "An officer-in-charge of a city is vigilant about his duties more towards the internal problems of the city while a charioteer, more towards the external problems of the chariot. While the former takes care to remove the impediments in the way of maintenance of peace in the city, the charioteer does so to avoid the external contacts of the chariot with the undesirable elements. A city may be destroyed by coming into contract with undesirable citizens living inside the city; the chariot, likewise, may get destroyed by falling into a pit or following an uneven path. Similarly, a wise man has to be attentive towards his body, not only towards his external needs but also towards the maintenance of internal stability."[274] Health and happiness are not to be bought, but they are to be known, they are to be earned and acquired. With this tremendous task the individual is not alone, the Science of Life is a reliable guide. Since the complete Ayurveda is not easy to be comprehended by an 'ordinary man', it was therefore necessary to incorporate many of its rules and prescriptions in the daily life of the people. These rules and prescriptions were made a routine so that all people could benefit from them. Religion was preferred to become the main carrier of many a rule of Ayurveda. Thus, it is not surprising to find 'preventive attitudes' and 'preventive modes of behaviour' all over India which all have their roots in Ayurveda or in any other ancient wisdom compiled in classical texts of knowledge.[275]

Besides being determined by the model of balance and the above mentioned fundamentals, prevention in Ayurveda is based on sets of regimen to implement the overall ideas. It is rich in rules, regulations and prescriptions for one's daily conduct and behaviour. Certainly many of them are outdated and should be only regarded in the light of history. That is why it is not justified to merely repeat them today. But there are also timeless instructions and advice how to maintain one's health and to prevent diseases. Among them, the knowledge about food and sleep is the most important. Besides the practice of self-control, which is spiritual and mental, the intake of wholesome food, which is material, is a second pillar of health. It occupies an essential positon if taken in proper quantity and at appropriate times.[276] It has to be taken as to the needs of a particular season[277], in an agreeable place[278], and according to its wholesomeness.[279] The ten rules of taking food[280] seem so modern that they could have been taken from a present textbook of nutrition: (1) Food should be warm when taken. (2) It should be unctuous when taken. (3) It should be taken in proper quantity. (4) It should be taken only after the previous meal is digested. (5) Food ingredients should not be contradictory in their potency. (6) Food should be taken in a pleasant place with proper accessories. (7) It should not be taken in a hurry, but (8) it should not be taken too slow either. (9) Food should be taken with concentration on the intake, and (10) it should be taken with knowledge of what is wholesome for oneself. Sleep, besides food and self-control, is the third pillar of health. Sleep is the most abolute form of rest for the mind and body. It is responsible for happiness and misery, nourishment and emaciation, strength and weakness, virility and sterility, knowledge and ignorance, life and death.[281] In Ayurveda, there are clear rules for sleep according to time, season and one's own constitution.[282]

There are plenty of other regimens in Ayurveda. But, once more, it should be crystal clear that several of these regimens are not or only partly suitable for modern life. There is little point in discussing them here in detail as some popular health books do today unless this is accompained by a critical analysis of the particular society in which they were should be used. But it was Ayurveda that has bestowed them with a prominent place in daily life so that they could help maintain health and prevent diseases. It is only in our time that many a science take a lot of pains again to re-discover some of them in the light of health and disease. Ayurveda has developed regimens for good health in relation to:

- The behaviour to achieve personal hygiene during day and night time as to the application of collyrium in the eyes, smoking, taking nasal drops, teeth brushing, tongue scraping, chewing, gargling, oiling of head and ears, massage, bathing, clean dressing, use of fragrance and ornaments, cleaning of feet and excretory orifices, caring for hair and nails, using foot wears, umbrella and hand stick.[283]
- The behaviour of how to deal with natural and unnatural urges as to urine, faeces, semen, flatus, vomitting, sneezing, eructation, yawning, hunger, thirst, tears, sleep and breathing

which all should not be suppressed; and those relating to rashness and evil deeds, greed, grief, fear, anger, vanity, shamelessness, jealousy, lying, violence, theft and addictions which all should be suppressed.[284]

- The behaviour of how to live during the various seasons and times as to the six seasons: shishira (late winter, January-March), vasanta (spring, March-May), grishma (summer, May-June), varsha (rainy season, July-September), sharat (autumn, September-November), and hemanta (early winter, November-January).[285]
- The behaviour of how to live in particular geographical areas and countries.[286]
- The behaviour of how to live according to normal and ethical norms.[287]

All these regimens will be consciously practised only by those who acquire knowledge and truth including the "knowledge of the self".[288] This will enable them to change rules and prescriptions where and whenever necessary according to their own needs.

6. An Assessment

We can now outline Ayurveda's concept of prevention. It stresses worldly approaches and goals. It is congruence between content (life) and form (Ayurveda) which is instrumental for the balance of total integration of prevention with life as its prime factor. To put this lofty ideal into practice, a human being needs an ideal personality, self-control, strength to pursue positive factors, and responsibility for his own health. Regimens in the areas of self-control, food and sleep help realize prevention in the daily routine.

According to William James' understanding of pragmatism, the meaning of an idea is to be found in the consequence to which the idea leads in action.[289] This would be an adequate approach to assess Ayurveda's concept of prevention. But the overview of health education in India has shown that Ayurveda is not at all part of health education in today's India. Thus, there are neither respective actions to be examined nor results to be evaluated. We can, however, try to examine whether the ideas of Ayurveda prevention *could* be transferred into actions today. For this, it is important to know whether the aims of modern health education would be open to Ayurveda's concept of prevention. In a second step we can, then, try to review some of the societal realities, whether they would allow Ayurveda's concept of prevention to be incorporated or not.

There is a broad consensus today, internationally and nationally, about what health education ought to be. One of the most widely used definitions is that it is "a process which affects changes in the health practices of the people and in the knowledge and attitudes related to such changes."[290] This definition implies that health education is not a single procedure or transmission of health information but a continuous process which is a lifelong one. The definition further contemplates that health education is concerned with knowledge, attitude and practices (the so-called KAP-formula) and finally alludes to the efforts to achieve a proper health behaviour. Among the aims of health education, the outstanding and most universal ones are: (1) Health education shall help people strengthen the *responsibility* towards themselves. This is possible when man has enough freedom to decide on this responsibility and to develop it in a lifelong process. (2) Another aim of health education is to promote *self-determination* through active participation of the people. Health education shall help people decide on their own health matters.[291] (3) Health education shall formulate positive aims which can *motivate* people to attain health. This includes answers to the questions 'What is health?' and 'What are its values?' Four explanations are generally offered as answers:

- ***Health as value.*** Health is obviously of high value for all people. There is a common health desire. But this value is often not strong enough a base for developing respective health behaviour.
- ***Health as knowledge***. Simply telling people about health is not enough-as knowledge is not automatically transferred into behaviour. On the other hand, the availability of knowledge is necessary to support positve health behaviour.
- ***Health as norm***. Values are of higher level than norms, the former legitimating the latter. Noms are rules of behaviour for concrete situations and are developed by a group or a society. Norms always imply sanctions. Through norms health is valued as an asset in the community. Norms are very helpful to establish certain firm health behaviours. This denotes that the KAP-formula as a linear process is too much of a simplification. Health education processes should be, and are, more complex.

- ***Health as behaviour***. This has to be based on firmly established values, a set of group or society norms, sanctions if norms are violated, and the availability of well-selected knowledge.[292]

Health education according to the humanistic school in psychology and education shall help people answer these areas of concern: self-identity, which is the question 'Who am I?', relationship, which is the question 'What is the quantity and quality of my relationship with others?', and concerns for power, control and influences, which is the question 'To what degree do I have control over what is happening in my own life?' Helping people gain greater insight into their own value systems is, as to this school, the ultimate aim of health education. The approach to this is called values clarification and is defined as "one approach to improving the quality of life that involves people developing cognitive, affective, active, and interpersonal skills".[293] It seeks to help people clarify their values, feel more valuable, and appreciate the lovability and capability of oneself and others.[294]

These aims of modern health education which are widely accepted in India[295] do really concur with many aspects of Ayurveda's concept of prevention. Ayurveda is very much in favour of positive ideas (for example, a healthy life is a happy life) and also stresses values (for example, of an ideal personality), norms and sanctions (for example, if there is no conformity with them, then there is ill-health, unhappiness), and knowledge. Ayurveda may start with questions on self-identity, control over one's own life and on one's relationship with others. But there is a frame within which values have to be clarified, viz. the four pursuits dharma, artha, karma and moksha with a stress on the more worldly ones among them. Prevention is happiness, happiness is life, and a happy life leads to renunciation. This is prescribed. In such a process a person is constantly asked to bear reponsibility for his own health and self. Apart from this frame, there is great, sometimes amazing, similarity between the aims of modern health education and Ayurveda's concept of prevention. And by no means is it necessary or envisaged that Ayurveda is leading to passiveness against the modern approach. Keeping one's balance is a steady process of being active, indeed. A person who wants to be healthy, has to be constantly on his toes in order to follow the rules and regulations of good health and not to get sanctioned. In principle, Ayurveda grants a high degree of flexibility in a given frame. This flexibility endowed to every person is substantial, and the frame is not too strict and does not prevent the extension of this responsibility to a wider comunity.[296]

It is, however, widely known that life in ancient India, and unfortunately in present India too though less, was regulated by the system of caste.[297] From this, we may infer that there was (and is) a barrier to Ayurveda prevention. It prevented people from following their own, maybe radical, path. The mechanisms were so tight that only a few would dare leave the path traced out by the community to which they belonged. The few people who did do so and who were successful enjoyed full admiration of their fellow people and the after-born (e.g. Buddha), but only a handful of admirers were ready and able to do the same. This has not changed in our time as the example of Gandhi shows. His life style and teachings are venerated but hardly followed. Ayurveda prevention with all its other flexibility might be able to be adopted in a modern form - if the structure of the present Indian society and the conditions of life prevailing in it favoured this. But here we have to raise doubts. If it is true that stability is more important for many than dynamism, then it will be doubtful whether Ayurveda's ideas of prevention can be fully exploited. If self-aspirations are regularly sub-merged to family and communal needs, then compromise and resignation will be favoured rather than challenge and liberation. Authoritarianism is an in-built structure of life in India's hierarchically organized society. "A socially endowed authority provides power, and power, rather than achievements, gives prestige. Lack of spontaneity is an adaption towards cohesion and conformity and not an ability to express feelings. Selective interdependence is the essence of family structure."[298]

Earlier the miserable health situation of the majority of the Indian population has been outlined, though progress cannot be denied. There are piles of reports, investigations and other documents proving again and again the pitiful situation of the millions of the poor in the country. All of them have one clear message: Proverty and with it its causes, above all oppression, has to be eradicated before a satisfactory state of health, let alone a complete state of health, can be achieved. We have to refer here, exemplarily, to the famous study of Indian proverty by V.M. Dandekar and N.Rath.[299] Though it appeared in 1971 with figures of the sixties, there is hardly any reason to believe that during the past 20 years the economic situation in the country has changed to the positive. It is true, the country is more industrialized today and wealth has been accumulated here and there, but the gap between the rich and the poor seems to have become wider though. There is still widespread oppression and distributive injustice. Dandekar and Rath regard three areas of policy and economy as crucial. Redistribution of land up to a certain meanigful extent is the first and foremost. They found in the 1960-61 census about 36% of the rural households without land of their own or with less than $^1/_2$ acre. Seven per cent of the total land was cultivated by about 57.6 per cent of the householders who owned between 0-2.5 acres each, whereas about 2.1 per cent of the households had more than 30 acres each available and cultivated, and by that owned about 23 per cent of the total land.[300] A study of more recent origin came to the conclusion that there was a 34 per cent increase of the core of the rural proletariat households against 16.6 per cent in respect to all rural households between 1964-65 and 1974-75.[301] Labour intensive technology and guaranteeing the right to gainful employment were the other crucial areas analysed by Dandekar and Rath.[302] On the basis of the 1968-69 consumer expenditure a per capita of Rs 324 per annum was to provide the minimum of existence for a person in rural areas, and a per capita of Rs 468 per annum for a person in an urban area.[303] Though these figures are completely outdated, it is instructive and revealing to read what the authors demanded from the well-off in order to achieve the only feasible and immediately available solution, namely "to offer and assure employment to all those who are willing to work on a minimum wage on works which can be immediately undertaken namely projects of land development, irrigation, afforestation, road construction, etc. This can immediately place in the hands of the poor incomes which may give them the desirable minimum living and in the process create community assets in improved land and water resources and needed infrastructure which in due course will improve the productivity in the economy and accelerate the process of economic development."[304] The expenses of these programmes had to be born by the rich: "A 15 per cent cut in the consumer expenditure of the richest 50 per cent of the rural and urban population and a 7.5 per cent in the consumer expenditure of the 5 per cent rich below them is all that is needed."[305] It is known that with the exception of some temporary massive work programmes this scheme of the two economists and others who have advocated similar ideas has never been put into practice. The rich did and do not share, and the poor did and do not get. Instead, the gap between them seems to be greater than ever, let alone an equal social and economic status in the long run. "Proverty... is the situation of the majority in this country, and not the fate of a minority." As the authors from the Young India Project Action Groups many other analysts think that the removal of proverty can only take place "if the existing socio-economic system based on private ownership of productive assets is superseded by a system based on social ownership".[306]

It is obvious that the injustice of the existing system producing social and economic inequality and disparity is a major impediment to Ayurveda's concept of prevention being permanently and widely implemented. It is finally the rigid structure of the Indian society which is instrumental for such a situation. This society has over centuries developed three generative sources of disadvantage, viz. (1) to have no consciousness which would relate to the perception or understanding of what goes on, (2) to have a self-concept which is highly self-centred around the family, and (3) to believe in the mythification of those who would possess knowledge and power as a gift of God.[307] Representative of this societal structure is the so-called 'spiritual Indian', a misconception of many an admirer (not only in the West) which has to be brought into sharp focus. The 'spiritual Indian' has developed a philosophy through which he becomes increasingly 'anthropocentric'. This may sound paradoxical, but "if the Absolute or Brahman is beyond all conceptualization, as the Upanishads teach, there is little to be said about it, except that it is invisible, inaudible,intangible, unimaginable, and transcending human thought. What can be referred to is man's relationship to the ultimate reality and the ways of approaching truth and union. In this sense the philosophy of the Vedanta might be described as anthropocentric, however odd the description may sound, for after all it is concerned with human liberation and salvation."[308] Copleston continues that man was not a purely wordly being "entirely definable in terms of his social relations".[309] He is of the opinion that both East and West were "threatened by the reduction of man to a purely this-wordly being."[310]

But has there ever been a real balance between wordly and non-wordly ideas in Indian philosophy and religion? There is today a strong criticism found among thinkers who argue that there was never this kind of balance. One of these critics is N.C. Chaudhari whose controversial study on Hinduism[311] is a vehement plea for the worldly character of Hinduism. He sees Hinduism primarily as a set of means to support and improve the existence of the people in this world: "The Hindus...make a distinction between this world (iha-loka) and the other world (para-loka), between things which belong to here (aihika) and those that belong to there (pāratrika). They also speak of salvation (moksha). But the unwordly have hardly any weight."[312] The notion of salvation was "wholly unreal and unattractive - a mere talking point." It has never been the "object of the religious observances and worship"; the main object had always been "worldly prosperity". The Hindus so "loved the world that they made the possibility of leaving it for good even after many cycles of birth as remote and difficult as possible."[313] Chaudhuri then asks what did the "Commons" gain from this religion and way of thought. His answer is that they gained in four fields: (1) The belief in support in the world through gods. (2) Consolation but not "freedom from sorrow, because sorrow was a real emotional enjoyment to them,... even the grief from bereavement they kept alive as long as they could by hanging up a photography of the lost father, mother, husband, or child, adding it to the collection of twenty pictures of Krishna or Kali".[314] (3) Joy of life through religious festivals; and (4) personalization of the support from religion by a guru: "The extent to which this is done is astonishing, and the subserviency is not paralleled even in the political sphere where the Hindus have always submitted to autocracy. In fact, they become almost slaves of the Guru."[315] Against this, he puts the gains of the "Lords" which are in two major areas of life. (1) They enjoy power: "The secular rulers shouldered the responsibility for protecting the life and property of their subjects, whereas the religious rulers had the advantage of keeping all the practical gains from power to themselves, giving nothing more than psychological confidence to the men whose minds they dominated."[316] (2) They enjoy the gift of freedom from "the compulsion of work for food", "from the bondage to soil which agriculture has imposed on man", "from the compulsion to find houses and wear clothing", and from staying "anywhere longer than they pleased".[317]

What does this mean to Ayurveda? We have to note that Ayurveda itself is based on some of the criticised ideas and values. It believes in authority, in the instruction by a guru, in the organization of a class society; it supports mystification, and it is an 'expression' for its underlying religion and philosophy and their - wordly - character after all. Ayurveda as a system of thought is certainly a product of the Indian society and is not meant to deviate too much from its norms. Moreover, it must not be regarded as a tool which can change the system that has produced this very tool. But we may raise the question whether Ayurveda's concept of prevention and the conditions and values of this society can be re-assessed and re-shaped in order to give Ayurveda's ideas of prevention a fair chance of being realized in our time. There seems to be no either-or answer advisable. Both have probably to be re-assessed and changed, but there is at present little hope for a radical and quick reconstruction of the Indian society which is governed by a ruthless capitalistic mechanism (despite all declamations for a so-called 'mixed economy'). This mechanism is the root cause for a considerable degree of exploitation of the weak and the poor through the rich and the powerful. Politicians generally do not help because they belong to the "Lords" and very often join the plundering. The chances for a re-assessment and re-shaping of Ayurveda may be better. First, it has to be made again clear that the old rules of conduct are not at all a model for our time any longer. Their regular repetitions in modern Ayurveda books do not help but, on the contrary, establish needless obstacles to new and fresh thinking. Basking in the rays of the glorious past and its ancient concept of 'holistic prevention', as perfect as it was in itself, does not help solving today's urgent problems. This is escaping *from* life but not entering *into* life. Second, it is also obvious that Ayurveda is a product of Indian culture which is greatly based upon the religious context of Indian thought. Ayurveda is not a mere technique that can be changed and adopted to new situations arbitrarily, nor is it a monolithic concept of truth that is right for ever. A model of balance cannot be achieved when the perceptions for more equal social and economic conditions in a society have tremendously changed. At least in theory, there is an urgent desire in India to form an egalitarian society, to build up a classless society. Though Ayurveda's structure of thought is not contrary to this from the very beginning, it would have to develop new approaches to cope with this desire and to become one of the instruments of building up a 'new' society. Ayurveda prevention could provide a set of principles for health education which might be accepted as suitable for the improvement of the health (education) situation in the country.

Chapter 3

Modern Health Education, Prevention, Ayurveda

1. Modern Health Education

Health education in India is still two-fold. Its first practical aim is to improve sanitation and individual hygiene in order to reduce the menace of communicable diseases. Besides this, it is also aiming at imparting more knowledge about proper nutrition, regular medical check ups, etc. in order to prevent diseases and to detect them as early as possible. On a second level, health education is trying to influence the socio-psychic behaviour of people to prevent modern 'civilization diseases' such as cardio-vascular or diabetic diseases from occurring. Both these forms of diseases, simplified as diseases of poverty and of affluence respectively, are prevalent in India, though much less in the second group. Health education is therefore concerned with both of them. It is said that the individual himself is framing his life style, but we also know that this is not true for millions and millions in India. They are exploited, their human rights are neglected, and their participation in running the country is rejected. They are victims of a socio-cultural and socio- economic system which is either feudalistic or extremely capitalistic, i.e., which clearly marks out the oppressor and the oppressed. Accepting and pursuing rights for a free life is, amongst other things, to accept one's own self-identity and self-determination as supreme goals of one's own life. These two qualities are the starting point of health education as well. Becoming aware of one's roles and aspirations, of one's position in family and society, of one's duties and rights towards individual and social health, becoming aware of the necessities and possibilities to direct one's life and its environment to one's own satisfaction while taking into account the needs of a group, a community, a society - these are the first steps of a successful health education.

In earlier times, health education was incorporated in a 'culture of health', it was identical with the knowledge of life. Ayurveda is one of the finest examples of this form of ancient health education. It, along with other classical forms of medicine, had no systematic health education developed. This was felt unnecessary because life was set in a narrow frame of customs and beliefs in one's own caste and class respectively and ensured by this a peaceful coexistence of humankind with the environment.[318] This has changed drastically. Nowadays health education is found practised between a group of rival sciences from medicine to natural sciences, humanities and social sciences. The wholeness of the earlier health education function has gone and has been replaced by pieces of various specialist sciences. We may regret this but this development was inevitable due to the social development of modern societies and its scientific achievements. It is now widely acknowledged that health education, i.e., the help which is given in shaping one's own health environment, covers six major areas of life: proper cultures of nutrition, occupation, leisure, time. sleep, sexuality, and psycho-hygiene.[319] In the 1980 volume of the "international journal of health education" two fundamental schools advocated for different sciences as foundations of health education. The controversy centred around the criticism that health education was dominated by modern medicine and that health education personnel would only imply the mechanistic system of modern medicine. Instead, H.Vuori means that the educational and behavioural sciences should be accepted as the primary foundation of health education.[320] Opposing this, L.van Parijs represents the view that health education was already too much dominated by the behavioural and social sciences; he pleads for a deeper interdisciplinarity and co-operation among social and medical sciences.[321] Both the authors, however, agreed that health education should contain an important political component in order to be able, if necessary, to help change the values of people. Health education should attempt to prepare a suitable "climate" which would allow structural intervention to improve the health situation of a whole community or society.[322] In the former German Democratic Republic, for example, such an integration of health education into the political spectrum had become a major principle, and the whole society was responsible for health education and its connection to the main political tasks of the society.[323]

As was discussed in the Introduction, there is no concept of health education in India worth its name. It is true that India has entered the specialist stage in its training of health educators as against the "orderly" and diploma stages"[324], but the conceptualization and structure of health education in the country have not reached this specialist stage. Health education has hardly any impact on the health situation of the vast majority of the people and is highly bureaucratic in its administration. There is but a marginal reflection about its theoretical foundations and its socio-economic and political frame. Here we have to appreciate the authors of *Health for All* for their endeavours. In determining the objectives of health education, they have started from the principle that the individual is not the object but the subject of health, and that to acquire health is, in reality, a process of knowing, living, participating and being. They have defined these objectives as follows[325]:

Knowing

"The first step in health is knowing or cultivating a health-awareness. A health-conscious individual should know how his body functions, how it can be kept fit, how diseases are caused and how they can be prevented and cured. He should also know what he should or should not do, not only to keep himself healthy, but to ensure that his actions do not harm the environment or cause illness to others. He should also know how to nurse himself in illnesses and how to offer similar services to others when needed."

Living

"The second step in health is living or cultivating a life style which is promotive of health. For instance, the health-conscious individual has to take physical exercise, cultivate the right dietary habits, avoid excesses and observe a certain self-discipline. This is, of course, quite different from the consumerist attitude to health where an individual gives full licence to himself and then tries to buy 'health' through doctors and medicines."

Participating

"The third step in health is participating in or cultivating a social responsibility for health. An individual must realize that health has a social aspect, that an individual's attempt to be healthy will succeed only, and succeed better, if policies which strive to provide health for the individual is to be sought in the health of the society as a whole. He should, therefore, be aware of the social causes of illness and willing to play his role in remedying them."

Being

"Finally health is also a process of being or cultivating interests, attitudes, and values promotive of health. For instance, an individual will have to learn to emphasize promotive and preventive aspects of health and to look upon curative measures as necessary evil rather than as a prestige symbol. He will also have to develop the right attitude to pain, to growing old and to death. In short, every individual will have to develop his own 'philosophy' of health just as he will also have to develop a 'philosophy' of life. The two are obviously related because lack of adjustment in life does cause ill-health just as ill-health affects adjustment in life."

The authors conclude that health education like all other education is a three-fold process of giving information, of teaching skills, and of inculcating values. They suggest that health education programmes for the poor should cover seven basic and some specific content areas, viz. sanitary disposal of excreta and waste water, control of vectors, use of protected water, production of nutrient foods locally, encouragement of good health habits, and maintenance of good personal hygiene and debilitating infections such as tuberculosis, hookworm, malaria and filaria. They think that simple health messages communicated effectively would prove excellent results.[326]

But, against this, we know that the guru-shishya tradition is still prevalent in Indian life and education[327], and this pattern of communication seems to be a major obstacle for a modern two-way communication behaviour which is so decisive in education. We may assert that many health education programmes fail because of a routine, mechanical and status- conscious way of communication. We should therefore not be deceived by public words of politicians, officials of any sort, or educators. In practice, most of them stick to their desks and prefer a safe distance between them and the learners. They frequently propagate working and learning together, sharing and exchanging ideas, but in reality it is often the boring monologue poured over a mostly patient audience. It is very often a mere show that has the character of an inaugural function. There is not even the slightest chance to be successful in health education if this dominating attitude of patronizing is not changed. By and large, modern 'shoulds of teaching and learning' for adults are simple and down-to-earth: (1) Know the culture of the learners. (2) Start from where the learners are. (3) Give people learning experiences. (4) Motivate by linking the required behaviour with goals of groups and individuals. (5) Suggest specific behavioural changes which can be easily carried out. (6) Meet felt needs first, and (7) select a variety of learning ways.[328] But since health education in India is still ruled by a bureaucracy which not only does not give any help but prevents independent ideas from developing, these 'shoulds' will remain a dream for quite some time to come. Health is first of all an individual value, and its promotion by health workers, including those in administrations, is often not acknowledged by the people, and more so if forces of centralization are put up as obstacles to spontaneous and indigenous practices of 'health education' by the people - despite a gigantic structure of health care respective governments are envisaging and trying to set up.

The Government of India has accepted primary health care as the most important means to achieve health for all by the year 2000 - when the population of the country is expected to be around 920 million. Administrators and planners are convinced that they will be successful in achieving this goal. The machinery they want to establish is impressive: one health sub-centre for every 5.000 rural population, one subsidiary health centre for every 25.000 rural population, and one primary health centre for every 50.000 rural population.[329] It is reported that in 1985, about 83.000 sub-centres and 7.250 primary health centres were functioning.[330] Besides this, the Government has also accepted a Community Health Workers Scheme which, by 1990, should have one community health worker for a population of 1.000 or for a village. Altogether about 580.000 community health workers have consequently to be trained. According to the Minimum Needs Programme the target was to increase the number of health workers or volunteers from 140.000 in 1980 to 360.000 by 1985.[331] To bring about such a development in infrastructure, in other words a revolution in health organization, would probably need another political structure rather than the existing one, and a deep re-thinking of the values of political and social activities. A highly individualistic life-style within the strict boundaries of castes, classes, families, and professions is not a fertile ground for "Another Development" in health.[332] What the British colonialists introduced, namely modern medicine to strengthen the oppressive classes including a small fraction of the Indian population, is still in existence. And so is the orthodox view of medicine and society which culminates in three central but problematic assumptions: the determinants of health and disease are predominantly biological, medicine is a natural science only, and this scientific medicine provides the only viable means for mediating between health, medicine and society.[333] Health services are still handled down. Increasing commercialization and professionalzation of the health services are still the major elements of India's elite-oriented health services. There are no clear signs that despite revolutionary words the haves in the centres will change their attitudes and behaviour. D.Banerji concluded as early as 1973 that the "political leaders and the health administrators sought to secure an aura of social legitimacy for their actions by getting ill-defined or irrelevant issues raised by social scientists and health educators. Thus, social scientists dutifully compared 'modernization' with 'traditionalism' and 'urban culture' with traditional 'folk culture', and the comparisons were then used to justify the urban orientation for the health services in in India: the backward, superstitious, uneducated villagers would first have to be educated by a corps of 'well-trained' health educators from the cities, who would teach them the virtues of the 'modern' health services, with all their trappings of dependence promotion and profit orientation." Banerji's comprehensive investigation of the interaction between the health practices which are introduced through primary health centres and the pre-existing health practices is an eye-opener and clearly reveals that the ideal of the primary health centre exists only in name. The malady lies deep in the "Culture of the political leadership of the country - their lack of real commitment to the welfare of the weaker sections of the population."[334]

Also in the seventies, alternative models were discussed and being published. It was J.P.Naik, besides others, who was one of the moving spirits behind the large-scale questioning of the system and the continuous debate following out of it. Three key publications were instrumental for the discussion about Another Development in health.[335] They contain the following design for Health for All, or Another Health. There are three *basic issues* of development in general, and of health development in particular: (1) A decision has to be taken on the type of society which shall be created in India and the model of health care that shall be built up without transferring social models of others. (2) If an egalitarian society is the objective, the double-think and the double-talk should be abandoned. This means the talking of serving the masses of the people while in reality one is aggrandizing things for the benefit of one's own classes should be stopped. (3) If egalitarianism should be brought about, it is inevitable for the well-off to be prepared to share with the people and to cut down their conspicuous expenditure and unnecessary affluence. These basic shifts are deemed necessary for a system of health services that will have to be an integral part of programmes of abolishing poverty, of larger production, of better distribution of food, and of universal basic education.[336] Some *general considerations* for this system were put in a ten point programme: (1) Benefiters of the alternative system of health care must not be the rich alone. (2) Emphasis should be put on preventive and protective aspects. (3) The over-centralized, over-expensive, over-professionalized, over-urbanized and over-mystified medical technology should be replaced by a technology best suited to the interests of the people. This new technology should not expect the people to adjust themselves to the technology. (4) A de-professionalization of medical professions is necessary. The country needs the highly specialized expert as well as the locally trained man and woman from within the community in an appropriate combination. (5) The infrastructure which over-emphasizes the provision of hospitals and super-specialities should be changed. Encouragement should be given to a greater use of home treatment, to provision for small rural hospitals and to a radical change of medical education. (6) Production of fancy and costly drugs for the well-to-do should be limited and widely replaced by mass production and cheap sale of essential drugs needed by the common man.[337] (7) The masses should decide what is good in health for the people, not the buraucracy. (8) Health education for the people needs a "spiritual basis of health". This is desirable because there is no purely technological answer to the basic (health) problems in life.[338] (9) Many pilot projects are necessary to adopt a pragmatic approach which allows trial and support to several viable alternatives. (10) The choice of alternatives will depend on their financial implications. The existing expenditure has to be increased, at the same time costs of health services have to be brought down by only a limited increase of services where the benefit goes to urban or well-to-do people. The largest share should go to rural areas or to the depressed sections of the society.

There are two models which graphically depict the traditional and the alternative approaches in health care[339]:

Health Pyramid A: Traditional Model

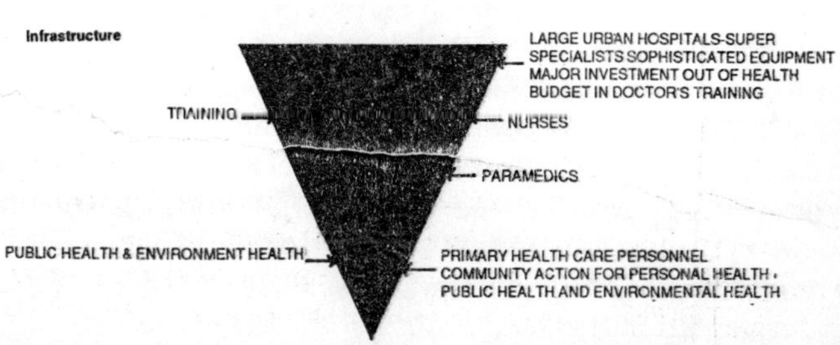

Health Pyramid B: Alternative Model "Health by the People"

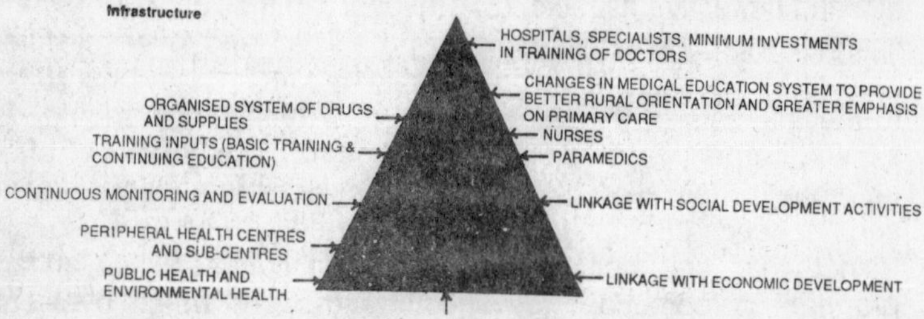

The alternative model should strongly root in the community, integrate promotive, preventive and curative aspects, provide adequate, efficient and equitable referral services, and combine the valuable elements of India's culture and tradition with the best elements of Western systems. It should also be more economical and cost-effective and should concentrate, above all, on expanded and improved maternal and child health[340], the eradication and control of communicable diseases, training of community health volunteers, the production of drugs in accordance with the disease pattern, an administration of good leadership, research related to all these priorities, and a rise in health expenditure by 8-9 per cent a year (at constant prices) to reach about 6 per cent of the GNP by the year 2000. Success in these programmes would depend on the capacity to create a mass movement to work for alternatives in development and health.

To integrate Ayurveda Health Care and Ayurveda Health Education into this new understanding and structure will be difficult since Ayurveda was never keen on developing a 'system' to influence people. This is, on the one hand, an advantage since a self-confident human being does not like too much of guardianship in health by so-called superiors he very often does not understand. Centrally-directed modes of behaviour, if enforced, can destroy man's self-confidence. This is what is happening today in many an educational and social field (including health). This is not only not helpful but influences people finally to reject health education at all. Ayurveda seems to be free from such an arrogant approach by those in power. Whether this is the result of the existence of inherent values of its philosophical background or merely the consequence of the long standstill or simply the lack of opportunities does not matter; its abstinence from bureaucratic rule is a fact and will, I do hope, not change. People of all walks of life are able to get all the vital things they need, including health, provided they have a fair chance to acquire them. But political preconceptions and modern administrative and development machineries with their traditional guru-shishya pattern restrict this fair chance considerably. Building up a minimum infrastructure in health is good and a must for Ayurveda, but to let it run by people whose sole aim is to make money and to rule other people (these are reported motifs of personnel in health education) will be disastrous. Self-identity and self-determination imply the development of one's own ideas about one's own needs and desires. Thus, the lacking of a positive infra-structure of health education in general and of Ayurveda in particular is mirrored in a low level of self-identity and self-determination towards health among the majority of India's population. Some isolated crash programme in health education are not going to change this. There where it is existing, even if only in theory as in the example below, health education in Ayurveda is often highly sophisticated and elite-oriented.

The example of the administration of rasayana which is one of the most important treatments for cure and at the same time a measure of prevention is taken for illustration. In a suggestion by a prominent Ayurveda physician[341] the individual and social implications of this kind of health education become obvious. P.R. Warrier distinguishes two main divisions of rasayana administration, kuṭipraveshika and vatatapika. "In 'Kuṭīpraveṣika' the person enters into a specially constructed KUṬĪ or house for the treatment and stays there till the treatment is completed. This method is the best in view of the totality of the effect. But, it is suitable only to persons who observe all the meticulous details of the elaborate treatment in respect of diet, routine etc. One should have absolute freedom to devote sufficient time to complete the full course of the treatment depending upon the nature of the individual case."[342] Vatatapika does not impose so many restrictions. The period of treatment is shorter and the essential facilities necessary are less than for kutipraveshika. Literally, vatatapika means to allow the patient's exposure to wind and sun.[343] The kuti or house shoud be situated on the North-Eastern side of a city. "It should not have access to wild poisonous creatures, wicked persons and erotic elements."[344] Only good-natured and humble persons and kind physicians are allowed to reside in it. About its architecture the author is enthusiastic: " The Kuṭī should contain a main room situated in the innermost place with specific dimension where the patient has to remain during the whole course of the treatment. It should be enclosed by two adjacent outer apartments having good and concealed ventilation and impenetrable to smoke, direct sunlight, dust etc. which will disturb the tranquility and purity of the atmosphere. The innermost room allotted to the patient should be very comfortable with all the amenities and equipment giving protection to the patient from the prevalent seasonal and climatic conditions. All kind (s) of medicine, accessories and attendants necessary for the treatment should have accommodation provided in the 'Kuṭī' so that the patient need not leave the place till the end of the treatment. The furnishings should also be pleasant to the patient."[345] Before admitted to the kuti for the rasayana treatment, a person should be prepared through panchakarma treatment, the renowned methods of extirpation and detoxication.[346] A large number of diets and drugs are recommended for rasayana according to their curative or preventive nature. But it is always a treatment of considerable length. The author gives an example of treatment with pippali medicine which can last between 19 and 38 days.[347]

P.R.Warrier thinks that a preventive treatment with rasayana, comprising complete relaxation of both mind and physique with strict regimen in the daily diet and routine, would be the only answer to the present day health problems. By this he even wants to prevent the "radiation menace" which is caused by the various types of nuclear experiments conducted in many places of the world. Another success would be the fight against the stress of our modern industrialized world.[348] Here the author certainly demands too much from a single means of prevention in Ayurveda, and his argumentation is conspicuously devoid of political analysis. Besides this, he does not argue consequently according to Ayurveda's principles which stress that the root of the case has to be eliminated in order to cure a person or to prevent health problems. The nuclear menace, for example, and the stress of modern life have their roots in a 'philosophy' of violence and a 'philosophy' of monetary power. To cure or to prevent their effects through kutis and rasayana available only for a few privileged would not help uprooting the roots. The author admits that the method "requires a reorientation to suit the modern trends of living" but fails to provide this reorientation. He dreams of the installation of some well-equipped kutis in various parts of the country "at appropriate centres blessed with picturesque scenery and salubrious climate free from the humdrum multicoloured bewildering stream of life."[349] The medicinal and psychological effects and virtues of rasayana cannot and shall not be belittled, but to build a string of kutis all over the country would involve large amounts of public funds which are not available because of the allopathic orientation of today's medical care and health education; that is why allopathic systems get the biggest share of the health allocation. It would involve people only who could afford this preventive treatment from the point of time and money, certainly a minority. It would also require a process of conscientization to accept this kind of prevention and health education; this is not an easy task and would demand the full cooperation of the public and the individual which seems hardly possible today among health functionaries and the common people.

In all we may conclude, that Ayurveda is structurally not integrated into the health care system of the country, particularly not in the alternative one though this is, at least, being discussed today.[350] This is not only the fault of the political hierarchy but also based on the reluctance of the responsible people who organize and administer Ayurveda to discuss critically Ayurveda's concepts of health care and health education; this critical thinking would then have to take into account the condition of today's Indian society and the goals of how to improve it if found necessary.[351]

2. Levels of Prevention and Strategies of Intervention

Self-identity and self-determination are surely not sufficient to establish a scientific base of health education. Each science needs a theoretical framework and methodology of research and practice. Though health education is one of the youngest branches of the science of education it has tried hard to have a theory and a methodology of its own. The theoretical framework of health education consists, besides its goals and objectives, mainly of the levels of prevention and the principles underlying its practical approaches. The research side is not dealt with here, whereas the other two fields are now being discussed while comparing them with the ideas of Ayurveda.

There is a unanimous agreement among health educationists that health education, as every other form of education, is troubled by two questions, a question of content and a question of style. What shall be imparted, acquired in which way and time? is the basic question of every kind of education. Health education has arrived at a scheme that may help answer this question. It is a three-tier scheme of prevention: primary, secondary and tertiary prevention. The agreement upon this scheme is almost world-wide and is, for example, accepted in countries like Switzerland and Germany, England, the U.S.A. and India.[352] Only a few decades ago, health education was "more illness education than health education".[353] But in the seventies,the emphasis shifted from disease to health after re-discovering that real prevention has to start before the outbreak of a disease. It became apparent that health promotion is prevention. In the Western industrialized countries, a number of areas were formulated which were regarded important for the maintenance of health. These areas were adequate nutrition, mental hygiene beginning at an early stage, adequate housing, moderate and well-balanced personal habits including personal hygiene, a useful and productive role in society, general education and education specifically for health, a safe and healthy working environment, recreation opportunities and facilities, a sense of personal security including access to health services and provision for income maintenance during disease.[354] Health educationists arrived at the conclusion that there were many homogenic diseases, diseases which are caused by man. They are normally caused by an upset of the balance of the ecosystem in which man lives and in which "he may inadvertently create conditions in which new diseases may increase".[355] General improvements in the standard of living and the eradication of poverty were recognized as important measures of prevention and major contributions to a decline of disease. The scope of prevention became a multipurpose one.

The present three-tier scheme of prevention can be explained by the example of prevention of schistosomiasis (also called bilharziose) where man becomes infected by the larval forms of one of the species of the worm schistosoma while bathing in infected water. The worm breeds in the infected person's veins and the eggs are excreted in both faeces and urine. Vectors of the first larval form are certain species of snails. The larval form leaves the snail after several weeks and is able to infect man once more.[356] This chain of causation can be broken and the disease,prevalent in many parts of Africa, can be prevented in a number of ways: (1) Faeces and urine can be disposed so that they will not contaminate water. (2) Land drainage can be improved so that the breeding grounds of the snail will be reduced. (3) Chemicals can be used to kill the snails. (4) Protective footwear and clothing can be provided for those exposed to contaminated water. (5) Separate uncontaminated water for drinking and washing can be supplied. (6) People at risk can be educated, and (7) all infected people can be treated.[357] The first three ways of prevention (disposal, drainage, chemicals) belong to primary prevention, the second pair of three (footwear, water,'risk education') belong to secondary prevention, and the last way is tertiary prevention (treatment).

What is meant by these levels? In short, the following definitions may be useful: *Primary prevention* attempts to prevent a disease or disorder from occurring. It has to be done before particular symptoms of a disease or disorder are to be found. *Secondary prevention* attempts to identify and treat at the earliest possible moment so as to reduce the length and severity of a disease. This prevention has be imparted when certain risk factors of a disease or disorder have been identified. *Tertiary prevention* attempts to reduce to a minimum the degree of handicap or impairment that results from a disease that has already occured. It has to be applied when a certain disease has been partially or fully treated.[358] Park and Park describe these levels in detail and conclude that primary prevention would consist of health promotion and specific protection, this phase would be identical with the period of pre-pathogenesis. Secondary prevention, to them, would be early diagnosis and treatment; and tertiary prevention would comprise disability limitation and rehabilitation. The second and the third levels were identical with the period of pathogenesis.[359] These three levels of prevention are now examined a bit closer.

Primary prevention is not directed at any particular disease but is intended to improve the general health and well-being of an individual and/or a community. Its first step, health promotion, aims at an ideal, a striving after perfection, Many practices fit into it such as adequate nutrition, provision of sanitary environment, provision of safe working conditions, personal hygiene, sex education, physical education, genetic counselling and the improvement of the standard of living of the people.[360] The second step of primary prevention is specific protection. The ideal of a disease-free community can hardly be achieved by health promotion. Therefore specific protection against dangers have to be introduced, for example immunizations, use of specific nutrients, protection against occupational hazards and accidents, protections against carcinogens, and avoidance of allergens.[361] Primary prevention in industrialized countries has accomplished great successes.

Smallpox and cholera are eradicated; typhoid, diphtheria, poliomyelitis and tuberculosis are considerably reduced. "A number of chronic diseases, particularly those associated with certain occupations, have been amenable to primary prevention - e.g. cancer of the lung among chromate workers, cancer of the scrotum among chimney sweeps."[362] 'Target group' of primary prevention is the healthy person. A wider understanding of primary prevention which gains more and more ground today is advocated, amongst others, by N.Kisnerman. To him a medical social worker should also conduct the following functions in primary prevention or first level of prophylaxis as he prefers to call it: "To provide information about citizens' rights and duties concerning health. To study the incidence of the socio-economic and cultural variables involved in the causes, distribution and development or health problems. (...) To participate in the study of the quality and quantity of the health services and measures. To inform and educate the community about the use of institutional measures which can help to secure a higher standard of living."[363] This understanding of primary prevention is much more structural and political than , for example, the one of Park and Park. It is widely hoped that this understanding which takes into account the socio-political nature of primary prevention will soon replace the medicine-oriented dominance in primary prevention.[364] For India especially, this seems to be an urgent necessity because primary prevention is the most important level of prevention.[365]

Secondary prevention is based on the knowledge that early detection of a disease is the cornerstone of prevention. Park and Park regard secondary prevention as "the domain of curative medicine."[366] Health educationists prefer to operate with risk factors and symptoms which are actually not a disease and therefore more prone to educational efforts and interventions. For instance, hypertension is regarded as a major risk factor for a potential heart disease. When 'treated' early and regularly through, e.g.,less intake of salt in one's diet or through regular physical exercises or through particular drugs, it may not lead to a heart attack or stroke. It is finally a matter of definition whether this kind of early detection and treatment is called prevention or medical treatment. Park and Park argue for curative medicine "because the disease has already commenced in the host: but in modern technology, treatment is also considered part of prevention."[367] Secondary prevention is important in respect of diseases like leprosy, tuberculosis, cancer, veneral diseases and cardio-vascular diseases. 'Target group' of secondary prevention is the person who is strongly endangered by a certain disease, whether the disease has already commenced or not; it is the person at risk who has to follow the regimens of secondary prevention. Secondary prevention can be criticised from the point that it invites people to find an arrangement with the existing system which eventually causes or supports their diseases. Secondary prevention may be successful within a short span of time but very often does not tackle the real problem underlying a disease. On the other hand, primary prevention would try to bring about structural and institutional changes if necessary. Or to put in this way, risk behaviour would often try to avoid conflicts in small groups of a society and would therefore be dangerous for health in the long run because suppressing of particular urges would start the chain of, in particular, psycho-somatic diseases.

The objective of tertiary prevention is to halt the disease process by instituting adequate treatment and thereby to limit the disability, prevent further complication and, if possible, postpone death.[368] Tertiary prevention is mainly part of rehabilitation. It helps restore functions (= medical rehabilitation), restore the capacity to earn a livelihood (= vocational rehabilitation). restore family and social relationships (= social rehabilitation), and restore personal confidence and dignity (= psychological rehabilitation).[369] Tertiary prevention adopts the measures and efforts of special experts after necessary medical treatment. It also helps reduce the dangers of relapsing into a disease again, "Target group' of tertiary prevention is the sick person.

These levels of prevention in modern health education fit well into the inherent understanding of health education in Ayurveda. Promotion of health in Ayurveda is supported by an increase of immunity and resistance. Ayurveda's focus is on primary prevention, more than ever envisaged in modern health education and medicine. We know that traditional societies did not need a concept of specialized prevention since they were not so much individualized and constituted homogenous groups. But it is difficult to attain complete health in Ayurveda. It is the interwoven knowledge of the disease process as well as the factors of variation which make an identification of clear steps practically impossible.[370] The steps of pathogenesis in Ayurveda are six in number. It is important for prevention and health education to break or check the spread of vitiated doshas from the beginning, or before the disease manifests itself. Once the disease is established it has to be cured, or relief has to be obtained before it becomes chronic or complications start. If the disease has become chronic, then Ayurveda works for the limitation of disability or for rehabilitation, similar to modern medicine in structure.[371] C.P. Shukla has explained the similarity of Ayurveda prevention with the modern three-tier model of prevention in a table which is reproduced below in slightly different from[372]:

	Ayurveda		Modern medicine
1.	sanchya	pre-pathogenesis	promotion of health
2.	prakopa/prasara	early pathogenesis	specific protection
3.	stanasamsraya	demonstrable early disease	early diagnosis and prompt treatment
4.	vyakti	advanced manifest disease	specific treatment
5.	bheda	chonicity	limitation of disability and rehabilitation
6.		convalescence	rehabilitation and rejuvenation

According to this model, 1 and 2 of the table are equal to primary prevention, 3 and 4 to secondary prevention and 5 and 6 to tertiary prevention. Step 2 may be eventually regarded as secondary prevention as well. But Ayurveda is extremely diversified. It attempts to take into account the slightest variations in spiritual, mental, physical and social life since the concept of health in Ayurveda is covering all the four components of a living organism, viz. body, senses, mind and spirit, as well as his environment and social group.[373] This diversification applies to cure and prevention. These variations are not easy to grasp, if at all, and therefore make an organized health education programme almost impossible. This is evident form the list of variations below. While commenting on the subtleness of the factors determining the result of treatment, based on Cakrapani Datta, the following variations are given in the Caraka Samhita[374]:

Variations relating to doshas: "The quantity of doṣas may either get diminished or aggravated or may remain in equilibrium. The doṣa may vary according to their upward, downward or sideward movement or according to their location in the periferal, central or middle path. Doṣas may also vary as they are aggravated in their place of origin (svadeśa) or elsewhere (paradeśa) or as their aggravation primary (svatantra) or secondary (paratantra). The aggravation of a doṣa might vary in terms of its particular aspects.

For example, aggravation of vāta might sometime be mainly related to the aggravation of coldness, lightness, etc. Doṣas might also vary according as they vitiate different dhātus. Similarly these doṣas might vary according to season, constitution of the patient and dhātus affected."

Variations relating to drugs: "The drug may vary in its effect as it is young, old, green, dry, combined with some other drugs and different forms of preparation. They also vary as they are effective for the doṣas of the body by virtue of their rasa (taste), vīrya(potency), vipāka and prābhava (specific action)."

Variations relating to place: "Places vary as they are marshy, arid, ordinary or most suitable."

Variations relating to time: "Time may vary according to the change of seasons or as it is forenoon, noon, afternoon, etc., or according to the periodicity of the diseases like the duration of fever for eight days etc."

Variations relating to strength :"The strength of the patient may vary as it is inherent, acquired or affected by time (season, age, etc.). It might also vary as it is superior, mediocre or inferior."

Variations relating to the body: "The body may be fatty, compact or porous. It may also be differentiated according to the vital organs, eye, etc. which are to be protected very carefully."

Variations relating to diet: "It may vary according to its nature, method of preparation, combination, quantity, etc."

Variations relating to wholesomeness: "It may vary depending upon the locality, time (age and season), disease, constitution, nature and habits."

Variations relating to mind: "It may vary as it is associated with fear, grief, sorrow, happiness, etc."

Variations relating to constitution: "There are variations in bodily constitution as it is initiated by vāta, etc."

Variations relating to agni: "There may be variations in the individual according to his age, viz. child, youth, old and their different stages."

Another example confirming this extreme diversification is this of rain water as described in the Caraka Samhita's chapter on the properties of diets and drinks[375]; here are only examples on the nature and kinds of rainwater: "While falling and also after fall from the sky, the properties of water vary depending upon the time and space.(...) While falling from the sky water comes in contact with the moon, the air and the sun - all ordained by the time. Similarly, after its fall on the earth, it gets in touch with the proximal properties of the earth, like cold, heat, unctuousness, ununctuousness etc. (...) By nature rain water has...qualities, viz. coldness, purity, benevolence, pleasantness and clearness.(..) After it has fallen down on the earth, its properties are determined by the place of its fall . If it falls on the earth of white colour, it becomes astringent in taste, on yellowish white earth it is bitter; on brown earth it is alkaline, on saline soil it is of saline taste; on the mountain valley it is pungent in taste and on the black soil it is sweet in taste. These are the six properties of rain water after it has fallen on the ground. Tastes are not manifested in the rain water, hailstone or snow water.(...) The water which is slightly astringent and sweet in taste, exceedingly thin, non-slime, light, soft and non-greasy is best to be taken. "After that the quality of rain water during the different seasons is described. Later it is concluded that water collected from untimely rains is undoubtedly unwholesome. This attitude towards a basic sustainer of life, water, is far more sophisticated than today's towards potable water which is only divided into clean and unclean, safe or unsafe.

From these two examples, variations and water, we can see how difficult is is to develop a design of practical health education on the lines of the pure Ayurveda. But shall we really aim at this pure health education? When taking into account the water problem in India alone and thinking of the majority of people having no access to potable water, then it would be a luxury to follow Ayurveda's advice. Ayurveda's classification of water and the suggestion how to use it are then too much of an ideal for our time. This ideal cannot be achieved, But the examples make it abundantly clear that there is an overall predominance of primary prevention in Ayurveda. That is why prevention in Ayurveda may be called 'holistic prevention'. What is true for primary prevention is also valid for the other levels of prevention. This is shown in the case of the examination of a patient. Such an early and thorough examination as described below would surely detect symptoms early enough. But we have to add the inevitable: Where and when in present-day India could such a system be widely practised? The patient shall be examined "with reference to his prakṛti (physical constitution),vikṛti (morbidity), sāra (excellence of dhātus...), saṃhanana (compactness of organs), prāmaṇa (measurement of the organs of the body), sātmya (homologation), sattva (psychic conditions), shāraśkti (power of intake and digestion of food), vyāyāmśakti (power of performing exercise) and vayas (age) in order to ascertain his strength and the intensity of the malady."[376]

Apart from the levels of prevention, the strategies of intervention in modern health education are important. There are two basic strategies used. (1) *Communicative interventions* which in their widest sense mainly aim at promoting a healthy psycho-social life. Communication covers promotion of interpersonal relationships and/or interventions which may lead to reduce disorders in a whole community. In practising health education there is often no clear distinction between information and communication in the instructional process. The significant difference is that communication is more two-way oriented than information and by this tries to include the learner in the process of his own education . (2). *Structural interventions* contribute to an effective infrastructure of preventive measures, i.e., the provision of sufficient facilities and respective laws.[377] The corresponding methods to these interventions are either individual, group or mass media work.[378] A balanced combination of these methods is believed to be the most promising way in health education on a practical level. In order to specify some of the aims in the field of communaicative intervention we may refer here to the theory focussing on values clarification which shall help people develop skills in fours areas: the cognitive (thinking), the affective (feeling), the active (behaviour) and the interpersonal (communication).[379]

Cognitive skills are, amongst others:

choosing freely,
choosing from among alternatives,
choosing with an awareness of the consequences of one's choices,
being aware of patterns in one's life,
thinking critically, i.e., analysing, synthesizing, drawing inferences, and
ideating, i.e., the ability to generate ideas and alternatives.[380]

Affective skills are, for example :

identifying and acknowledging feeling as one source in making decisions,
legitimizing one's intuition as another possible source in making decisions, and
focussing on what one prizes and cherishes.[381]

Active skills are, for instance:

acting on one's choice,

goal setting, and

culling out the inconsistencies between what one would like to do and what one is likely to do.[382]

Interpersonal skills are, amongst others:

publicly affirming one's choices where appropriate,

sending 'I' messages,

empathic listening, resolving conflict situations,

asking clarifying questions,

community building , and

validating, i.e. , focussing on the positive in self and others.[383]

This list of skills indicates that prevention as the core of health education is a normative process. It is future-oriented because decisions have to be taken on a day to day basis. Consequently, prevention is always a selection because demands can only be partly fulfilled at any time, and is therefore implicit 'repressive' for not all the possibilities can be realized.

There is nothing in Ayurveda which can match the systemacy of the strategies in modern health education. Such comprehensiveness and interrelationship of strategies and their corresponding methods were, however, not necessary at the time when Ayurveda was postulated and developed. Communities and individuals had their established roles and places in societies and there was less imbalance since subjects and societies did not change their relationships rapidly. There was no insecurity in values either because values were provided by religions and imparted by religious and worldly authorities in a fixed manner. The individual was not invited to participate in the decision-making process on a larger scale. This picture changes when we regard certain fundamentals of the teaching and learning process. Here Ayurveda shows a remarkable resemblance to modern pedagogy (or vice versa) as the discussion of the fundamentals, which have been given in the preceding chapter, will show.

The first fundamental-*Know the culture of the people*-is fully covered by Ayurveda ideas. Ayurveda can only be implemented successfully when the culture of a person is known in its widest sense, the place where he lives, the physical and psychological nature of the person, etc. Ayurveda is wholly culture-oriented, and it can be assumed that Ayurveda physicians advised their patients by what is today called "Health Education by Appropriate Analogy", i.e., "Using the Familiar to Explain the New ".[384]

The second principle-*Start from where the people are*-is also fully met by Ayurveda ideas. The individual is the decisive factor. The norm of health and disease is first set by the individual and not by the community. The prakriti of a person decides,amongst other things, on the specific means for the maintenance of health. How deep Ayurveda demands people to go in order to realize this fundamental is clear from its differentiating between the physical constitutions and the types of mind[385]: "Mental faculty is of three types - sāttvika, rājasa and tāmasa. The sāttvika one is free from defects as it is endowed with auspiciousness. The rājas type is defective because it promotes wrathful disposition. The tāmasa one is similarly defective because it suffers form ignorance. (...) Each of the three types of mental faculty is in fact of innumerable variety by permutation and combination of various factors relating to the body, species and mutual interactions. Sometimes even the body follows the mind and vice versa."[386]

The third, fourth and fifth fundamentals-*Give people learning experience/Motivate by linking the required behaviour with goals of groups and individuals/Suggest specific behavioural changes which can be easily carried out*- are also applied by Ayurveda. The example of giving up addictions step by step hosts all the three of them: "A wise person should give up by and by unwholesome practice of which he is addicted and he should correspondingly adopt ones which are wholesome. The schedule for the same is given below .(...) On the first day one should give up a quarter of the unwholesome practice (still maintaining 3/4 of it) and correspondingly adopt a quarter of wholesome. On the second day half of the unwholesome practice is to be given up and half of the wholesome one is to be adopted; this is be continued for the third day also. On the fourth day, 3/4 of the unwholesome practice is to be given up and 3/4 of the wholesome one is to be adopted. This process is to be continued on the 5th and 6th day also. The process of giving up of the unwholesome practice is completed fully on the 7th day."[387]

The sixth salient feature-*Meet felt needs first*- was believed to be known to Ayurveda physicians when they practised their prime duty of prevention. Though a limitation has to be passed on for the knowledge of life which was available to the physician was much more comprehensive than this one of a non-physician. That is why an Ayurveda physician was able to recognize premonitory symptoms much earlier in a common man than this man himself.

Preventive recommendations of a more sophisticated nature may thus have been prescribed; they probably focussed on the potential disease about which the 'patient' was not at all aware. Hence, the physician met needs first which were not always felt by the people first.

The seventh fundamental-*Select a variety of learning ways-* was not systematically covered by Ayurveda practices. Health education in Ayurveda was not promoted as an organized teaching and learning process but was, instead, an in-built value, hardly questioned by the people. Various methods of teaching and learning were not found wanted. Probably the Ayurveda physician thought it fit to follow the general norm for 'students',i.e., learners in ancient India, viz. that a 'student' learnt only one-fourth from his teacher and the other three-fourths in equal portions by himself, from his fellow students and by experience in later life.[388] Moreover, the physician could feel rest assured that the 'patient' would try his level best to learn because he certainly knew that health (swasthavritta) stressed equally swa ("individual self, i.e., a particular being in its natural state"), stha ("maintenance or stabilization") and vritta ("course of action or observance of particular procedures by the individual").[389]

In all, there is, despite variations and limitations, obviously a high degree of similarity between the fundamentals of teaching and learning in modern health education and Ayurveda's design of practical prevention. Ayurveda not only fully shares the three-tier system of the levels of prevention with modern health education, but also some fundamentals of modern pedagogy: knowing the culture of the people, starting from where the people are, giving people learning experiences, motivating through concrete goals, and suggesting specific behaviour changes. The main difference between modern health education and Ayurveda prevention lies in their stages of organization. Modern health education is a highly structured process suited to the needs of a modern industrialized and fragmented society. Health education ideas and procedures in Ayurveda are part of a fixed Science of Life which does not resort to special theories to impart health knowledge since everybody was asked to follow the rules and regimens for his own sake; a corrective or an additional 'programme' was therefore not deemed necessary. These rules and regimens were aimed at preventing the causation of diseases. This provided the most promising opportunity for prevention and health education. The causes of the diseases were understood either as wrong utilization, non-utilization or excessive utilization of time, mental faculties and objects of sense organs. The reason for false utilizations was adharma, i.e., not following one's own spiritual and social existence. "The source of adharma is Prajnaparadha (intellectual error) which is unrighteous conduct due to error of Prajna (thinking, restraint and recollection).[390] And vice versa, diseases are "destroyed by dharma", and this good conduct would act as rasayana.[391] By time, the three seasons (winter, summer, rainy season) were meant. "The objects of sense organs are sound, touch, vision, taste and smell as well as their accessories like matter (dravya), quality (guṇa) and action (karman) which are utilised through the sense organs". The commentary then distinguishes the three as to their order of importance: "Time is the most important factor inasmuch as it is indispensable in character. Then come the mental faculties that lead to the defects in the objects... Thus, even though, the abuses of the objects of sense organs arise out of the defective mental faculties, still owing its proximity to the psychosomatic diseases, the former is categorised separately. The abuse of mental faculties on the other hand leads to the somatic, oral and psychic ailments."[392] This description is an indication again that Ayurveda has always tried to uproot the roots, an idea which gets more and more popular in modern health education.

3. Ayurveda and Lifelong Education

We may now assert that, though in spite of differences, modern health education and educational ideas and procedures in Ayurveda are built on self-identity and self-determination, the there levels of prevention namely primary, secondary and tertiary, and an individualized type of non-formal teaching and learning.

We have said earlier that health education in Ayurveda was not organized. This is true when we understand organization as a process which is planned, conducted and evaluated by an outside agency. Ayurveda neither contains a *curriculum* of health knowledge, nor does it maintain particular *institutions* imparting knowledge about how to maintain one's health.[393] Health education in Ayurveda was never of an institutionalized type. But this is not the same as non-organized as becomes clear when we consider some of the organizational structures of Ayurveda in relation to health education. They centre around the terms responsibility, self-education and lifelong education.

We have earlier concluded that responsibility in Indian (Hindu) life was very much existent, at least for oneself as the nucleus and starting point for more society-oriented responsibilities and activities. Ayurveda is a typical example for this kind of responsibility. The simile on personal vigilance cited above illustrates this. According to our hypothesis of congruence between content and form, responsibility for one's own health consequently embraces only one's own responsibility. To Ayurveda, congruence between content and form, that is health = content and responsibility = form, can only be achieved in oneself. Hardly any other person can help in this process. It is the individual who has to control his health, though others may have provided the rules for this, but they are authorities who are not questioned and whose work is over. The individual has now to look after his health and happiness, he himself is completely responsible for his behaviour and the practice of positive health. He is, of course, supported by the physician who knows the connections between right behaviour and health better than others, and who can advise whenever needed. But the decision whether to practise the transformation of the rules and regimens into his life is nevertheless left with the individual. The 'teaching' of the physician is only on the occasion when he is consulted. His 'teaching' is functional at a particular hour and not intentional over a stretch of time. Thus, a modern statement that health education was the basis of health services[394] could be accepted by Ayurveda but without its implication to a self-contained aspect of institutionalization.

In adult education, there are four basic forms of relationship between teacher and learner are distinguished[395]: (1) the "relationship of patronage" which gives full authority to the teacher and regards the adult learner as an immature; (2) the "relationship of mission" which tends to accept a learner only when he accepts the only truth which is available with the teacher; (3) the "relationship of subject competence" which gives the teacher only an authority for a certain topic or subject; and (4) the "relationship of partners" which aims at sharing knowledge among equals. The last two forms are regarded, in Western countries, as the most adequate for health education of adults. Ayurveda tends to cover the first two forms, instead. But the total superiority of the Ayurveda physician as a 'teacher' is neutralized by the deep-rooted responsibility of the'patient' or learner for himself, and of the physician for himself. A teacher (physician) can only become a good teacher when he himself follows the path of rules and regimens perfectly. This has saved health education in Ayurveda from becoming a total process of instruction with one technical source of knowledge (teacher) on the one side and an 'ignorant' learner on the other. Educational activities were strictly understood as means to an end guided by the capacity of self-determination, i.e., the capacity to set goals for oneself and act accordingly. This was supported by the pre-occupation of the physician with himself.

Modern health education is organized on five levels: family, education (school) system, mass media, adult education and health services. There, and through these institutions, health education takes place. Ayurveda knew only the family as an agency of health education besides the occasional advice of the physician. That is why in the ultimate analysis we cannot say that the ancient Indian concept of medicine covered all that what modern health education wants, namely to help people help themselves in achieving health.[396] Though we have to admit that the 'family approach' in adult education in so-called developing countries may become more important in future; no other than G.Myrdal has advocated it strongly and has called for entirely fresh approaches: "The whole pattern, transmitted from the urbanized countries in the West, of segregating children in schools and then perhaps having 'classes' for adults should be questioned. It is quite possible that a program of teaching families or whole communities together would be more effective."[397] But as far as we know Ayurveda did not provide a creative educational environment which is characterized by participating in decision making (not only for oneself), by granting freedom of expression and availability of information, and by endowing mutual responsibility in defining goals, planning, identifying activities and evaluating.[398] Ayurveda as an authority-based way of life and learning was never in the position to structure health communication on those lines. It never identified steps for an effective teaching-learning situation of which we know, today, six in number:[399] (1) "helping the learners discover their needs in a given situation" (diagnostic function), (2) "discovering the present level of development and what is needed to improve the situation" (planning function), (3) "assisting the participants to set their own learning goals" (motivation function), (4) giving the identified goals and determining what techniques will function best (function of selecting appropriate techniques), (5) giving the available resources and assigning specific responsibilities (function of selecting appropriate resources), and (6) evaluating "what has been learned and what are the future needs and interests of the learners" (function of re-diagnosis). Thus, efforts in Ayurveda which may be described as rudimentary forms of health education are less *help* but *aids* and *rules*. Help allows the individual to go his own way and to consult a person or institution whenever necessary, but rules and aids do not allow this; they have to be complied with, otherwise the balance of a system will be disturbed. At this point, the value of responsibility in Ayurveda suffers a severe setback compared with modern health education. Ayurveda's understanding of responsibility is narrower since its frame, the system, is narrower. This is, however, not unusual. Prevention and health education practices are social practices, and we have to regard them historically as they always change their social functions.

Ayurveda's rules and aids are notwithstanding the stimuli for *self-education*, i.e., "the requirement to form oneself, within the framework of the *possible*".[400] The very concept of self-education points out that there is no *one* true pedagogy for all. There is no one real elixir of pedagogic life either, hence there is no one true health education. Health education as to Ayurveda philosophy has to be chiefly self-education. This too explains to a certain extent why there is no infrastructure of health education in Ayurveda, it would be sheer impossible to organize it for each and everyone. It was not only Ayurveda's philosophy, however, which prevented an infrastructure of health education but also India's "small zone communication networks with people sharing similarities in language, religion, kinship and ethnicity", with each zone evolving its own media and strategies of communication.[401] Again, organization of the small zones would have been a nearly impossible task for one educational function. Instead, in a traditional society, people reproduced and transmitted culture as a personal matter and "they had to spend much more attention and effort personally ensuring that the details of form were correctly maintained. This meant naturally that relatively few forms could be kept available, and those forms that were available had to be maintained and used more intensively then we are accustomed today."[402] Health behaviour or health form accompanied a person throughout his life, it was maintained in a lifelong process. That is why it is justified to speak of Ayurveda health education practices as lifelong education. This we find also as a popular idea in modern health education. The Ayurveda physician was asked to look after his own lifelong health promotion and an increase in his professional knowledge. He was obliged to continuing education as the fourteenth rule for a disciple reads: "You should always make efforts for the upliftment of your knowledge and adoption of such methods as would give you good health."[403] Ordinary people were urged to look after their health at any time, not only when they feel ill but, more important, when they feel well and healthy, and that throughout their life.

It seems that this inherent health education practised in Ayurveda was a classical example of today's concept of lifelong education. This may become more obvious when considering the present understanding of lifelong education in the words of one of the foremost thinkers in this field today.[404] To P. Lengrand, the concept of lifelong education is a circular one. There can only be lifelong education worth its name if people receive a fair and rational education in childhood.[405] (This was, at the time of Ayurveda, certainly restricted to a (Brahmin) minority.) Adult education and lifelong education are distinguished by the author (adult education is the "locomotive"[406] seen in the context of lifelong education), but both are "education in freedom, for freedom and by freedom".[407] The author means by lifelong education "a series of very specific ideas, experiments and achievements, in other words, education in the full sense of the word, including all its aspects and dimensions, its uninterrupted development from the first movement of life to the very last and the close, organic relationship between the various points and successive phases in its development."[408] Lifelong education, to Lengrand, is needed because of the challenges modern man face, such as the acceleration of change, demographic expansion, evolution of scientific knowledge and technology, political challenge, information, leisure, crisis in patterns of life and relationships, the body awareness, and the crisis in ideologies.[409] In contrast to this, the (well-developed) educational system of the past was far removed from the problems of everyday life: "Everyday life had a pattern and a rhythm of its own, and with agriculture as the main occupation of the people, the pattern of life was set largely by the nature cycle. The concerns of education were almost entirely divorced from these mundane affairs of everyday life. They were related to the sublime and the spiritual. In any case education was meant only for the elite groups in society who, by their social and economic standing, were protected from the routines and realities of the work-a-day world."[410] P.Lengrand regards the current responsibilities of education as (1) "the setting into place of structures and methods that will assist a human being throughout his life span to maintain the continuity of his apprenticeship and training", and (2) "to equip each individual to become in the highest and truest degree both the object and the instrument of his own development through the many forms of self-education."[411] Despite the necessity of conveying knowledge, the essential part of education 'is a change in the human being who in a sense becomes the content of his own education."[412] Therefore, self-education would be the main object of training. Such a lifelong education would be "only morally defensible as a voluntary undertaking" and the "only satisfactory upbringing", argues J.White.[413] Lengrand opines that life with its needs, conditions, rhythms and expressions should be regarded as the supreme guide in all the educational ventures, and that the accent of education should be placed on the individual human being respecting the importance of difference because no two things were identical.[414]

Ayurveda's concept of prevention and in-built ideas about health education have much in common with these last reflections of Lengrand. They are pleas for personal freedom, personal self-expression and overall development (in the given framework) as well as a warning against too much of istitutionalization and organization. Ayurveda's abstinence from building institutions may be criticised and regarded with much scepsis in a time of steady and rapid change, but it also provides a chance to avoid mistakes which modern health education (whose results are not at all impressive) has often made. Doubts about ready-made solutions by present-day technologists, even in some of the humanities, have to be raised. We are very quick in assuming that we know what people ought to want. But: "Do you spend money on creating facilities that people do not want and probably will not use, just so that you can educate people slowly to begin to use tnem? Alternatively, can you educate in the absence of facilities, until you have created a consumer demand? Much the same situation arises over the sanitary disposal over excreta. Do you build latrines and hope to educate people to use them, or do you educate people first to demand them?"[415] Many of these chicken-and-egg situations are common in health education. They deserve a careful analysis before obtruded to people. In spite of this, we may conclude that many aspects of Ayurveda's ideas towards health education are timely, actual and necessary, above all self-identity, self-determination, individualized non-formal teaching and learning, self-education and lifelong education.

Chapter 4

Ayurveda Health Education and People's Education

1. Ayurveda Health Education

In the forgoing analysis, I have attempted to work out the components of the concept of prevention in Ayurveda, whereas in this chapter I shall try to interpret this analysis and use this interpretation for a speculative reconstruction of a theory of Ayurveda Health Education. It is one of the central conjectures proposed in this study that the hypothesis of congruence between content and forms in Ayurveda can help arrive at conclusions for this theory. The leading question for these conclusions is: Can Ayurveda's concept of prevention and its ideas of health education be utilized for the benefit of the present health (education) problems in India? I hope to end up with a set of ideas which support the role Ayurveda Health Education could possibly play in the present health system.

The *first conclusion* is that Ayurveda Health Education can be defined though there is, in fact, no practical health education available in India which is patterned on the ideas and experiences of Ayurveda. Thus, Ayurveda Health Education is a theoretical construct. But is there any use in a theoretical construct without the possibility of verification or falsification through practice? It is my belief that we have to learn not only to dismantle but also to reconstruct; we have to learn not only to analyse, that means to break down material into its constituent parts and to detect relationships of the parts and of the way they are organized, but also to synthesize, that means to put parts or elements together in order to form a coherent whole. This is often wishful thinking and ends up too often in vague assumptions. Despite this limitation, from which this inquiry is not free either, I think it can be important to contribute to the reconstruction of one field of Indian education, simply to produce new ideas which then can be used for a clearer picture of the discipline we are dealing with. Reconstruction does not imply uncritical examination, and it is not resting on the belief that all what is old is good. On the other hand, we should not try to pass judgement either on achievements and attainments of our time without examining them.

Ayurveda Health Education is not only not found in practice, but has so far not attracted more than a handful of people to think about it either, which is not surprising when taking into account that such a discipline does virtually not exist on theoretical and practical levels.[416] Ayurveda Health Education is only a concept consisting of principles which may be able to establish a corresponding subject area one day. Another weakness has also to be mentioned. The present practice of Ayurveda in the country does not help much in arriving at a corresponding discipline. In practice, we find that except some institutions "the practitioners of the indigenous systems of medicine...have gone commercial".[417] But not only that, Ayurveda today is not at all the all-pervading and all-embracing medical science, let alone a Science of Life, which would be able to comprise all the existing medical treatments. It has been reduced to a medicine of more or less successful herbal cures. That is why we have solely to rely on the traditional and classical ideas, a substantial limitation when linking Ayurveda Health Education to modern conditions. Hence, we cannot refer to data or sources which would document actions after the ideas.[418]

Ayurveda Health Education is first determined by interdisciplinarity, integration and life-orientation of its basic science Ayurveda. In it, health is considered to be a vehicle, a carrier to achieve other, more comprehensive goals, viz. happiness, usefulness and, later, self-realization by liberation and emancipation. Ayurveda Health Education is consequently not disease-oriented but health-oriented, it is not only patient-oriented but oriented to the healthy human being. It not only aims at health but also at a happy and useful life. Such a health education cannot simply be divided into subjects but stipulates educational, social, psychological, philosophical, religious, medical and biological perspectives to meet the needs of a healthy and happy life.

The centre of Ayurveda Health Education is its concept of prevention. This is designated by a complete congruence between content and form which means that Ayurveda Health Education is the equilibrium while aiming at the equilibrium. It is an equilibrium of biological, spiritual, ecological, social, economic and political elements. This comprehensiveness is, at the same time, the flexibility to realize the universal preventive utility of matter. Through this, Ayurveda Health Education would become, indeed, universal health education which would be health education not bound to a certain country, time, populace, etc. but which would have a universal insight into health and life. Assigned to this understanding of prevention are the following fundamentals: responsibility for one's own health, strengthening of positive factors in health achievements and life, self-control, and the striving for an ideal personality which is characterised by health, wealth and self-realization. Ayurveda Health Education, through these ideas and principles, is an individualized health education with an openness to one's own environment and community. It will strive for a healthy and happy life of the whole community from which every individual would benefit. By this, Ayurveda Health Education would also lay emphasis on creating opportunities for every human being to realize his self-identity and self-determination and would concede full participation of the individual in decisions and programmes of health promotion. Ayurveda Health Education consists of three levels of prevention, primary, secondary and tertiary. They would cover every possible variation in tissue elements, locations, time, food, relations, etc. There would be a clear predominance of primary prevention for Ayurveda Health Education aims at the maintenance of health first, and at the removal of obstacles (=risk factors or pre-monitory symptoms) second. The ideal of Ayurveda Health Education would be a complete state of primary prevention, that is an all-around healthy life. This would be implemented by three chief means of prevention, diet, sleep and regimens for daily conduct and self- control.[419] Moreover, it would contain effective means for secondary prevention like, above all, panchakarma and rasayana. Besides these, it would be open to change regimens and treatments according to the needs of a person. Ayurveda Health Education would be directed by teaching and learning which can best be described as an idiividualized lifelong non-formal process. The learning would take place according to the ability and exprience of a person, he would be stimulated to seek for his own self-education throughout his life.

Out of these characteristics, a tentative definition of Ayurveda Health Education can be given: It is an interdisciplinary preventive science aiming at a healthy, happy and useful life (= content) while being a 'healthy', 'happy' and 'useful' science (= form). It is built on an awareness of self-responsibility, self-identity and self-determination of the human being. By that it invites participation in health affairs of a community. It prefers primary prevention through balanced diet, sleep and regimens as its chief means. It is self-education and stimulates further self-education throughout the life of a human being.

2. Community Health Education

The *second conclusion* is that Ayurveda Health Education should become community health education. The problem will be of how to make use of Ayurveda Health Education in order to change the dismal situation of health in India. Though the health situation has been analysed earlier, some of the salient underlying issues of the economic situation have to be recalled in order to be close to reality.

Poverty is the principal cause of many a disease in India. It is the main determinant of the health and disease pattern, "rather than a warm climate."[420] Poverty is regarded as the "single largest cause of ill-health" in India."[421] Social injustice is "probably the main reason that poverty continues to exist."[422] The Indian society is described as a dual society of a few rich and many poor people. Modern medicine with its dependency on high technology would support this dual society and sustain the elite, its technology would not be neutral.[423] In 1977-78, 48.13 per cent of India's total population were regarded as below the poverty line; 50.83 per cent in rural areas and 38.19 per cent in urban areas.[424] These estimates were derived by using the all-india poverty line of Rs 65 per capita per month of consumption expenditure at 1977-78 prices. This corresponded to a daily calorie requirement of 2.000 per person in rural areas. Rs 75 per month were taken in urban areas corresponding to a daily requirement of 2.100 calories.[425] Later, in the Sixth Plan Period (1980-85), the poverty ratio based on new estimations for requirements (namely a calorie intake which is equivalent to Rs 6.400 per year per household or about Rs 100 per person per months) had declined to 37.4 per cent in 1983-84. During the Seventh Plan (1985-1990), the Planning Commission envisaged a target of 25.8 per cent.[426] Even if we considered this to be achieved (what nobody at the time of writing can say for sure), there would be above 200 million people in the country living in distress and misery.[427] The per capita annual earnings of factory workers 1978 and 1982 provide a more precise (though in terms of actual figures outdated) picture. They ranged from a low of Rs 2.999 (1978) and Rs 4.568 (1982) respectively for workers in wood factories via a medium of Rs 5,606 (1978) and Rs 6.726 (1982) for workers in rubber, plastics, petroleum and coal product factories to a high of Rs 6.922 (1978) for workers in basic metals and alloys factories and Rs 9.193 (1982) for workers in electricity factories respectively.[428] The number of unemployed persons in India is only vaguely known because there is no proper registration. But the known figures are appalling enough. In 1980, there were 16.2 million applicants on the live registers of 567 employment exchanges.[429] This figure had risen to 30.25 million on 755 registers in 1987.[430] The magnitude of the problem becomes more evident when we also think of those millions of people who are, particularly in agriculture, chronically underemployed for which the Planning Commission has used the term and measurement of "person-day unemployment".[431] It is discussed that the figure of the registerants at the exchanges is to be taken twice to three times in order to know the actual number of unemployed and underemployed.[432] This would have meant for the end of 1987 60-90 million people. One of the strong critics of the Indian governments' employment policies argues that in this context politicians not really wanted these people to join the mainstream because a "poor man on a subsidy or charity is a sure vote (for) whosoever he thinks is feeding him."[433] Unemployment as one of the symptoms of poverty poses a tremendous personal and national problem. There is no quick solution, and it will not be solved by simply stamping up investment and the overall growth rate of national income. To cope with it effectively, first, the basic structural processes at work in economy and society have to be analysed. May be the conclusion is as it is often supposed today: "Only to a very limited extent are unemployment and poverty the result of individual causes such as lack of skills or wrong value systems. They are basically a social phenomenon and have to be dealt with in social terms."[434] J.Dubashi, on the other hand, also remarks that today too much of focussing is "on the poverty syndrome", people would lay too much of emphasis on poverty (alleviation) while forgetting modernization; only modernization would offer a chance for growth and, later, for more equally distributed wealth. He criticizes Indian planners who had never explained what they would mean by self-sufficiency, and unless this question had been answered the country would continue to be mired in poverty.[435]

Again, on the other hand, the example of Kerala is well-known. It is called the "social conscience" of India[436] where one finds better sanitation "though Kerala does not spend more on public health than many other states do, but what it spends is more evenly distributed".[437] Better health has set the traditional chain of demographic transition in motion by increasing life expectancy (64 years in Kerala against an all-India figure of 51 years in 1978), by declining the death rate (7/1000 against 14.1/1000), by declining the infant mortality rate (54/1000 against 132/1000), and by declining the birth rate (24.5/1000 against 31/1000)[438], let alone the famous general literacy rate of 70.4 per cent as to the 1981 census. All this amounts to a "Physical Quality Life Index" (PQLI), which is regarded (by the U.S. Overseas Development Council) as a new indicator of the level of progress achieved by any country in meeting basic human needs, of 68 for Kerala (minimum of the PQLI is o, maximum is 100). This is somewhat surprising because Kerala's average per capita GNP 1970-75 was only US Dollar 110 compared to the all-India figure of 133 and a PQLI of only 41, or compared to Iran's US Dollar 1.260 and a PQLI of 52.[439] Like many other authors, A.Pacey attributes Kerala's astonishing advancement in health, even in the absence of much economic development, to its universal primary education (the enrollment on primary level is near to 100 per cent) and its adult literacy in which it is leading in India. He states that the acquisition of literacy "sometimes makes people more innovative and more self-aware."[440]

These and many other contradictions are well known in the functioning of the Indian societies and economies. It was Amartya Sen who has recently pointed them out again. To him, this dichotomy of strengths and weaknesses is the crucial point in assessing how India is doing: "It is doing quite well in many specific respects - for instance, in breaking the pre-independence stagnation and achieving a respectable growth of income per person, in guaranteeing mainly traditional liberties, in developing science and technology and higher education, in putting more dynamism into agriculture, in meeting... the world recession". But he also maintains that the basic weakness of India, the persistent inequity, has not been conquered so far. The elitist character of the Indian society would "permit endemic malnutrition and hunger that is not acute, so long as these happen quietly; it does not permit a famine both because it would be too acute and because it cannot happen quietly. It permits the injustice of keeping a large majority of the people illiterate while the elite enjoys the benefits of the vast system of higher education. It tolerates the continuing disadvantages of those who formerly suffered from explicit discrimination even though such discrimination is now made illegal, and even though 'positive discrimination' promotes a small number from the bottom stratum to positions of power and influence as new recruits of the elite. The election, the newspapers, and the political liberties work powerfully against dramatic deprivation and new sufferings, but easily allow the quiet continuation of an astonishing set of persistent injustices."[441]

Here,we should now turn back to one of our fundamental questions, viz. whether Ayurveda could really be an alternative system of medicine and a relief for the health problems connected with poverty and social injustice of the Indian society. Ayurveda is sometimes glorified as the saviour of the poor.[442] This view does not take into account properly that an alternative to the elite-oriented Allopathy should be able to tackle the health problems of millions of underprivileged people. Today we generally distinguish three forms of medical systems, the modern (allopathic) medicine which in a country like India is often elite-oriented and costly, then the traditional or original or classical systems like Ayurveda or Siddha which are hardly less costly today and which are often reduced to some forms of standard aids, and lastly the socially-oriented 'basic medicine' which consciously tries to work on grass-root level. This basic medicine should work from within the society, and it is supposed to integrate modern medicine with indigenous systems. This is C.R.Bijoy's theoretical claim also for Ayurveda in order to develop towards social health. But, he concludes, Ayurveda today would not represent such a form of community medicine.[443] This view is shared by P.R. Krishnakumar who gives ample evidence of how Ayurveda has still been neglected during the last decade by the existing bureaucratic power structure of the present medical-research system, the national development programme and the national planning systems.[444] He suggests that non-governmental organizations involved in the promotion of the traditional systems of medicine together with concerned individuals, researchers, educational and people's organizations, should create a "third system" as distinct from the inter- or intra-governmental organizations and the transnational corporations. Its role would be to struggle "for a more humane alternative in areas of alternatives as information and media, health care, energy, science, technology, finance, development etc."[445] The author regards Ayurveda as one amongst those alternative social action groups which seem to be one of the few institutions today which really try to help the downtrodden and the oppressed.

Like adult education, community medicine or social health cannot be politically neutral. According to the experiences of D.Werner, after examining 40 health programmes all over the world, only small non-government efforts are community-supportive programmes, namely those "that favourably influence the long-range welfare of the community, responsibility, initiative, that build upon human dignity".[446] For the large regional or national programmes, the author found only "a minimum of effective community involvement and a maximum of dependency-creating handouts, paternalism and superimposed, initiative destroying norms."[447] Community health is the need of the hour. It is most probably the only way to achieve health for all by the year 2000. It is widely accepted as a "balanced integration of curative, preventive and promotional health services. Its primary commitment is more to promotion of well-being (physical, mental and social) than to relief of suffering, to a reduction in the incidence of load of disease and disability in the community through preventive and promotional activity. It is concerned with motivating individuals and groups to change patterns of behaviour as to take such action, including seeking of medical care, as would enable them to achieve optimal health. It involves co-ordinated group-activity on the part of a team representing a number of disciplines...with varying levels of technical skills and competence."[448] This is at best a careful definition affirming how much of paternalistic thinking is found in the medical profession. The authors, throughout their textbook, consider the physician as the leading person of all activities who has to direct and to decide. This corresponds with the overall situation in India where there is hardly any people's participation in community health projects.[449] We have to repeat it again that the elite in health with the physician on top throughout the hierarchy is not really committed to change.[450] This elite is quick in defining what one should do, but it is extremely slow, if not unwilling, to make itself do, viz. (1) "tackling real problems und unifying people, instead of dividing and ruling" (for politicians); (2) "working to get results, not only to get rewards" (for bureaucrats); (3) "learning and continuing to learn, in order to be able to teach" (for educators); (4) "being industrious, creating productivity and rewarding productivity, instead of speculating and looking for sheltered markets" (for industrialists); (5) "pursuing their profession faithfully, neither bending to win rewards from the wealth nor to share privileges enjoyed by power holders, maintaining a mastery over one's subject" (for managers and technocrats).[451]

There are authors who are doubtful whether community health which has to cover 580.000 villages can be achieved by 'barefoot' approaches. They argue that only "heavy reliance on advanced technology and managerial systems" would help tackle this stupendous problem efficiently. Reversion to sentimentalism would result in "regression to primitivism, impracticality and total failure".[452] But the experiences so far made in India and abroad with advanced communication technology in education for development purposes have all miserably failed like the SITE- programme in 1975. Instead, barefoot approaches of a different nature seem to be more and more successful. A successful example is reported by S. Kaithathara who, after 14 years of experience in community health, is convinced "that the most realistic solution for providing health care to the vast population of the rural areas is to have community health workers trained from among the people. Health care cannot be imposed on the people. It should begin from and by the people."[453]

She wants the community health worker, who is also a community health educator[454], to be trained in such a way so that she or he is able to listen to people and to learn from them[455], to analyse the society in which she or he lives and which is also the society of her or his community, and to regard *health as an entry point* "to help the people think beyond questions of mere health, and to awaken, especially among the women, a new sense of social responsibility. The auhtoress continues that community health "should also be a way to motivate and mobilise the people to resist the domination of the traditionally powerful". Community health would offer "an effective way to bring people together to discuss their day-to-day problems and take responsibility for them."[456] (This is, of course, a much more radical definition of community health than the physician- and status quo-dominated one given by Park and Park.) Community health and community health education work for justice and against exploitation. The four-phased community health worker's training programme by S.Khaithathara with tribal women in Orissa is reported to be highly successful. Women are preferred as community health workers and educators because they are able to communicate well with everybody and they have more access to families than men.[457] Further, they have proved to be excellent health educators and home nursing instructors: "There is no predetermined time and place for health education. It may be when they have some free time in the village, or are at work in fields, in the forests, or while gathering firewood. They sing songs related to health and diseases, and talk to their own group about the wonders they learned."[458] Later in their programme, health education becomes a process of awakening to situations of poverty and ill-health, low wages and bondedness. Men are involved and an awareness about injustices in their villages is created.[459] In the last stage of the training, different laws and acts related to mortgage, land reform and revenue are studied as well as legislation on credit and interest rates. Techniques and skills to organize and orient the community to action are also trained.[460] Many of theses women health workers and educators later become eager participants in other adult education programmes and even resource persons for those.[461] At this point, community health and community health education have reached a stage where "there can be no conceivable remedy for education apart from radically changing society" as already advocated in the legendary UNESCO report "Learning to be" about two decades ago.[462]

This experience in Orissa is confirmed by many a contribution in a collection of case studies analysing various entry points to community work and community change.[463] Whether taking formal education, women's work, social housing or relief work in case of a natural disaster, the authors are unanimously convinced that only "a process of genuine education can change the present oppressive situation".[464] This kind of education should be non-formal and the key to any social transformation.[465] It is also named as authentic education which is aiming at making a human being fully and truly human[466] and enabling him to practise "people-based development" which is "the self-conscious, self-planned, self-reliant and sustainable progress of a community in all aspects of its life functions and relations which leads it towards a more human existence in terms of the fullest flowering of the potentialities of all its members and in terms of contribution towards cultural enrichment, peace and a viable future for all mankind."[467] This is also claimed by D.Werner and B.Bower who distinguish between three practical approaches of education for development, namely the conventional style whose major objective is to conform, the progressive style whose major objective is to reform, and the liberating style whose major objective is to transform.[468] They clearly consider the last one as the most adequate for development work that is truely people- based and in which any subject authority, e.g. in health, is derived from the people and in which "health awareness must become a people's movement,a people's programme."[469] From these experiences it becomes obvious that any form of popular education needs people's organization. It does not matter what is first, whether popular education arouses people's organization or vice versa, all what matters is that it is there to protect the rights and duties of people who are so far not used to having any rights. Demanding a "more equitable social order", no other than the philosopher of idealism, S.Radhakrishnan, long ago wrote that education had to be planned properly "and (to) strive to eliminate the sources of iniquities and injustices" and to reconstruct the society. For this, we had to have in view "the development of each and every individual as producer, as citizen, as a human being."[470]

We may conclude this chapter by asserting for Ayurveda Health Education, though it is first and foremost education which systematically aims at getting people "to perceive the world in a certain way"[471], that it should become community health education in order to make people conscientious about their own situation and to help them create new social circumstances. Out of this dialectic process a new consciousness and new form of living could emerge.[472] Ayurveda Health Education should dare enter this dialectic process in its field of health promotion and prevention.

3. Ayurveda Health Education and Community Health

The *third conclusion* is that Ayurveda Health Education should modernize itself in order to become an entry point to community health which rests heavily on social responsibility. Generations of observers have noted that responsibility for another community beyond one's own was hardly known in India otherwise the country with all its resources and talents would not be in the deplorable state it is.[473]

In view of Ayurveda Health Education this problem of social responsibility has to be examined critically. How can there be social responsibility when the basic assertion of Indian philosophy is that "man is declared to be an indescribable non-corpo-reality", that "all empirical relationships are declared to be chimerical", and that "the empirical world itself is declared to be non-existent"[474]? Can there be a deep-rooted feeling of social consciousness, of social responsibility in a society that, in the views of not so few, does not even exist? What has ethics to do in such a 'non-existing' world? If there is only pure consciousness, then there will be neither the poor nor the rich, neither the exploited nor the exploiter, neither the starver nor the opulent, neither the sick nor the healthy, neither the unhappy nor nor the happy, and so forth. Obviously, this philosophical background is not that strong in Ayurveda since Ayurveda was a very practical and worldly science which dealt with empirical matter and which did not subscribe to the pure version that only Brahman, the pure consciousness, exists. Ayurveda's aims of happiness and usefulness were and are goals of this world. But could the man of the hoary past internalize both, the abstract and the concrete? Could he combine the non-existent and the existent? Could he believe in the Upanishads which told him that the world in which he lived was an illusion? Could he believe in Ayurveda which promised him, at the same time, a healthy and happy worldly life? Were the people able to understand these considerations which lastly prepared the ground for many a ruler to suppress the people? This is not the place to try to answer all these questions but they shall finally lead to a reflection on the society of a time when many of the ancient philosophical texts, including those of Ayurveda, were formulated.

Following A.Shourie's argumentation, we end up at the same conclusion N.Chaudhuri proposed, viz. that Hindu philosophy was (and is) basically of worldly character. There was the society of primitive production, which was not integrated. There were only sporadic, infrequent contacts among the people who lived in geographically isolated communities. The productive activities of one unit were, within a community, not greatly dependent on those of another.[475] In such a community rule had to be maintained by an organized consent which was left to private initiative and appeared to be voluntarily given. This hegemony was not established by force but by means of an ideology,"a world -view that is anchored in each individual and is one that reproduces itself permanently".[476] This was achieved by internalization which acquired an imperative character and determined conduct. Once this had been done, the rules needed did not perceive the lack of freedom, they were even regarded as a pre-condition for 'inner freedom'. Thus the subjects did the work for the rulers, they repressed themselves. The system appeared to be tolerant and non-violent, but was hard to break since it did not admit any overt attack.[477] The ancient world-view, the ideological superstructure, was highly articulated inasmuch as in it every element was perfected to reinforce the other; rules of social conduct, ritual, family life and religion were ensuring the internalization of details. Three elements of the world-view had to be manipulated: "man's view of nature,man's view of the social world - using the world 'social' in its comprehensive sense to cover all of man's relations with his fellow men - and man's view of man himself".[478] As soon as man had internalized that the empirical world did not exist it affected his views of nature, of the social world and of himself. He was neither aware that laws could be used by man to autonomously create relationships nor that these relationships could be under his control and remoulded by him. The philosophical texts helped the ruler and their ideologists "of having the populace rationalize, accept and internalize the empirical order in which it finds itself trapped".[479] They used vulgar and even distorted forms to convince the common folk and maintained that it had all been explained in these texts. They attributed anything that suited them to those texts and derived the convenient from them.[480] Shourie is concerned that this philosophical tradition will continue to help the ruling class maintain its power, whatever the ruling class of the day is, unless this tradition would be abolished. Here Shourie meets, though from a completely different angle,with many other thinkers, for example A. Schweitzer who is of the opinion that people have to develop a positive attitude towards life in order to master life.[481] There is also the view of the psychoanalyst that this "meta-reality" of the Hindus and its underlying instinctual and cultural imperatives would create tension and "dis-ease" in case they are denied. "For such a meta-reality is not a system of abstractions, to be more or less hazily comprehended during the adult years; it is a part of the actuality of psychology and culture, absorbed by the child in the relationship with his adult care taker from the very beginning of life as the underlying truth of the world in which he will spend his life".[482] This explanation only supports Shourie's argument of internalization of "truth" which was convenient for adults,say rulers.

Though Ayurveda has always stressed its worldly character, it nevertheless belongs to the (philosophical) tradition Shourie has (sociologically) analysed. It is evident that a breakthrough to community health can only be achieved if Ayurveda liberates itself from the heritage of this traditional philosophical pattern. This means liberation form the deep-rooted belief that there have to be powerful and powerless, knower and unknower, rich and poor, educated and uneducated, and so forth. It is the liberation from this early internalization of a hegemonic rule. It means liberation form the caste ideas, that is "the refusal on the part of many to regard 'other' groups,classes or individuals as possessing the same worth and rights as they have, as being entitled to the same treatment."[483] Ayurveda health workers would have to develop the conviction that moulding life to satisfy one's own needs is possible, that everybody including oneself in a community is able to mould one's life. In principle, Ayurveda according to its definition as a comprehensive Science of Life should be open to this. And despite the strong criticism and charges levelled against the conservative character of Indian philosophy in general Ayurveda and its philosophy behind could follow the best of its tradition, viz.- the more one evolves, the greater does one identify oneself with the interests of all. If it is a choice between individual interests and social interests, the right course for one would be to choose the latter. The rule is, the wider the better."[484] Similarly argues S.Gopalan who stresses an "integrated pattern" in HIndu social philosophy. "If a balanced approach to material possessions had been developed, it would have averted all the social and political ills which the world at present is witnessing. Social coherence would have been an accomplished fact; progress of society would not have been retarded; and above all, the dynamic and reciprocal relationship between the individual and society would not have been lost sight of."[485]

A first step to accept full social responsibility is to accept "the primary disease" in India which is inequity of wealth, of land, of educational opportunities, of access to health care services, of political representation, and of basic human rights.[486] If Ayurveda health workers, suppose they were available, conducted predominantly social activities combined with reliable medical aid, then this approach would be more 'holistic' than the stressing of the commonplace relationship between mind and body, then people would bring up this science which is inviting their participation to improve their life. When, on the other hand countries like India today show so much of interest in the revival of their traditional medical systems, then it is also because of a certain degree of chauvinism.[487] By using the standard argument, prevention is more important than cure, they only safeguard the medical profession's monopoly of curative medicine by looking down upon ill-taught and ill-equipped health workers.[488] Such health workers could never become the much needed "germ of social change".[489] It has to be said again, the role of a village health worker and that of a health worker in deprived urban communities is that of a liberator who works preventive in the fullest sense. An Ayurveda health worker (educator) should have, conceptually, no difficulty to become such a liberator who tries to put an end to oppressive inequalities not only from outside exploitation but from the people's own shortsightedness, futility and greed as well.[490] He should have to ask the question 'Where shall prevention begin in a world of greed?' to which D.Werner replies that if "the building of latrines bring people together and helps them look ahead, if a nutrition centre is built and run by the community and fosters self-reliance, and if agricultural extension rather than imposing outside technology, encourages internal growth of the people towards more effective understanding and use of their land, their potential and their rights...then, and only then, do latrines and nutrition centres and so-called extension work begin to deal with the real cause of preventable sickness and death."[491] This is the idea of people's education by the people which is also known as "popular education".[492] Once it was hoped that adult education could be the vehicle of this process of empowering people by helping individuals and groups analyse the sources of their major problems and determine which solutions lie within their own hand.[493] , but we know now that this was a futile hope.[494] It is fallacious to regard adult education as the liberating force as long as educational and public life in India is ruled by double-standards, as put by K.L. Shrimali: "We advocate rational theories in public behaviour but our daily life is guided by rituals and superstition."[495] This behaviour is "schizophrenic" and divides people not so much between modernity and tradition but between passivity and action, between ennui and commitment, between the practical and the intellectual".[496]

What then about Ayurveda Health Education? There are plenty of myths which have to be abolished. First, it is highly unrealistic to state that Ayurveda is conducive to a "socialistic pattern of society" because Ayurveda pharmacies would create employment possibilities.[497] This seems to be naive and one of those coffe-table arguments we so often hear from highranking Ayurveda officials who think that they have to think like that and who feel it opportune to write such and similar statements intheir books which are not more than (certainly helpful) summaries of the classical scriptures.[498] Second, we have to be aware of a tendency among health and health education experts of find an easy, a 'technological' solution in order to escape the basic problems of poverty and inequality and the reasons behind. It is naive to believe in a "combination of traditional healing and modern medicine" as "the most promising appropriate solution for the health care problems facing the developing countries". [499] We should not be deluded into such a simplistic solution which would be of a mere technocratic nature and which would never help people get imbued with a strong sense of self-reliance and of control over their own lives and their own health. [500] There is no evidence today that Ayurveda has really left its ivory tower of exclusiveness, and the proposal to simply rehabilitate it will become an overly ambitious and unrealistic endeavour. Ayurveda can, no doubt, improve the medical care available in India but it cannot do very much to improve the health situation as a whole[501] because it has not changed yet from a maybe eternal Science of Life of the past to a down-to-earth political instrument of changing the health (and economic) sufferings of the weak.[502]

Why has it not changed? Change follows a learning process in which "the learner must expose himself to the threat of failure and loss of self-esteem". [503] Ayurveda physicians were certainly afraid of losing their power over the people, of losing their major social position in chiefly rural societies. It seems that Ayurveda has not solved a problem, obviously as old as humankind - people in power do not want to lose their status that gives them security in relationship and finance and aggrandizement. Maintenance of this status becomes in the end more important than the acceptance and adoption of the changing world around. Ayurveda has consequently avoided this challenge of the changing world. But change is the pre-condition of modernization. An economist's argument reveals (surprisingly?) that Indians are not adverse to the idea of change but that they change all the time. In economy this is as immediately visible as it is in health, here in terms of money and economic growth, there in terms of illness and personal and community health growth. J.Dubashi thinks that the Indian resistance to the idea of Westernization is basically its form of resistance to the idea of change; very often the two would be mistakenly equated with each other.[504] But how can modernization be brought about without

Westernization? he asks. This would be a modernization consistent with India's social, moral and cultural ethos (as was achieved by Japan). The author offers a solution which is already practised - satyagraha, the traditional Indian way by simply slowing down the rate of modernization so that change is absorbed with as little disruption as possible. He writes that India has "a genius for this kind of system: movement without actually moving, activity without much action, furious work without immediate tangible results" and means that in a fast changing world this was "the only way to survive" and that the Indian society had precisely "survived for centuries" in this way "without loosing much of its essence".[505] Dubashi gives as an example the so-called "Hindu rate of growth" which is, economically, on an average around 3.5 per cent a year. Whether big plans, whether bumper years or dwindled year, the rate seems to be fixed to this figure. Indians would prefer "to adjust oneself to change from within, which is what development is all about, than to change imposed from without, which is growth without development". As to the psychological block of Indians against Western technology or Western political institutions, he states that there was no reason why the hangover of the recent past should not be overcome by a future generation without the faintest memory of Western interference in the lives of the Indians.[506]

But by modernization we do not only have in mind the modernization paradigma in development theory of the fifties whose central element was economic growth simply by capital accumulation. Here, I like to use modernization much more in its original meaning, namely to adjust oneself or someone to a new situation and vice versa. This adjustment includes the openness of man to innovation and change and his readiness for new experiences.[507] This understanding of modernization is certainly not simply social welfare which never analyses the causes of poverty; it is not satisfied either with mere measures of improving structures of institutions to deliver more and better services; this understanding of modernization should, instead, aim at structural changes, even if as slow as the 'Indian rate', in socio-political and economic structures.[508] Such understanding is difficult to get accepted and realized in the development model of capitalism. In order to be successfully implemented, it probably needs the framework of a model which contains many more forces which act cooperatively and /or collectively to achieve structural changes and to maintain them, by breaking the vicious cycle of poverty and low productivity.[509]

Community health is certainly closely related to modernization in the above understanding since it can only be successful when collective efforts achieve and maintain structure changes for a more equal and humane society in relation to other development areas. Community health activities are probably becoming more and more radical if the progress is too slow. Once people have understood that their health and disease situation is interlinked with their social and economic situation, then there is no look back. Then community health will initiate real prevention, and real prevention has first and foremost to do with improvement in the standards of living of the whole community. For this process, health can be used as an entry point. And this is also the entry point for Ayurveda Health Education, whose aims and values have to be connected with the economic and social status of the people. In Ayurveda Health Education, there is the seed for becoming a valuable instrument for community health and for popular education. This means, if Ayurveda Health Education succeeds in realizing its theoretical and practical potential, which is centred in its basic principle of congruence between content and form, then it will attract people again. But what does this realization mean? Simply aiming at healthy and happy people with the help of 'healthy' and 'happy' knowledge? How can this knowledge become a 'healthy' and 'happy' instrument of education which is generally regarded as a dull and boring venture? And how can a science work 'healthily' and 'happily' when the subjects and objects of it are usually in dreary conditions? How can happiness be brought about by people who are suffering from diseases due to maltreatment by an oppressive system? Mere techniques and methods, even the most sophisticated ones, will not help. Sooner or later would they be used by the haves against the have-nots or, at the most, become well-intended welfare measures by the haves *for* the have-nots. Repetition of old Ayurveda advice will not help either. Day, night and season regimens even when applied to modern Indian conditions will never be able to change the health situation substantially. It is naive to hope that a simple recourse to traditional forms[510] would help, say, change the problem of malnutrition or unequal land distribution. It is not helpful either to be proud of the ancient heritage without analysing its suitability for today.[511] Nor would the situation change through big government programmes and interventions which usually contain only lots of 'shoulds' for which nobody feels responsible. What seems to be necessary is a radically alternative strategy for social health through Ayurveda as, for example, proposed by C.R. Bijoy in the following points:

1. Providing "the theoretical tools for understanding and analysis of health problems, thenceforth the formulation of policies of the alternative social health strategy."[512]
2. Providing "practical training towards becoming social health planners through a direct involvement in the local action for health improvement."
3. Providing for "the implementation of social health plans, co-ordinating (the) health sector with other development sectors of the locality for a more humane environment intended to evolve low-cost methods of health care delivery."
4. Providing for "community based action through the direct participation of the community themselves, by their training in Āyurvedic practices through indigenous methods by demystification of the health science."
5. Providing a "decommercialised, deburaucratised, decentralised democratic pariticpatory system through community self-reliance in health practices and appropriate medical technology."
6. Providing for the "organisation of the community to effectuate the direct transfer of people's health, in people's hands, positive rural biased in character with the ensuing responsibilities."[513]

In the words of the authors of the Centre for Social Action, Bangalore, who have tabled the "Potential of Various Health Involvements", it would be an approach of "Conscientisation" with Community Health Care/Community Development; this would mean "less direct health & economic benefits... but direct action towards structural changes".[514] Only such a *nonclinical* approach to community health would ensure emphasis on structural changes which no amount of resources would bring about.[515]

In sum, we may now conclude that in order to become an entry point to community health, Ayurveda Health Education is

- to help develop in persons a strong feeling of social responsibility,

- to liberate itself from the heritage of the traditional philosophical pattern which is taken as the rationale for oppressing rather than liberating people,
- to accept the reality of the many inequalities in the present society,
- to change, that means to risk its delusive status and position,
- to help people become aware that their health and diseases are interlinked with their social and economic situations, and
- to work for the improvement in standards of living by using (health) education as an entry point.

These demands, put into practice, may then transform not only the society but also Ayurveda Health Education itself into a movement of popular education, and an ancient Science of Life into a modern instrument of helping create a just society.

4. Ayurveda Health Education and People's Education

The *fourth conclusion* is that Ayurveda Health Education could become an integral part of people's education.

Is it a way out of the ups and downs of life to say that human life need not be a problem because the problem we want to solve is absurd?[516] This argument by a psychotherapist who was much influenced by the East sounds harsh and pitiless. But is it really so? What he later explains in his study on psychotherapy in East and West is that it is impossible to solve life through other means than life, or relaxation through other means than relaxation.[517] This would mean that health can be achieved only through health, happiness only through happiness usefulness only through usefulness. In other words, it is the principle of congruence between content and form which is proposed by A. Watts (without naming it in this way) in order to share ways to solve human problems. In the language of E. Fromm, it is the mode of *to be* instead of this of to have, it is the mode of loving instead of this of death, it is the mode of loving through love and not through that what today is often pretended to be love, viz. masochism, sadism, selfishness. From m distinguishes these two fundamental modes of existence as two different kinds of orientation towards the self and the world, as two different kinds of character structure which determine the totality of a person's thinking, feeling and acting. In the having mode of existence, a person's relationship to the world is one of owning and possessing, one in which everybody and everything, including oneself, is made one's property. In the being mode of existence, there are two forms of being. One means aliveness and authentic relatedness to the world, this is in contrast to having. The other refers to the true nature of a person or a thing, its true reality, this is in contrast to appearing.[518] But Fromm does not deny the mode of existential having for survival in order to fulfill the biologically given desire to live.[519] He points out that having would refer to things which are fixed and describable, being instead would refer to experience and would not be describable, because words were not the experience. Hence being would be only communicable by sharing one's experiences.[520] In an earlier work[521], he had already furnished a concept by which the mode of being could be achieved, the concept of love. To Fromm, love is the answer to the problem of human existence. It is the answer to a society of greed which can be changed only through love. Love arouses internal growth which is the foundation of changing a community to a healthy, happy and useful one. Only love can abolish inequality, not laws alone. Only love can develop social responsibility, not recommendations alone. Only love can provide an education for oneself and the community, not technocratic thinking by teachers alone. Let us therefore have a closer look at this concept as developed by Fromm.[522]

The author starts with the assumption that mature love is "union under the condition of preserving one's integrity, one's individuality."[523] Love is active, it is primarily giving and receiving. It is giving without the feeling that one should give. "Giving is the highest expression of potency. In the very act of giving I experience my strength, my wealth, my power. This experience of heightened vitality and potency fills me with joy. I experience myself with overflowing, spending, alive, hence as joyous. Giving is more joyous than receiving, not because it is a deprivation, but because in the act of giving lies the expression of my aliveness."[524] But Fromm is also sure that poverty beyond a certain limit makes it impossible to give. This would be degrading because of the suffering it causes directly, and because of the fact that it deprives the poor of the joy of giving.[525] However, the most important sphere of giving is not that of material things, but the giving which lies in a specifically human realm. "What does one person give to another? He gives of himself, of the most precious he has, he gives of his life. This does not necessarily mean that he sacrifices his life for the other - but that he gives him of that which is alive in him; he gives him of his joy, of his interest, of his understanding, of his knowledge, of his humour, of his sadness - of all expressions and manifestations of that which is alive in him."[526] He enriches the other person by this giving, and he enhances the sense of aliveness in the other. Giving is in itself joy, therefore he does not give in order to receive. "But in giving he cannot help bringing something to life in the other person, and this which is brought to life reflects which is given back to him. Giving implies to make the other person a giver also and they both share in the joy of what they have brought to life. In the act of giving something is born for both of them. Specifically with regard to love this means: love is a power which produces love".[527] Besides this element of giving, true love implies the basic components of care, responsibility, respect and knowledge. About care, Fromm says that love "is the active concern for the life and the growth of that which is love. Where this active concern is lacking, there is no love."[528] By responsibility, not the duty is meant which is imposed on a person from outside, but an entirely voluntary act as a response to the needs, expressed or unexpressed, of another human being. "To be 'responsible' means to be able and ready to 'respond'".[529] The third component, respect, saves responsibility from deteriorating into domination and possessiveness. It is no fear and awe but denotes the ability to be aware of the unique individuality of a person. "Respect means the concern that the other person should grow and unfold as he is. Respect, thus, implies the absence of exploitation."[530] Care, responsibility and respect are guided by knowledge. Knowledge has a fundamental relationship to love. "The basic need to fuse with another person so as to transcend the prison of one's separateness is closely related to another specifically human desire, that to know the 'secret of man'. While life in its mere biological aspects is a miracle and a secret, man in his human aspects is an unfathomable secret to himself - and to his fellow man. We know ourselves, and yet even with all the efforts we may make, we do not know ourselves. We know our fellow man, and yet we do not know him, because we are not a thing, and our fellow man is not a thing. The further we reach into the depth of our being, or someone else's being, the more the goal of knowledge eludes us. Yet we cannot help desiring to penetrate into the secret of man's soul, into the innermost nucleus which is 'he'."[531] The object of love is not primarily the relationship to a specific person but an attitude "which determines the relatedness of a person to the world as a whole, not toward one 'object' of love": "If a person loves only one other person and is indifferent to the rest of his fellow men, his love is not love but a symbiotic attachment, or an enlarged egotism, yet, most people believe that love is constituted by the object, not by the faculty. In fact, they even believe that it is a proof of the intensity of their love when they do not love anybody except the 'loved' person."[532] These people would not see that love is an activity, a power of the soul, and it is not enough to find the right object and hope that everything would go by itself afterwards. "This attitude can be compared to that of a man who wants to paint but who, instead of learning the art, claims that he has just to wait for the right object, and that he will paint beautifully when he finds it. If I truly love one person I love all persons, I love the world, I love life."[533]

Ayurveda Health Education, in order to modernize itself and to become an entry point to community health and to become in this process an integral part of people's education could focus on this understanding of love as the truest form of congruence between content and form. In it love would arouse love through giving, caring, responding to others, respecting the other's unique individuality, and searching to know oneself and the other. It would be certainly attended with health, happiness and usefulness in the life of humankind. Love is the feeling which is inherent in all human beings, for which all human beings are longing, it is universal. But it has to be used and implemented. This promotion could be one of the main tasks of Ayurveda Health Education. This would cover all the aspects we can find in this form of health education and would help create a form of health education which, in fact, would not be the rather conventional answer to health problems caused by an unjust society and economy structure. Its lifelong endeavours would not only have a powerful impact on the individual in the long run but on all men in a community. Community health should start with 'community love' as an entry point. Ayurveda as the Science of Life, and not the science of some herbal cures and many an old regimen of conduct only, should include love as the basic principle of education to achieve health, happiness and usefulness, rather than through mere rules which would be complied with, if ever, only mechanically. Love is health, happiness, usefulness, life. Such a master concept of Ayurveda Health Education would recreate, i.e., continually modernize, a real Science of Life. Ayurveda (Health Education) could perhaps become part of those sciences B. Russell had probably in mind when he analysed the links of science and progress. "There is only one road to progress, in education as in other human affairs, and that is: Science wielded by love. Without science, love is powerless; without love science is destructive."[534]

But we are still left with the question of how to practise love, health, happiness, usefulness, life. It might be through productiveness. According to Fromm, the mode of being "implies the faculty of being active". Activity is "socially recognized purposeful behaviour that results in corresponding socially useful changes."[535] Fromm understands this activity as a "nonalienated activity" in contrast to the alienated activity which is mere business and which is actually passiveness. But activity is a "process of giving birth to something, of producing something and remaining related to what I produce." This kind of activity is a manifestation of one's powers. He calls this activity "productive activity". It is not the capacity to create something new or original that matters but the quality of activity. "Productive activity denotes the state of inner activity" which has not necessarily a connection with the creation of something.[536] Productive persons would animate whatever they touch. They would give birth to their own faculties and bring life to other persons and to things.[537] This is productiveness. For this process Fromm has coined the term "productive love" which is genuine love rooted in productiveness.[538] Realization of productive love is realization of art. Fromm upholds that the practice of every art is based on certain general requirements. First of all, it requires discipline, not only in the practice of a particular art (e.g. love, health, productiveness), but as a "discipline in one's whole life".[539] The second condition is concentration which is even rarer than self-discipline.[540] The third essential factor is patience; yet this is also difficult to attain particularly in an industrialized world which is fostering exactly the opposite, viz. quickness of production. And "as in so many other aspects, human values have become determined by economic values. What is good for machines must be good for man - so goes the logic."[541] The fourth condition to learn an art is a "supreme concern with the mastery of an art":"If the art is not something of supreme importance, the apprentice will never learn. He will remain, at best a good dilettante, but will never become a master. This condition is as necessary for the art of loving as for any other art."[542] There is sometimes a misunderstanding between love and fairness. Love is inseparably connected not only with the personal but also with the social realm. "There is no 'division of labour' between love for one's own and love for strangers. On the contrary, the condition for the existence of the former is the existence of the latter. To take this insight seriously means indeed a rather drastic change in one's social relations from the customary one's.[543] Contrary to this, relations in a capitalist society despite all lip-service to love your neighbour is determined by, at best, fairness. This modern fairness ethics "means not to feel responsible... but distant and separate; it means to respect the rights of your neighbour, but not to love him."[544] But are true love and secular societies ruled by competition and consumption not basically incompatible? Fromm tries to give a balanced answer. First, he confirms this incompatibility, but then he argues that modern society has to be seen as a complex phenomenon in which a "salesman of a useless commodity, for instance, cannot function without lying; a skilled worker, a chemist, or a physician can. Similarly, a farmer, a worker, a teacher, and many a type of business man can try to practice love without ceasing to function economically. Even if one recognizes the principle of capitalism as being incompatible with the principle of love, one must admit that capitalism is in itself a complex and constantly changing structure which still permits of a good deal of non-conformity".[545] He, however, sums up that people who are capable of love in our present societies are the exceptions, not so much because many occupations would not permit a loving attitude, "but because the spirit of a production-centred, commodity-greedy society is such that only the non-conformist can defend himself successfully against it." Thus, if love is to become a social phenomenon, then "important and radical changes in our social structure are necessary".[546] But love is a means without an end whereas economic goals necessarily are means with an end. Love is a need which is generally absent in its comprehensive form today due to certain social and economic conditions which may be affluence *or* poverty. But more important, future hope is the rational faith "in the possibility of love as a *social* and not only exceptional-individual phenomenon".[547]

But we have to keep asking whether love is too much of an idealistic concept and by this unfit for Ayurveda Health Education because idealism can induce man to self-deception and can very often lead him to the concept of help *for* the people and not to help *by* the people. Consequently, it would lead in Ayurveda Health

Education to health *for* rather than to health by *the* people, to happiness *for* rather than to happiness *by* the people, to usefulness *for* rather than to usefulness *by* the people, to productiveness *for* rather than to productiveness *by* the people, and would by this disregard the rights of the people again. Love, according to Fromm, is, however, not only idealism but also a representation of realism. It is able to set the chain of health - happiness - productiveness in motion. It is the inspiring force of the desire to live. This desire gets, through love, its constant justification, and this justification is important for man in the present time (whereas the classical Indian idea of the quest for life was aimed at the emancipation in future lives). The latter one was idealism, whereas love as the motif for the desire to live is a realistic objective. Nobody is excluded from it regardless of caste or class. Love in this wide sense is a day-to-day challenge, whereas moksha is a future challenge. Thus, it may be argued that love is a help now which can overcome "moral aloneness" of man.[548] This aloneness is the lack of true relatedness to values, symbols or patterns now. By that it can be even regarded as a means of prevention because we know that "moral aloneness" is one major cause of many a health problem on the mental plane. We have stated that love can set the 'chain of health' in motion, and that love is a realistic concept. This would be in accordance with the other parts of health (happiness,usefulness, productiveness) which are also realistic concepts. In principle, Ayurveda's flexibility in adopting means for education is beginningless and endless. It is not at all necessary that it must stick to the old values, traditions and regimens but can define new priorities which its inherent educational corpus can try to realize; love would be such a priority. It can, for example, easily adopt P. Freire's idea of "dialogue" which could not exist "in the absence of profound love for the world and for men. The naming of the world, which is an act of creation and re-creation, is not possible if it is not infused with love. Love is at the same time the foundation for dialogue and dialogue itself."[549] On the basis of dialogue, communication emerges, and through this true education is built up.[550]

In Freire's theory of liberation education, we can possibly find the second base of true popular education. His ideas of dialogue and conscientization, for the growing movement of popular education in Latinamerica, have already become proven fundamentals.

This form of popular education "has been based on, and has developed, the theory of the relations between class struggle, political strategy, and educational action."[551] Freire's first and foremost conviction is that *every* human being "is capable of looking critically at his world in a dialogical encounter with others. Provided with the proper tools for such an encounter, he can gradually perceive his personal and social reality as well as the contradictions in it, become conscious of his own perception of that reality, and deal critically with it. In this process, the old, paternalistic teacher-student relationship is overcome. A peasant can facilitate this process for his neighbour more effectively than a 'teacher' brought in from outside."[552] The tool for this is "problem-posing education" which can break the vertical pattern of oppressive "banking education" (which, amongst other things, fails to acknowledge men as historical beings) by constantly unveiling reality[553] through critical perception of "*the way they exist* in the world" and by this taking man's historicity as its starting point.[554] In such a process a "teacher is no longer merely the-one-who-teaches, but one who is himself taught in dialogue with the students, who in their turn while being taught also teach."[555] The main technique in such a process is the dialogue which is based on love for the world and for men and which requires faith in man, faith in his power to make and remake, to create and re-create, and faith in his vocation to be more fully human.[556] Dialogue is then an investigation process into the people's "thematic universe" which is the complex of their "generative themes" and searches and elaborates by this a programme content for "education as the practice of freedom".[557] In the course of this thematic investigation, conscientization of man's situation emerges which can/should lead to intervention.[558] Conscientization "refers to the process in which men, not as recipients, but as knowing subjects, achieve a deepening awareness both of the socio-cultural reality which shapes their lives and of their capacity to transform that reality."[559] It is "brought about not through an intellectual effort alone, but through praxis - through the authentic union of action and reflection."[560] This intervention is called by Freire "cultural action" whose main characteristics is "dialogical action" which consists of cooperation, unity for liberation "in order to transform the world", organization one of whose essential elements is "*consistency* between words and actions" (which is part of our understanding of congruence between content and form) and "cultural synthesis".[561] By the last one Freire means : (1) "... the actors who come from 'another world' to the world of the people do so not as invaders. They do not come to *teach* or to *transmit* or to *give* anything, but rather to learn, with the people, about the people's world." (2)"... the actors become integrated with the people, who are co-authors of the action that both perform upon the world." (3)"... there are no spectators; the object of the actors' action is the reality to be transformed for the liberation of men."[562]

Returning to Ayurveda Health Education, we may now have a justification to assume that if Ayurveda Health Education followed those outlines of love (Fromm) and praxis (Freire), it would have a chance to become a part of true people's science [563] and people's education

- in which, first, each and everyone has the right and opportunity to acquire critical knowledge about himself and his society, and
- in which, second, after historical analyses, people develop deliberate forms of actions to free themselves from the oppression and exploitation of those who do not want the world to be named.

This would then be popular education (form) in accordance with its principles (content). It would be based on love which would be the seed of health and happiness, which would close the cycle by being the soil for usefulness, productiveness, knowledge, and praxis (reflection plus action). All these concepts - love, health, happiness, usefulness, knowledge, action - are not only interlinked with each other but also dependent on each other. If one were omitted, the'chain of health' would collapse. But as such they are able to form a perfect chain of man's complete well-being. Popular education, for example in the form of Ayurveda Health Education, would be an entry point to this chain. Yet it remains doubtful whether this kind of popular education can be realized within the present structure of the Indian society. K.G Saiyidain has analysed that the basic password in the thinking of the humanists among the Indian educational thinkers (Rabindranath Tagore, Mohammad Iqbal, M.K.Gandhi, Maulana Abul Kalam Azad, Sarvapalli Radhakrishnan and Zakir Hussain) was reconciliation in a society where there is so much of social and cultural diversity as in India. For those thinkers, the maintenance of a proper balance was of the utmost importance, a balance "between tradition and experiment, between the national heritage and the human heritage, between the claims of reason and the light of intuition, between science and technology and religion and vision, between activity and contemplation, between power and compassion, between the world of matter and the world of spirit".[564] On the other hand, he found a common feature in their thinking that would leave enough scope for change, may be radical change which would drop the balance (at least for a movement), viz. "a high vision of potentialities of man, who is looked upon not as a passive creature of circumstances,... but as a creative and original individual, a spiritual being in whom there are infinite inner riches still waiting to be developed."[565]

Completing this thread of thought, I my finally formulate a less tentative definition of Ayurveda Health Education: Ayurveda as a science has inherited an educational component which is responsible for imparting ideas on health and helping people realize them. This educational component is of an in-built nature and is aiming at health while focussing on the art of living. Love as the basic attitude sets adequate actions in motion in order to achieve health, happiness, usefulness, productiveness, knowledge and praxis. This is then complete prevention. According to Ayurveda's basic principle of congruence between content and form, all the means of Ayurveda Health Education are to be devised like that - self-identity generates self-identity, self-education generates self-education, and so forth. Thus, Ayurveda Health Education has less of a teaching character (in the traditional sense) but more of a living character (in the sense of Freire). By this it can become a part of popular education, that is education *by* the people and not for the people.

Conclusionary Note

I hope the major argument in the forgoing inquiry, i.e., from preventive rules in traditional Ayurveda to a possible Ayurveda Health Education discipline, has been plausibly unfolded, and the speculative reconstruction of Ayurveda Health Education for our contemporary society has been made in such a way that it can be reproduced and by that improved by others. In which direction this will happen, I do not know, and I do not want to give advice and suggestions because my way of thinking is pre-determined by the close contact I have had over years with the material, and by my biased thinking which is still inclined towards idealism. I am sure this inquiry will be read by others, if it has any reader at all, in a completely different way, certainly more detached and by this more critically. And this is a must in order to foster progress in science and thought.

Today, I am far less sure whether the main ideas I have pursued in this inquiry some years ago are really that "main". The hypothesis, for example, could be taken as a thought which is too worn out for a fresh consideration. And is the concept of love by Fromm really that powerful to help change societal structure by influencing values of people? Even Freire's seemingly revolutionary dream of an epistemological pedagogy, is it not the old dream of change from outside rather from within? (Freire has never made it clear what to do with those who are oppressing, how they could be involved in the process of a more humane, just and equal society.)

If we understand philosophy as a discipline aiming at the state of critical awareness, then our speculative reconstruction may be of value for discussing pragmatic considerations though we should not go to the full length and suggest immediate practical implications. Practical utility is not the goal of philosophic thinking but, at the most, a consequence of those. I do not consider Ayurveda Health Education an urgent necessity for social change in the health field, but the speculation about it and its theoretical reconstruction might help in getting clearer about the health field in India and the present endeavours to improve it. (A volume which I find helpful in the general discussion about philosophy and social utility is the recently published "Philosophy and Social Change", edited by D. Goel.)

The reconstruction of Ayurveda Health Education might be of use even for another purpose. It is known and widely lamented that in India there is hardly any philosophy of education worth its name. The going back to the same old names like Tagore and Gandhi in modern times or to the revered (blindly?) concept of the gurukula system of ancient India for example, does not help much today when there is a shift of emphasis necessary because we are confronted with different problems and perspectives. There is hope that those in the philosophy of education who try to make it into a contemporary discipline may be successful in the end by combining in their reflections old with new ideas, by re-considering the old ideas in the light of the change of time and circumstances, and by considering the new ideas humbly as a follow-up of that what has been thought before. There is only a little of that what we think today which is really new, if at all a little. If therefore my try of concept formation in this inquiry could be seen in this way, I would be more than satisfied and would accept my efforts as a brick in an eventual system. A humanistic Philosophy of Education would be such a system.

Notes

1 If this process in education is conducted by an indifferent teacher who is governed by feelings of duty, and not by commitment, failures have to be expected. This is not new and has been known since the beginning of systematic thinking about teaching and education. Johan Amos Comenius, as one amongst many, said in the 17th century that teachers should be all what they expect their students to become. They should be able to show their students the vision towards which they can direct their efforts of self-education. R.R. Rusk/J. Scotland: *Doctrines of the Great Educators,* n.p., Macmillan, [5]1979, p.73

2 Knowledge and teaching as content are here used in the general understanding of Sociology, the "sum total of elements and processes which constitute an object or a phenomenon". On the other hand, life as form is the widest "mode of existence and expression of the content". B.P. Singh: *A Dictionary of Modern Political Sociology,* Delhi: Mittal, 1987, p.62

3 What Strawson applied to metaphysics, we should also utilize in our field of study, viz.: "If there are no new truths to be discovered, here are old truths to be rediscovered." P.F.Strawson: *Individuals,* London: Methuen,1977 ([1]1959), p. 10

4 W.H.Greene/B.G.Simons-Morton: *Introduction to Health Education,* New York/London: Macmillan, 1984, pp. 44-45

5 The modern term primary prevention resembles at its centre the age-old Indian understanding of a "true philosopher" who "does not believe in certain theories which cannot be carried into practive in everyday life" and who lives upto that what he believes. S.Abhedananda: Hindu Philosophy in India, in: S. Radhakrishnan/J.H. Muirhead (eds.) :*Contemporary Indian Philosophy,* London: Allen & Unwin, 1958 (1936),pp. 49-64; here:p.5

6 Here I do prefer to quote a verse fro m the ancient Tamil classic "Kural" in order to illustrate this assumption (though eventually more learned comments by Aristotle, Plato or Vivekananda could be given too): "There is no bigger fool than the man who has acquired much learning and preaches the same to others,

but who does not control himself."*Kural.* The Great Book of Tiru-Valluvar. With English Translation and Notes by C.Rajagopalachari, Bombay; Bharatiya Vidy a Bhavan, 1981, p.17

7 Shiv Sharma: Health Services - Other Systems of Medicine, in: India, Government of - The Planning Commission (ed.): *Encyclopaedia of Social Work in India,* Vol. I, New Delhi: Ministry of Information and Broadcasting, 1968, pp. 373-378; here: pp. 373-374

8 The two historical primay sources of this study are the two great books of Ayurveda, the *Caraka Samhita* and the *Sushruta Samhita.* They have, by and large, the same contents with identical or analogous divisions. The Sushruta Samhita is richer in the field of surgery than the Caraka Samhita which, on the other hand, appears to go deeper into internal medicine. The Caraka Samhita is more extensively dealing with theoretical and philosophical aspects. The teachings of these two sources are presented in an extremely condensed form, but because of the abundance of matter both the works are nevertheless voluminous. Their didactic texts are in prose or verse of varied metres, but the English translations to which this study refers throughout are entirely in prose. I have found it appropriate to use the English translations rather than the Sanskrit originals since this study is essentially deveoted to education and not to Ayurveda or Indology. It is meant to be a contribution to the theory of education rather than a philological study of Ayurveda texts. The translation of the Caraka Samhita is completely available in English, as is the Sushruta Samhita, but I have opted for a new translation of the Caraka Samhita which is not yet complete; at the time of writing only three of its four volumes have so far been published, but they contain the main section for our analysis: the Sutra Sthana. Moreover, this new translation of Agnivesa's Caraka Samhita by R.K.Sharma and B Dash is provided with a critical exposition by the translators based on the learned commentary by Cakrapani Datta of the 11th century. I have selected the Sutra Sthana as the main section because it contains the essential ideas of Ayurveda and its major regimens for health in a nutshell. In fact, the Sutra Sthana is considered to serve as the brain of the whole treatise. It deals with the fundamental principles of Ayurveda, both for the prevention and the cure of

diseases. I have prefered the Sutra Sthana of the Caraka Samhita to that of the Sushruta Samhita in the version originally published between 1907 and 1916 by K.K. Bhishgratna because it distinguishes scholarly between translation and commentary. This is not so in Bhishgratna's work which is a mixture of translation, commentary and interpretation. Of the Great Trio of Ayurveda texts (Caraka Samhita, Sushruta Samhita and Ashtanga-hridya by Vagbhata), the Caraka Samhita is considered to be the most authoritative for it represents an authentic thesaurus of various aspects of Ayruveda.

9 B.Russell: *My Philosophical Development,* London: Unwin, 1975, p.197

10 G.Z.F. Bereday:*Comparative Method in Education,* Calcutta: Oxford & IBH, 1967, p.28

11 W.J.A.Harris: *Comparative Adult Education,* London: Longman, 1980, p.163

12 B.Tibi: "Development Policy is no Field for Exotic-Romantic Yearnings".*Development and Cooperation,* 3/1982, p.23

13 L.Kolakowski: "Wo sind die Barbaren?"*Der Monat,* 2/1980, No.277, p.70

14 M.Muller: *India. What can it teach us?* Delhi: Munshi Ram Manohar Lal, [2]1961,p.13

15 B. Griffiths: *The Marriage of East and West,* London: Fount, 1983,p.9

16 J.Salmi: "Educational Research on the Third World: a view from the South".*IDS Bulletin* (Sussex),15:4 (1984),p.9

17 L.Elvin:*The Place of Commonsense in Educational Thought,* London: Allen & Unwin, 1977, p.138

18 M. Polanyi: *Knowing and Being,* London: Routledge & Kegan Paul,1969,p.54

19 K.Thompson: *Education and Philosophy,* Oxford: Basil Blackwell, 1972,p.89

20 G.J.Mouly:*The Science of Educational Research,* New Delhi: Eurasia, 1964,p.64

21 John S.Brubacher/Velorus Martz: Philosophy of Education, in: W.S. Monroe (ed.): *Encyclopedia of Educational Research,* New York: Macmillan, 1956, pp. 817-820; here: p.817

22 *Ibid.,* p.817

23 *Ibid.,* p.818

24 B.Morris: *Objectives and Perspectives in Education,* London: Routledge & Kegan Paul, 1972, p.64

25 L. Hudson: *The Cult of the Fact,* London: Jonathan Cape, 1972,p.76

26 E.R.Emmet: *Learning to Philosophize,* Harmondsworth: Penguin, 1968, p. 79

27 W.Dilthey: Die Entstehung der Hermeneutik, in: S.Oppolzer (ed.): *Denkformen und Forschungsmethoden der Erziehungswissenschaft,* Vol.1, Munchen: Ehrenwirth, 1966, pp.13-24; here: p.16

28 K.R. Popper: *Objective Knowledge,* Oxford: Clarendon, 1973, p.182

29 *Ibid.*, p.186

30 India, Government of (ed.): *Report of the Health Survey and Development Committee,* Vols. I-IV, Calcutta/New Delhi/ Simla: Government of India Press, 1946

31 *Ibid.*, Vol. IV, pp. 5-6 (emphasis mine)

32 *Ibid.*, Vol. II, p.2

33 *Health for the Millions,* VII:4 (1981),p.5

34 L.C. Jain: "The drag". *Seminar,* No.307, March 1985, p.23

35 D. Banerji: Formulating an Alternative Rural Health Care System in India, in: J.P.Naik (ed.): *An Alternative System of Health Care Services in India,* Bombay: Allied, 1977, pp.31-47; here: pp.35-36

36 The Constitution directly and indirectly reflects on the provision of health for the people. Several of its economic rights are the bases for good health, so, for example, provision of adquate means of livelihood, fair distribution of wealth, employment, living wage, and public assistence in the case of unemployment, old age, sickness, disability and other cases of undeserved want. Besides that, there is the direct call for raising the level of nutrition and the improvement of health. The fundamental rights of the Constitution are equally important for the health of the people. The rights to equality and against exploitation, if vigorously implemented during the past four decades, would have improved the health status of millions. And in a Directive Principle of the State Policy, article 38 of the Constitution demands from the states, which are responsible for the health services, "to secrure social order for the promotion of welfare of the people", and in particular "to minimise the inequalities of income, and endeavour to eliminate inequalities in status, facilities and opportunitiess". India, Government of - Ministry of Law, Justice and Company

Affairs (ed.): *The Constitution of India,* New Delhi: Government of India Press, 1981, pp. 6-8, p.11, p.17

37 India, Government of - Ministry of Health and Family Welfare (ed.): *Health Statistics of India 1985,* New Delhi: Government of India Press, 1986 (hereafter referred to as HSI 1985), p.172. The "Health Statistics of India" (later "Health Information India"), published annually by the Ministry of Health and Family Welfare, attract attention to 17 sections from population statistics via public health statistics to international comparative statistics. These publications are truly outstanding: the highest administrative authority in the field reveals there year after year a clear statistical picture about the state of health and disease in the country. It is a good tradition in Indian administration to point out its achievements as well as its weaknesses pitilessly, very often, however, buried in boring and wooden reports which will be read only by a handful of people. Moreover, the reliability of the figures reported has to be taken with a pinch of salt; often they document certainly only fractions of the real picture and show, at best, trends in the field.

38 *Ibid.*, p.172

39 *Ibid.*, p.176

40 India, Government of - Ministry of Information and Broadcasting (ed.): *India. A Reference Annual,* New Delhi: Ministry of Information and Broadcasting, 1980, p.90

41 *HSI 1985, op.cit. p.184*

42 *Indian Express,* 30.7.1982

43 The Tuberculosis Association of India (ed.): *Diagnosis, Treatment and Prevention of Pulmonary Tuberculosis for Practitioners,* New Delhi: TAI, [2]1981,p.1

44 *HSI 1985,* op.cit., p. 185. It might be worth mentioning that c. 60 years ago, in colonial India, the Public Health Commissioner once wrote that tuberculosis was "one of our biggest problems and will... be tackled in the near future by a suitable organization. The keynote is not 'sanatoria', but education." S.Read/S.T. Sheppard (eds.): *The Indian Year Book 1932-33,* Bombay: The Times of India, n.d., p.570

45 India, Government of - Ministry of Health and Family Welfare (ed.): *Health Statistics of India 1981.* Nasik: Government of India Press, 1982, pp. 136-137 (hereafter referred to as *HSI 1981)*

46 *HSI 1985, op.cit., p.188*

47 India, Government of - Ministry of Information and Broadcasting (ed.): *India 1985. A Reference Annual,* New Delhi: Ministry of Information and Broadcasting, 1986, p.147

48 *HSI 1985,* op. cit., p. 186

49 K.M. Pillai/P.R. Dutt: "Sociology of Medicine and Social Change in India". *Bulletin of the Gandhigram Institute of Rural Health and Family Planning,* X:3 (1976), p.72 and R.Chengappa: "Sexually Transmitted Diseases".*India Today,* VIII:14 (1983),p.57

50 *HSI 1985,* op. cit., p.191

51 L.Baric et al: "cancer education in Kancheepuram".*internationales journal für gesundheitserziehung,* XVII:1 (1974), p.34. Chengappa reports about estimates in1984 that three lakhs Indian would die every year from cancer, and that currently there were 1.5 million Indians stricken by the disease, a figure which is supposed to increase to 4.5 million in the year 2000. R. Chengappa: "Cancer. A Growing Threat". *India Today,* IX:19 (1984),pp. 42-43

52 *The Illustrated Weekly of India,* 27.12.1981

53 *HSI 1985,* op. cit., p. 194; see also S.C. Seal: "Present Health Status and Some Suggestions for the Future Action".*Indian Journal of Public Health,* XXVI:4 (1982), p.221

54 A. Verghese/A. Beig: "Neuroses in Vellore Town". *Indian Journal of Psychiatry,* 16:1 (1974), p.7

55 *Indian Express,* 8.6.1983

56 *HSI 1981,* op.cit., pp. 148-155; unfortunately the HSI 1985 does not give this kind of table any more.

57 J.D.Sethi: "India's Bigological Decay".*Indian Express,* 5.12.1982, p.5. The author concludes his article by stating that at the present rate of expansion 'it will take more than 100 years before the public health care reaches the poor." (p.5) The high number of sick people was confirmed by a model investigation of the South Kanara District in Karnataka in 1977. It showed that out of 443 respondents, who accounted for more than one million of the entire rural population which was about 50% of the total district population, only 22 did not mention any disease. According to frequency the order was: dental ailments, skin disease, malaria, tuberculosis, mental ailments, leprosy, filaria. C. Aranha: *Report of the South Kanara District Health Survey,* Mangalore: The South Kanara

District Unit of the Voluntary Health Asociation, Karnataka, 1978, p. 59. See also J.G. Gill: "A Morbidity Survey for Chronic Illness by the Household Interview Technique". *Indian Journal for Public Health*,XXVI:1 (1982), who reported that 160 persons in a New Delhi middle class population of 1302 were found to be suffering form 201 chronic diseases; that is a prevalence rate of 123 chronically sick (or 154 chronic sicknesses) per 1000 population (p.55).

58 India, Government of - Ministry of Information and Broadcasting (ed.): *India 1987. A Reference Annual*, New Delhi: Ministry of Information and Broadcasting, 1988, p.171

59 *HSI 1981*, op. cit., p.409; *HSI 1985*, op.cit., p.79

60 C.B. Joshi: "Health Planning Structure in India". *Bulletin of the Gandhigram Institute of Rural Health and Family Welfare Trust*, XVI:2 (1981),p.81

61 P.O.George (ed.): *Health Care Administration Manual -II*, Kalamassery: Kerala Voluntary Health Services, 1986, pp.7-19 and 20-43

62 R.S. Arole: Community Health as Tool for People's Organisation, in: W.Fernandes (ed.): *People's Participation in Development*, New Delhi: Indian Social Institute, 1981, p.28

63 The International Conference on Primary Health Care at Alma Ata (USSR) in 1978 recommended in its well-known Declaration that primary health care is the key to attaining health for all. In seven points the Declaration defines what primary health care is, namely it

"1. reflects and evolves from the economic conditions and sociocultural and political characteristic of the country and its communities and is based on the application of the relevant results of social, biomedical and health services research and public health experience;

2. addresses the main health problems in the community, providing promotive, preventive, curative and rehabilitative services accordingly;

3. includes at least: education concerning prevailing health problems and the methods of preventing and controlling them; promotion of food supply and proper nutrition; an adequate supply of safe water and basic sanitation; maternal and child health care, including family planning; immunizations against the major infectious diseases, prevention and control of locally endemic diseases; ap-

propriate treatment of common disseases and injuries; and provision of essential drugs;

4. involves, in addition to the health sector, all related sectors and aspects of national and community developement, in particular agriculture, animal husbandry, food, industry, education, housing, public works, communications and other sectors; and demands the coordinated ettorts of all those sectors;
5. requires and promotes maximum community and individual self- reliance and participation in the planning, organization, operation and control of primay health care, making fullest use of local, national and other available resources; and to this end develops through appropriate education the abilities of communities to participate;
6. should be sustained by integrated, functional and mutually- supportive referral systems, leading to the progressive improvement of comprehensive health care for all, and giving priority to those most in need;
7. relies, at local and referral levels, on health workers, including physicians, nurses,midwives, auxiliaries and community workers as applicalble, as well as traditional practitioners as needed, suitabily trained socially and technically to work as a health team and respond to the expressed needs of the community."

World Health Organization (ed.): *Alma-Ata 1978. Primary Health Care,* Geneva: WHO, 1978, pp.4-5

64 H.Mahler: "The meaning of health for all by the year 2000'.*World Health Forum,* 2:1 (1981), pp. 5-20

65 ideas and action (ed.):"Towards a Rural Health Development Strategy". *ideas and action,* No.145,1-2/1982, p. 49. A typical example of this autocratic approach is represented by V. Natarajan who advocates for the creation of a "health communication" which he seems to see in a better way of transmitting health knowledge focussing on do's and don'ts. V. Natarajan:"Health Education In Policy Formulation".*FIRH and FWT Bulletin* (Gandhigram), XVII and XVIII (1982-83), p.80

66 D. Banerji: *Health Education and Community Health Behaviour,* New Delhi: Voluntary Health Association of India, n.d.(special print),p.1

67 See for example Central Health Education Bureau (ed.): *Resource Book on Health for Teachers,* New Delhi: CHEB,

1973 and V.N. Bhave et al (eds.): *You and Your Health*, New Delhi: National Book Trust, [2]1979

68 V.T.H. Gunaratne:"health for all by the year 2000". *international journal of health education,* Supplement to Vol.XXIII, Issue No.1, 1980, pp. 5-6

69 C.M.E. Matthews et al: "education to overcome malnutrition in rural pre-school children". *international journal of health education,* Supplement to Vol. XX, Issue No. 4, 1977, pp. 2-3

70 An excellent example is the movement of adivasis at Junglepati in Maharashtra. This movement, called Bhoomi Sen, has worked since 1970 for liberation from oppression and for the establishment of people's power. The method of the Bhoomi Sen consists of (1) mobilization, (2) consientization and (3) organization (as opposed to spontaneous action). G.V.S. de Silva et al: "Bhoomi Sen. A Struggle for People's Power".*development dialogue, 1979:2, pp. 55-62*

71 swasth hind (ed.); "Central Health Education Bureau. Landmarks 1956-1981". *swasth hind,* XXVI: 3-4 (1982), pp.82-83

72 K. Deb:*Rural Development in India Since Independence,* New Delhi: Sterling, 1986, p.230

73 The following of the print media published by the CHEB are glaring examples: "Against Vitamin'A' Deficiency" (1977), "Role of Peripheral Health Institutions in Tuberculosis Control" (1979), "Measles" (1980), "Japanese Encephalitis" (1981), "You Can Prevent Typhoid" (1981), 'You Can Prevent Lathyrism" (n.d.). On the other hand, the teaching and learning materials of the Voluntary Health Association of India, an organization of voluntary hospitals and health assciations set up in 1974, are far better. They inhere a spirit of community orientation, and they are born out of experience, practice and commitment. The system of booklets, books, slide series, charts and flash cards enables health eduaction personnel to pursue a flexible curriclulum which does not give the lecture method a predominant place. Good examples are the slide series of the "Jamkhed Comprehensive Health Care and Agricultural Development Work" (1977, originally produced by the London based Fundation for the Teaching Aids at Low Cost) and the flash card set "Tuberculosis is Curable" (n.d.), and, above all, the set of various materials to guide the process of "Teaching Village Health Workers" inspired by the experiences of the Jamkhed project; and the Indian editions

of D.Werner/B.Bower: *Helping Health Worker's Learn* and D.Werner: *Where There is No Doctor.*

74 India, Government of - Ministry of Health (ed.): *Report of the School Health Committee,* Faridabad: Government of India Press, 1965, p.89

75 C.Aranha: *Report of the South Kanara District Health Survey,* op. cit., p.68

76 Central Health Education Bureau (ed.): *Health Education,* Vols.1-3, New Delhi: Directorate General of Health Services, 1972. Here are their topics (they are only slightly different in the different age groups): 1. Personal hygiene/health. 2. Environmental hygiene/health. 3. Control of (communicable) diseases. 4. Food and Nutrition. 5. Health conditions in town or village/community health. 6. Growth and developmeent. 7. Rest, sleep, exercise, posture, leisure time. 8. Safety and first aid.

77 For example K.Madhavankutty: *Arōgya Pāthāvali,* Trivandrum: KANFED, 1978 (in Malayalam)

78 L.S. Saraswathi: "The Content of Adult Education Programme". *Indian Journal of Adult Education,* 39:2 (1979), pp. 30-32

79 T. Dharmalingam: *Health Education in Hospitals,* Gandhigram: The Gandhigram Institute of Rural Health and Family Planning, 1980, p.7

80 India, Government of - Ministry of Health and Family Welfare (ed.) : *Health Information India 1988,* New Delhi: Ministry of Health and Family Welfare, 1988 (thereafter referred to as *HII 1988*), p.88, 135, 136

81 S.Nagaraj et al: "health education status in teaching hospitals and associated health centres in India". *internationales journal für gesundheitserziehung,* XVIII:3 (1975), p.157

82 T. Dharmalingam: *Health Education in Hospitals,* op. cit.

83 *Ibid.*, pp. 21-22: skin diseases 3.119, helminthiasis 2.078, enteritis and other diarrheas 1.468, deficiency diseases 893, sexually transmitted diseases 739, tuberculosis 583, gastritis 236, gastro intestinal tract infection 187 (classified were only diseases of an occurence of more than 175 per year for in-patients and out-patients).

84 But a note of caution has to be issued. The santiation situation in hospitals is hardly encouraging health education programmes. A study-project report by the Department of Social and Preventive Medicine of the Kanpur Medical College in 1979

revealed the disastrous sanitation situation in four big and renowned Kanpur hospitals. It established that these hospitals "have an incredibly high rate of infection and atmospheric contamination".*India Today,* VII:13 (1982),p.119

85 T. Dharmalingam: *Health Education in Hospitals, op. cit., pp.93-94*

86 *Ibid.*, p.100

87 R. Venkataratnam: *Medical Sociology in an Indian Setting,* Madras: Macmillan, 1979, p.252

88 S. Nagaraj et al: "health education status in teaching hospitals and associated health centres in India", op. cit., p.164

89 J. Magee/W.C.Cockburn:"The mass media - players or spectators?"*World Health Forum,* 3:2 (1982), p.133

90 V.A. Moss: Padhar Hospital Community Health Project, in: Indian Council of Medical Research (ed.): *Alternative Approaches to Health Care,* New Delhi: ICMR, n.d. (1976/77), pp. 80-86; here: p. 82

91 *Ibid.*, p. 82

92 C.B. Joshi et al: "An Evaluation of Domiciliary Health Care Rendered by the Trained MPHWS (Multipurpose Health Workers Scheme) in Maharashtra and Andhra Pradesh (1976-1978)".*Bulletin of the Gandhigram Institute of Rural Health and Family Planning,* XV:3 (1980), passim

93 R.S. Arole: Comprehensive Rural Health Project, Jamkhed, in: ICMR (ed.): *Alternative Approaches to Health Care,* op. cit., pp. 95-101; here: p.100

94 E.R. Ram: Integrated Health Services Project, Miraj, in: ICMR (ed.): *Alternative Aproaches to Health Care,* op. cit., pp. 114-123; here: pp.116-117

95 A valuable overview is given by C. Leslie: "India's Community Health Workers Scheme: A Sociological Analysis". *Ancient Science of Life,* 9:2 (1989-90), pp. 40-53

96 There is, of course, little evidence for this optimistic view in Leslie's overview. *Ibid.* On the other hand, it is surprising that he appears to have not taken into account much of the educational approaches in the health workers scheme.

97 Nevertheless a note of warning seems to be necessary. The debate in the WHO journal *World Health Forum,* in the middle of the last decade, on the village or community health worker has yielded more scepticism about the succesful role of this worker. The tenor of the debate was that government ad-

ministrators and health officials would probably expect too much from these workers who in the eyes of the villagers would still follow a top-down approach whereas the officials would believe that using village health workers was a bottom-up approach. It was also criticised that village health workers would usually support the selective approach in primary health care (working for a few selected programmes) rather than supporting the comprehensive approach which "emphasizes social control over health services". D. Banerji: "Primary health care: selective or comprehensive?" *World Health Forum,* 5:4 (1984), p. 314; see also to the debate M.Skeet: "Community health workers: promoters of inhibitors of primary health care?" *World Health Forum,* 5:4 (1984): M. Jancloes: "Could villages do better without their volunteer health workers?" *World Health Forum,* 5:4 (1984); and R.N. Ratnaike et al: "Village health workers and malnutrition: a project that failed". *World Health Forum,* 5:4 (1984).

98 Examples are the studies of L.Baric et al: "cancer education in Kancheepuram", op. cit., showing that only a minority of women have been attracted by cancer preventive tests; of K.K. Misra: "safe water in rural areas". *internationales journal für gesundheitsersziehung,* XVIII:1 (1975), finding that a better water supply would lead to less diseases; of S.K. Sandhu et al: "adoption of modern health and family planning practices in a rural community of India". *internationales journal für gesundheitserziehung,* XX:4 (1977), coming to the conclusion that personal communication was a better means of health education than mass communication; and of V. Ramadasmurithy et al: "nutrition education and SITE telecasts". *internationales journ al für gesundheitserziehung,* XXI:3 (1978), proving the poor attendance of the 1975 SITE nutrition telecasts.

99 V.T.H. Gunaratne: "health for all by the year 2000", op.cit., p.9

100 The curriculum of this second part of the course is available in L. Ramachandram/T. Dharmalingam: *A Textbook of Health Education,* New Delhi: Vikas, 1983

101 M.K. Gandhi: *The Nature Cure,* Bombay: Pearl, 1965, p.2

102 *Ibid.,* p.8

103 *Ibid.* p.9

104 This has led, for example the Central Council of Indian Medicine in mid-1983 to advertisements in the national press

under the headline "Beware of Fake Medical Institutions/Practitioners". *Indian Express,* 22.8.1983

105 See to this complex D. Banerji: *Health Education and Community Health Behaviour,* op. cit.; K.R. Prasad et al: "A Study of Infective Heaptis Outbreak in Tirupati Town". *Indian Journal of Public Health,* XXVI:1 (1982); J. Murali et al: "Pattern of Utilization of Health Care Facilities by a Selected Urban Community in Delhi". *Indian Journal of Prevention and Social Medicine,* 12:2 (1981); D.N. Kakar: "Indigenous and Cosmopolitian Medicine in a North Indian Town".*Bulletin of the Gandhigram Institue of Rural Health and FamilyWelfare,*XXI:1 (1981); K. Sharma et al: "A Bio-Medical House to House Rural Survey of Village Durgapur (District Patiala)". *The Journal of Research In Indian Medicine,* VIII:3 (1973); V.Kochar et al: Strengthening the Folk Health System, in: ICMR (ed.) : *Alternative Approaches to Health Care,* op. cit., pp. 201-217; P. Hockings: *Sex and Diseases in a Mountain Community,* New Delhi: Vikas, 1980 ; G.Djurfeldt/S. Lindberg:*Pills Against Poverty,* New Delhi: Macmillan, 1980; C.M.E. Matthews: Health and Culture in a South Indian Village, New Delhi: Sterling, 1980; K.P. Shukla: *Traditional Healers in Community Health, Varanasi: Gomati Krishna; P.H.Raj: "Image of Some Existing Medical Systems Among Indian Rural Communities".Ancient Science of Life, 9:3 (1989-90)*

106 M.L. Dwivedi: Historical Background of and Introduction to Ayurveda, in: Pandit Shiv Sharma (ed.): *Realms of Ayurveda,* New Delhi: Arnold Heinemann, 1979, pp. 86-99; here; p. 94

107 *Ibid.*, pp. 91-94 and V.B.Dash: *Fundamentals of Ayurvedic Medicine,* Delhi: Bansal,[2] 1980, p.4

108 To mention only one: the success of J.P. Deshpande in the surgery treament of fistula-in-ano with a technique already described in the Sushruta Samhita. J.P. Deshpande: The Ayurvedic Treatment of Fistuila-in-Ano, in: Pandit Shiv Sharma (ed.): *Realms of Ayurveda,* op. cit., pp. 181-194. On the other hand, even a post-graduate centre like that for Ayurveda at the B.H.U. has no facilities for panchakarma, one of the important treatments in Ayurveda.

109 J. Filliozat; *The Classical Doctrine of Indian Medicine,* Delhi: Munshiram Manoharlal, 1964, p.31

110 *Ibid.*, p.31

111 P.S. Sharma: *Ayurvedic Medicine - Past & Present,* Calcutta: Dabur, 1975, p. 184

+P.H. Raj: "Image of Some Existing Medical Systems Among Indian Rural Communities". *Ancient Science of Life,* 9:3 (1989-90)

112 R.J. Majumdar/A.D. Pusalkar (eds.): *The Bhāratiya Itihāsa Samiti's History and Culture of the Indian People.* Vol. I: The Vedic Age, London: Allen & Unwin, [3]1957,p.459

113 P.M. Mehta: History of Indian Medicine, in: Pandit Shiv Sharma (ed.): *Realms of Ayurveda,* op. cit., pp. 47-85; here: p.65

114 *Ibid., p. 68*

115 J. Filliozat; *The Classical Doctrine of Indian Medicine,* op. cit., p.18

116 *Ibid.*, pp. 11-12

117 *Ibid.*, p. 14

118 J. Mitra: *History of Indian Medicine form pre-Mauryan to Kuṣāṇa Period,* Varanasi: Jyotiralok Prakashan, 1974, p. 4. The dominant role of Buddhism, for example, in the development of Ayurveda in Kerala is mentioned by S.A. Menon: *A Survey of Kerala History,,* Kottayam: Sahitya Pravarthaka Co-operative Society, 1970, p. 93: Buddhism held sway in Kerala in the acient period, and Vaghbhata, the author of the Ashtanga-hridya, was supposed to be a Buddhist. It was a common practice that free medical aid was given by the dispensaries of Buddhist monastries. A.L. Basham: *The Wonder that was India,* Calcutta: Rupa, 1971, p. 501, is of the opinion that besides yoga, Buddhism encouraged medical knowledge considerably: "... the Buddhist monk often served as a doctor among the lay folk from whom he begged his food; morevover he was encouraged to care for his own health and that of his fellow-monks, and his creed tended towards rationalism and a distrust of the medical magic of earlier times."

119 P.M. Mehta: History of Indian Medicine, op. cit., p.76

120 But D.D. Kosambi: *The Culture and Civilisation of Ancient India in Historical Outline,* New Delhi: Vikas, 1988 (1964) holds the view that the degeneration of Indian science began much earlier, viz. after Ashoka, because of the absence of logic and the contempt for mundane reality besides "the inability to work at manual and menial tasks" and the "emphasis upon learning basic formulas by rote" (pp. 174-175).

121 Among the first who gave official recognition to the merits of Ayurveda and its suitability to the Indian condition were the rulers of Travancore. K.S. Menon: Ayurveda, in: T.K.K. Menon (ed.): *Progress of Cochin,* Ernakulam: Cochin Government Press, 1932, pp. 279-394: here: p. 388

122 V.B. Dash: *Fundamentals of Ayurvedic Medicine,* op. cit., pp. 13-14

123 W. Durant: *The Story of Philosophy,* New York: Simon and Schuster, n.d. (originally published in 1926), p.2

124 T.C. Jain: Ayurveda and its Basis in Samkhya Philosophy, in: Pandit Shiv Sharma (ed.): *Realms of Ayurveda, op. cit., pp. 285-296; here: pp. 285-286*

125 P.T. Raju: *The Philosophical Traditions of India,* London: Allen & Unwin, 1971, p.157

126 R.R. Pathak: Metaphysial & Philosophical Discussion in Ayurveda, in: Pandit Shiv Sharma (ed.): *Realms of Ayurveda,* op. cit., pp. 297-310; here: p. 298; and V.N.B. Pandya: "Fundamental Principles of Ayurveda". *Ancient Science of Life,* 2:2 (1982-83), p. 102

127 T.M.P. Mahadevan: *Invitation to Indian Philosophy,* New Delhi: Arnold Heinemann, 1974, p.407

128 M. Hiriyanna: *Outlines of Indian Philosophy,* London: Allen & Unwin, 1968, p.20, 24. In his Foreword to a collection of essays by Indian philosophers of the 20th century, J.H. Muirhead writes: "Contrary to what is usually thought of the remoteness from practice of Indian Philosophy, what here strikes one is the lively sense of its practical value." S. Radhakrishnan/J.H.Muirhead (eds.): *Contemporary Indian Philosophy,* op. cit., p. 15. In the introduction of another source book, S. Radhakrishnan and C.A. Moore give the criteria of the distint spirit of Indian philosophy as beliefs in (1) the spiritual both in life and philosophy, (2) the intimate relationship of philosophy and life and the practical application of philospphy to life, (3) the introspective attitude and approach to reality, (4) idealism, (5) the extensive use of reason while accepting intuition as the only method through which the ultimate can be known, (6) the acceptance of authority providing a continuity of thought, and (7) the overall synthetic approach to the various aspects of experience and reality. S. Radhakrishnan/C.A. Moore (eds.); *A Source Book in Indian Philosophy,* Princeton: Princeton University Press, 1967, pp. XXII-XXVIII

129 Recently an interesting opinion has been given by P. Bala who writes that Ayurveda physicians in pre-Buddhist days must have developed a materialist view of nature. Concepts of the Lokayata school of philosophy were borrowed by these Ayurveda scholars: "They observed a fundamental unity of man and nature. Since man was believed to be made up of the same stuff of which everything in nature was made, nothing in nature was considered irrelevant for medical purposes." P. Bala: "Indigenous Medicine and the State in Ancient India". *Ancient Science of Life,* 5:1 (1985-86), p.1

130 S.Dasgupta: *A History of Indian Philosophy,* Vol. I, Cambridge: C.U.P., 1973,pp. 62-76

131 S.Radhakrishnan in the introduction of his *Indian Philosophy*, Vol. I, London: Allen & Unwin, 1977, p. 48, explains that dṛś - to see may be either "perceptual observatlon", "conceplual knowledge:", "intuitional experience", "inspection of facts", "logical inquiry", or "insights of soul".

132 V.J. Thakur: Fundamentals of Ayurveda, in: Pandit Shiv Sharma (ed.): *Realms of Ayurveda,* op. cit., pp. 108-123 here: pp. 112-123

133 S.P. Gupta: *Psychopathology in Indian Medicine (Ayurveda),* Aligarh: Ajaya, 1977,pp. 23-26,

134 R. Safaya: *Indian Psychology, New Delhi: Munshiram Manoharlal, 1976, p.320*

135 V.J. Thakur: Fundamentals in Ayurveda, op. cit., p. 122. A. Roșu argues that the commitment to reason and the desire for rationality and, at the same time, the profound respet for the handed-down teachings was shown by the attempts of the ancient physicians "to harmonise the determination of karman with the raison d'etre of health care. They claimed that it was not only piety but also hygiene which could counteract the mechanism of karman in such a way that a full measure of life of a hundred years or more could be possible. The analysis of means of right knowledge (prāmaṇa) applicable in the diagnosis of the diseases and the procedure for medical academic debates bear witness to the concern of the physicians for logical accuracy in their reasoning. The work of Caraka includes something without equivalent in the history of medicine, a short treatise on logic for the use of practitioners." A. Rosu: "Medicine and Psychology in Ancient India". *curare.* 4:4 (1981), p.206

136 V.J. Thakur: Fundamentals of Ayurveda, op, cit., p.123

137 R. Safaya: *Indian Psychology,* op. cit., p.1

138 V.B.Dash: *Fundamentals of Ayurvedic Medicine,* op. cit., p.19

139 P.S. Sharma:*Ayurvedic Medicine - Past & Present,* op. cit., pp. 164-165

140 K.N. Udupa: Present Status of Research in Ayurveda, in: Pandit Shiv Sharma (ed.): *Realms of Ayurveda,*op.cit.,pp. 311-325; here: pp. 312-313

141 A.R.P. Trivedi: "Functions of Vata (Based on Caraka)". *Ancient Science of Life,* 1:4 (1981-82), pp.184-191

142 K.N. Udupa: Present Status of Research in Ayurveda, op. cit., p. 314

143 *Ibid.*,p. 316

144 J.E. Sigdell: "A Brief Review of Ayurveda". *Ancient Science of Life,* 1:3 (1981-82), p.127

145 R.Lobo in his introduction to G.G. Thakkur: *Ayurveda,* Freiburg: Bauer, 1977, p. 21

146 V.B. Dash: *Fundamentals of Ayurvedic Medicine*, op. cit., p. 28; and J.E. Sigdell: "A Brief Review of Ayurveda", op. cit., p. 127

147 V.B. Dash: *Fundamentals of Ayurvedic Medicine,* op. cit., pp. 36-41

148 *Ibid.*, pp. 41-47

149 *Ibid.*, pp. 49-59

150 P.S. Sharma: An Introduction to Ayurveda, in: Pandit Shiv Sharma (ed.): *Realms of Ayurveda,* op. cit., pp. 11-21; here: p. 13. The dominant character of the Indian outlook on life, all-inclusiveness, has been also expressed in the phrase "Bhumeva sukham, Nalpe sukhamasti; happiness lies in the totality, not in fragments". H. Kabir: *Indian Philosophy of Education,* Bomaby : Asia, 1964, p. 177

151 L.S. Bhatnagar: Ayurvedic Concept of Health and Disease, in: Pandit Shiv Sharma (ed.): *Realms of Ayurveda.* op. cit., pp. 95-107, here: p. 95

152 B. Bhattacharya: *The Science of Tridosha,* Calcutta: Mukhopadhyay, [2]1975, p. 83

153 L.S. Bhatnagar: Ayurvedic Concept of Health and Disease, op. cit., p. 101

154 V.B. Dash: *Fundamentals of Ayurvedic Medicine,* op. cit., p. 22; see also V.J.Thakur: "Evolution of Diseases i.e. Samprapti Vignana". *Ancient Science of Life,* 1:1 (1981- 82), pp. 16-17

155 P.S. Sharma: *Ayurvedic Medicine - Past & Present,* op. cit., p. 160; and P.S. Sharma: An Introduction to Ayurveda, op. cit., p. 15
156 P.S. Sharma: *Ayurvedic Medicine - Past & Present,* op. cit., p.160
157 P.S. Gupta: *Psychopathology in Indian Medicine (Āyurveda),* op. cit., p. 403
158 P.S. Sharma: *Ayurvedic Medicine - Past & Present,* op. cit., p. 159; and L.S. Bhatnagar: Ayurvedic Concept of Health and Disease, op. cit., pp. 104-105
159 J.E. Sigdell; "A Brief Review of Ayurveda", op. cit., p. 138; and L.S. Bhatnagar: Ayurvedic Concept of Health and Disease, op. cit., pp.106-107; and K.N. Udupa: Present Status of Research in Ayurveda, op cit., pp.321-323
160 B.B. Gaitonde: Pharmacological Screening of Ayurvedic Drugs, in: Pandit Shiv Sharma (ed.): *Realms of Ayurveda,* op. cit., pp. 24-72. A first volume of the Ayurvedic Formulary containing some 450 formulations has been published by the Ayurveda Pharmacopeia Committee under the Chairmanship of A.N. Namjoshi in 1978. A second volume with another 500 formulations is under preparation. But compared to the estimated number of 23.000 formulations of the 800 single drugs and 200 compound medicines given in the ancient treatises of Nighantu or books of pharmacopeia, this work is only a beginning. A. Namjoshi: Ayurvedic Pharmacopeia and Drug Standardization, in: Pandit Shiv Sharma (ed.): *Realms of Ayurveda* op. cit., pp. 217-247; here: p. 218, 230
161 P.S. Sharma: An Introduction to Ayurveda, op. cit., p. 14
162 A. Namjoshi: Ayurvedic Pharmacopeia and Drugs Standardization, op. cit., p. 228
163 V.B.Dash: *Fundamentals of Ayurvedic Medicine,* op. cit., pp. 23-38
164 *Ibid.,* pp. 59-63
165 V.N.S. Mooss: *Ayurvedic Treatments of Kerala,* Kottayam: Vaidya Sarathy, [2]1946
166 C.P. Shukla: Principles of Treatment, in: Pandit Shiv Sharma (ed.): *Realms of Ayurveda,* op. cit., pp. 166-180; here: pp. 166-167
167 *Ibid.,* pp. 172-173
168 *Ibid.,* pp. 173-179

169 M. Weiner/K. Goss: *The Complete Book of Homeopathy,* New York: Bantam, 1982, pp. 18-23

170 P.S. Sharma: Salient Differences between Ayurveda and Modern Medicine, in: Pandit Shiv Sharma (ed.): *Realms of Ayurveda,* op. cit., pp. 22-46; here: pp. 22-23

171 *Ibid.*, pp.23-24

172 *Ibid.*, p.25

173 *Ibid.*, pp. 25-35

174 *Ibid.*, pp. 35-38

175 *Ibid.*, pp. 38-39

176 *Ibid.*, pp. 39-40

177 *Ibid.*, pp. 40-42

178 *Ibid.*, pp. 42-45

179 The Sutra Sthana is quoted from the original prose text in R.K. Sharma's and B. Dash's translation. Where necessary further information is added based on the translator's elucidations of Cakrapani Datta's commentary of the 11th century: *Agniveśa's Caraka Samhitā,* Vol. I, 1976; hereafter referred to as *CS;* in the following, *Sutra Sthana* is abbreviated *SS* and the elucidations based on *Cakrapani Datta's* commentary *CD.*

180 Here a brief description of the whole content of the Sutra Sthana. The Vhesheja Catushka, the quadruple of durgs, contains the chapters I-IV. Its first chapter, entitled "Quest for Longevity" elucidates the foundations of Ayurveda. The other three chapters describe 28 varieties of gruel and the drugs in connection with the five elimination therapies (chapter II), 32 types of the most effective powders and ungents useful in different diseases (chapter III), and 600 purgatives along with their ingredients, various preparations of each one of them (Chapter IV). These chapters explain medicines for internal cleansing, external cleansing and for internal and external cleansing as well. The Svastha Catushka (quadruple on regimens for the maintenance of health) covers the chapters V-VIII. This quadruple is the most significant for practical aspects of the maintenance of health. Chapter V on "Quantitative Dietetics" does not only deal with food but conveys also a considerable number of rules of conduct. Chapter VI on "Qualitative Dietetics" describes the dietetics and regimens for the six seasons of the year. Chapter VII on "Non-Suppression of Natural Urges" enumerates thirteen natural urges which should not be suppressed and the urges which should be

suppressed if one wants to avoid diseases. The chapter also contains rules of how to prevent endogenous and exogenous diseases. The last chapter (VIII) of this quadruple gives a "Description of Sense Organs"; sense organs play a crucial part in the concept of prevention. The chapter, however, begins with an elucidation of mind; mind according to Ayurveda is not included under sense faculties. The third quadruple, the Nirdesha Catushka, deals with instructions of therapeutics. It contains the chapters IX-XII. There is first a brief chapter on the quadrate of therapeutics (chapter IX) describing the physician, the medicament, the attendant, and the patient. The topic is continued in chapter X with more details. Chapter XI on the three basic desires in life answers the question:For what one should live if one has attained good health? This is followed by an elaboration of the merits and demerits of vata, the major dosha (chapter XII). The Kalpana Catushka is the quadruple on the therapeutical process. It comprises the chapters XIII-XVI which explain the various therapeutic measures helping the alleviation of the vitiated doshas. Oleation therapy (chapter XIII) is considered to be the best remedy for alleviating vata. Chapter XIV expounds fomentation therapy which generally follows oleation. Fomentation is useful for all diseases caused by the vitiation of both vata and kapha. Elimination therapies always follow oleation and fomentaion. In chapter XV the requirements of a physician in relation to elimination therapies are being described. In chapter XVI the duties of a physician who is really qualified to administer these therapies are being explained. The next quadruple is Roga Catushka. It describes diseases in the chapters XVII-XX. It covers head diseases, heart diseases, the states of doshas in different permutations and combinations, abscesses, the course of movement of doshas (chapter XVIII)); three types of swellings, the normal function of doshas and signs and symptoms of doshas and signs and symptoms of diminished and aggravated doshas (chapter XVIII); eight types of abdominal diseases (chapter XIX); classification of diseases, enumeration of diseases caused by vata, pitta and kapha (chapter XX). The sixth quadruple, the Yojana Catushka, explains the administration of various therapies in its chapters XXI-XXIV. While expounding the pathophysiology and treatment of obesity and emaciation, chapter XXI also lays emphasis on the effects of good and sufficient sleep. Chapter

XXII describes the six therapies of reducing, nourishing, drying, oleation, fomentation and astringent therapy. Chapter XXIII explains the refreshing regimen. The last chapter (XXIV) elucidates blood formation and the regimen therefor. The seventh and last quadruple, the Annapana Catushka, deals with diets and drinks in its chapters XXV-XXVIII. In chapter XXV various theories relating to the origin of man and diseases are initiated especially with a view to determinig the qualities of wholesome and unwholesome diets and regimens. Chapter XXVI expounds at length the taste (rasa) and potency (virya) of diets, and the taste of the food after digestion (vipaka); the chapter also includes an excursus on matter in order to explain the formation of the six-fold tastes out of the five proto-elements. In chapter XXVII specific properties of twelve groups of diets and drinks are being described in detail. Chapter XXVIII elaborates the process through which transformation takes place in food so as to sustain vital breath (=life). The separate chapter XXIX expounds the ten resorts of life - the two temples, the three vital parts (heart, bladder, head), throat, blood, semen, ojas, rectum - and the qualifications of a good physician. The last chapter (XXX) of the Sutra Sthana gives a complete summary of the whole treatise.

181 *CS, Vimāna Sthāna*, VIII: 6-7, p. 218

182 *CS, Vimāna Sthāna*, VIII:3, pp. 216-217

183 *CS, SS*, I: 15-17, p. 19

184 *CS, VImāna Sthāna*, VII: 8, p. 219

185 W.A. Sodeman (ed.): *Pathologic Physiology*, Philadelphia/London: Saunders, [3]1966

186 *Ibid.*, p. 617

187 *Ibid.*, p. 252

188 *CS, SS*, IX: 24-25, p. 190

189 *CS, SS*, XXIX: 6-7, pp. 587-588

190 *The Sushruta Samhita*, Vol. II, 1981 (originally published in 1911)

191 *Ibid.*, pp. ii-iii

192 *Ibid.*, p. iii (emphasis mine)

193 *Ibid.*, p. vii

194 *Ibid.*, p. v

195 *Ibid.*, pp. ix-x

196 *Ibid.*, pp. x-xi (emphasis Mine)

197 *The Sushruta Samhita*, Vol. III, 1963 (originally published in 1916) Uttara-Tantra, XIX:15, p. 105

198 *The Sushruta Samhita*, Vol. II, 1981, p.ii (originally published in 1911)

199 According to S. Radhakrishnan, Being is the foundation of all existence and as that "not something like a stone or a plant, an animal or a human individual. Whenever we say that anything is, we make use of the concept of Being. It is therefore the most universal and the most comprehensive concept. We unfold the nature of Being by the study of existences, though we cannot prove it. It is self-evident. If Being were not, nothing can possibly exist. Being is in all that exists. We live in the world of existence, we think of some kind of existence or other, but in metaphysics we get beyond the sphere of daily life, the objects of science, and rise to the transcendent conception of Being itself. Being posits everything but is not itself posited. It is not an object of thought, it is not the result of production. It forms an absolute contrast to and is fundamentally different from all that is. If anything exists, then Being is." S. Radhakrishnan: Samsara or the World of Change, in: Y.H. Krikorian/A. Edel eds.): *Contemporary Philosophic Problems*, New York: Macmillan, 1959, pp. 323-336; here: pp. 328-329

200 *CS, SS*, V: 13, p. 110

201 *CS, SS, CD*, V, p. 110

202 *CS, SS*, XXVI: 12, p. 453

203 *CS, SS*, XI: 4, p. 203

204 *CS, SS*, XXX:15, p. 596

205 *CS, SS*, XI: 14-15, p. 209

206 *CS, SS*, XXX: 24, pp. 599-600

207 V.V. Vyas: "The Scope and Nature of Ayurveda". *Ancient Science of Life*, 1:3 (1981-82), p. 135

208 So, for instance, the same author: "Our tradition records a very long era (the Satya or Kṛtayuga) when the whole of the mankind was totally free from all the physical diseases. If such an age ever returns, the other systems of medicine will lose all their utility, but Ayurveda will not, because it will begin treating mānasa vyādhis or mental diseases. And if mānasa vyādhis too should disappear, then there is the treatment of natural diseases, namely hunger, thirst, sleep and the cycle of birth and death." *Ibid.*, p. 136

209 Take for example the various requirments of a hospitals: "First of all, an expert architect should design a good building. The building should be strong and it should not be exposed to winds. However, it should be so constructed as to allow wind only through one passage. It should provide for a comfortable moving space. The building should not be situated in a mountainous place nor should it be located near a bigger building. Besides the building should not be exposed to smokes, the sun, water, dust or undesirable noise nor should it have undesirable contacts, tastes, sight or smell. The building should be well equipped with a water reservoir.....latrine, bath room and kitchen." *CS, SS,* XV: 6, p. 289

210 O.P. Jaggi: *Indian System of Medicine*, Delhi: Atma Ram, 1973, pp. 80-81

211 R.J. Majumdar/A.D. Pusalkar (eds.): *The Bhāratiya Itihāsa Samiti's History and Culture of the Indian People*, Vol. I: The Vedic Age, op. cit., p. 581

212 S.L. Bhatia: *A History of Medicine with special reference to the orient*, New Delhi: Medical Council of India, 1977, p. 3

213 K.G. Namjoshi: *Health and Population Education*, Ahmedabad: Nandadeep Prakashan, 1979, p. 4

214 S.S. Sivananda: *Practice of Ayurveda*, Rishikesh: The Yoga Vedanta Forest University, 1958, p. 76

215 O.P. Jaggi: *Indian System of Medicine*, op. cit., p. 81

216 e.g. *CS, SS,* I: 53, p. 39 and IX: 4, p. 184

217 *CS, SS, CD*, IX, p. 184

218 *Ibid.*, p. 184

219 *Ibid.*, p. 185

220 *Ibid.*, p. 185

221 *CS, SS,* XXVIII, p. 581

222 *CS, SS, CD*, XXVIII, p. 581

223 The pathway to this is described as follows:

- Visit the preceptor, i.e., the one imparting instruction on salvation.
- Carry out his instructions.
- Exclusively serve to the fire.
- Follow the prescriptions of the religious scriptures.
- Understand the meaning of such scriptures.
- Have patience as described in the scriptures.
- Perform acts as prescribed therein.
- Devote yourself to the noble.

- Shun the company of the wicked.
- Dissociate with the wicked.
- Make statements which are true, useful for all and not harsh. These statements should be made after proper examination at appropriate time.
- Look at all creatures as if they represent yourself.
- Avoid all acquisitions.
- Wear loin cloth.
- Wear saffron coloured dress.
- Have a needle case for the sewing of a robe.
- Have a water pot for maintaining cleanliness.
- Have a sacred stick.
- Have a sacred begging bowl.
- Take prescribed food only once a day just to preserve your life.
- Have a bed consinting of dry leaves, grass, etc. just for rest.
- Use a wooden resting plank for meditation.
- Live in the woods without having any home.
- Avoid Drowsiness and laziness.
- Avoid attachment and hatred towards the objects of sense organs.
- Initiate actions like sleeping, staying, going, seeing, eating, enjoying, movement of the various limbs with a sense of recollections of the nature of your soul.
- Maintain serenity in the face of honour, praise, criticism and insult.
- Stand the onslaught of hunger, thirst, efforts, labour, cold, heat, wind, rains, happiness, miseries, and sensory contacts.
- Be not disturbed by sorrow, misery, respect, perturbation, vanity, greed, attachment, envy, fear, anger, etc.
- View pride as a disturbing factor.
- Remember the identical nature of creation, of the self, and the Universe.
- Be afraid of postponing actions conducive to salvation
- Have confidence in yogic practices.
- Be optimistic about spiritual attainments.
- Direct intelligence, patience, memory and strength to salvation.
- Restrain sense organs in the mind, restrain the mind in the self and finally the self in Himself.

- Realize different organs of the body as composed of dhatus (doshas).
- Realize that everything caused is miserable, ephemeral and not belonging to the Self.
- View all attached actions as sinful.
- Consider renunciation aspotent factor for happiness.

CS, Śārīra Sthāna, II, V: 11-12,pp.420-422

224 In this connection we should not forget that the birth of Ayurveda occured under very practical circumstances, namely to heal the wounds of soldiers they got in wars. R. Lobo in C.G. Thākkur: *Ayurveda*, op. cit., pp.28-30

225 *CS,Śārīra Sthāna*, Vol. II, V: 23-24, p.424

226 S.P. Gupta : *Psychopathology in Indian Medicine (Ayurveda) op. cit., pp.386-387*

227 *CS, Śārīra Sthāna*, Vol. II, V: 6-7, pp.416-417

228 *Ibid.*, VI: 3, p.426

229 *CS, SS*, XI: 35,p. 220

230 *CS, SS*, XXVII: 345-347, p. 564

231 *CS,SS*, XXVII: 349-350 and XXI:, 36-38. pp.381-382

232 *The Oxford English Dictionary*, Vol. VI, 1961, p.897

233 *Ibid.*, Vol IV, p. 458, 459

234 V.E. Reddy/P.Sandeep: *Communication For Adult Education And Development in Rural Context,* Hyderabad: Department of Non-Formal Adult Education, Osmania University, 1983,p.28

235 in J.Ritter (ed.): *Historisches Wörterbuch der Philosophie*, Vol. 3, Darmstadt: WBG, 1974, p.559

236 *Ibid.*, p. 559. The "single thing" of content and form is, in another context, analysed by R. Panikkar as such: "The Gospel injunction not to put wine into old skins is more than a simple request for prudence... It means, at least to me, that life in its constant novelty cannot be squeezed into an old farmework, that change cannot be measured by an obsolete gauge. It also means that content and form constitue a single thing so that any content which could not create, as it were, its own form would be a kind of existential lie, just as any form which expresses a content other than its own becomes mere hypocrisy. (..) Nevertheless, if people feel the need for a new wine (a better one) - that is, if life is change and movement- there will be some tension and polarity between content and container, symbol and symbolized, *nāma-rūpa* and *avyakta* .

A living content, despite the fact that it depends for intelligibility on its form, will eventually have to break this selfsame form. Likewise, though united with a particular content, a form which is to remain alive will sooner or later fail to satisfy its own content. Yet what appears to be a *vicious* circle is in fact a *vital* circle. As the *Epistle to Diognetes* said long ago, it is not so much that the body contains the soul which contains the body...(...) Have we not observed all too often how the spirit is suffocated when it is encapsulated , how an ideal is limited when it is formulated in logical terms and how the message of a prophet is diluted when his vision is transferred to the written page or his call for reform is transferred into organizations (however necessary such things may be at the time)?" R.Panikkar: *The Unknown Christ of Hinduism*, London: Darton, Longman & Todd, 1981, pp.9-10

237 S.C. Dhyani: The Pharmacological Aspect of Ayurveda, in: Pandit Shiv Sharma (ed.): *Realms of Ayurveda*, op. cit., pp. 200- 210; here: pp. 202-203

238 *The Oxford English Dictionary*, Vol. VI, 1961, p. 249

239 *Ibid.*, Vol. IV, p.459

240 C.R. Bijoy: *Health: Emerging trends and Indian reality*, 1982 (mimeographed), p.8

241 C.R. Bijoy: "Ayurveda, an Appropriate Strategy for Social Health". *Ancient Science of Life*, 1:2 (1981-82), p.99

242 *CS, SS, CD*, I, p.25: Life is either hita (useful), ahita (harmful), sukha (happy) or dukha (unhappy).

243 *CS,SS*, I: 42, p.25

244 *CS,SS*, I: 46-47, p.33

245 *CS, SS*, VIII: 15-16, pp.169-170

246 *CS,Śārira Sthāna*, Vol. II, X: 42, p. 232

247 *CS, SS*, XXVI: 10, pp.451-452

248 *CS, SS, CD*, XXVI, p.453

249 *CS, SS*, IX: 26 p.191

250 *CS,SS,CD*, X,p.195

251 See S. Radhakrishnan's Introductory Essay to his translation and commentary of *The Bhagavadagītā*, London: Allen & Unwin, 1956, pp. 12-13

252 *The Oxford English Dictionary*, Vol. XII, 1961, p. 90; it is interesting to note that the Germanic adjective "whole" has the original meaning of "uninjured, sound, healthy, entire, complete" *Ibid.*, p.89

253 *CS, Sarira Sthāna*, Vol. II, I: 59-62, pp. 326-327
254 V.B. Dash: *Fundamentals of Ayurvedic Medicine*, op. cit., p.53: "What cause these differences among the several categories of matter? It is the state of mind and sense organs which are responsible. A piece of metal even though composed of the same conscious material, does not react to a stimulation in the same way as a human being, because in the former, the mind and senses are latent. In plants, where there is some reaction, but not the same as in animals and human beings, the mind and senses are in a semi-manifested or sub-latent form. In animals, the mind and senses are fully manifested but not to the same extent as in human beings."
255 S.P. Gupta: *Psychopathology in Indian Medicine (Āyurveda)*, op.cit., pp.357-358
256 *CS, SS*, XI: 3,p.202
257 S.P. Gupta: *Psychopathology in Indian Medicine (Āyurveda)*, op.cit., p. 374
258 *Ibid.*, pp. 374-375
259 *Ibid.*, pp. 376-382
260 *Ibid.*, p. 387
261 M.M. Pandya: "Prakrtivada or Inherent Constitution of an Individual". *Ancient Science of Life*, 1:4 (1981-82), p.218
262 *CS, SS*, VIII: 27, p. 179
263 *CS,SS*, I: 54, p. 39
264 *CS, SS*, XXX: 15, p. 596
265 *CS, Vimāna Sthāna*, Vol. II, VI: 14, p.203
266 V.B. Dash: *Fundamentals of Ayurvedic Medicine*, op. cit., pp.xi-xii
267 *Ibid.*, p. xii
268 P.R. Warrier: "Problems of Aging. Jara Cikitsa-The Ayurveda Treatment for Preventing and Curing Senility". *Ancient Science of Life*, 1: 4 (1981-82), p.211
269 *Ibid.*, p. 212. According to V.S.S. Shukla, rasayana should be applied from the age of sixteen before the decay of body tissue; he regards its application beneficial "only on pure and healthy body and mind". V.S.S. Shukla: "Consciousness and Its Profound Elevation with Ayurveda and Yoga". *Ancient Science of Life*, 2:2 (1982-83), p. 90, a view which is certatnly not undisputed.
270 P.R. Warrier: "Problems of Aging", op. cit., p. 212

271 "Constitutional strength is the one which exists in the mind and body from the very birth. Temporal is the one which is based on the division of seasons and the age of the person. The acquired strength is one which is achieved by the combination of diet and other regimen." *CS, SS*, XI: 36, pp.220-221

272 C.K. Ramachandran: "Gcrontology in Ayurveda". *Ancient Science of Life*, 5:1 (1985-86), p.6

273 *CS, SS*, V: 103, p.128

274 *CS, SS, CD*, V,p. 128

275 Cf. e.g. the tenfold law in the Laws of Manu: "Contentment, forgiveness, self-control, abstention from unrighteously appropriating anything, (obedience to the rules of) purification, coercion of the organs (control of the senses), wisdom, knowledge (of the supreme self), truthfulness, and abstention from anger (form) the tenfold law." S. Radhakrishnan/C.A. Moore (eds.): *A Source Book in Indian Philiosophy*, op. cit., p. 175

276 *CS, SS*, V: 3-4, pp. 105-106

277 *CS, SS*, VI: 6-48, pp. 132-143

278 *CS, SS*, VIII: 20,pp. 175-176

279 *CS, SS*, X̄XV: 38-39, pp. 423-425

280 *CS, Vimāna Sthāna*, Vol. II, I: 25/I-X, pp. 128-131

281 *CS, SS*, XXI: 36-38, pp.381-382

282 *CS, SS*, VI: 9-48, pp. 135-143

283 *CS, SS*, V: 18-102, pp. 112-127

284 *CS, SS*,VIII: 3-37, pp. 146-153

285 *CS, SS*, VI: 4-48, pp. 130-143; and *Vimāna Sthāna*, Vol. II, III: 9-20, pp.145-147

286 *The Sushruta Samhita, Sūtra-Sthāna*, Vol. I, XX: 24-27, pp. 192-193 and XXXV: 46-48, pp. 325-327

287 "One should not deviate from generally approved principles nor one should break any code of conduct; one should not walk during the night nor in an inappropriate place. One should not indulge in taking food, sexual relation or sleep during the dawn or dusk . One should not make friends, with children, the old, the greedy, the fools, persons under affliction or the enuchs. One should not have any iclination towards wine, gambliing or prostitutes. One should not insult anybody. One should not be conceited, undextrous, unfriendly nor one should back-bite. One should not insult the brahmanas nor one should beat the cows. One should not use harsh words

towards the old persons, teachers, persons, grouped together or kings. One should not speak too much nor one should oust kins folk, persons attached, persons who had helped during the time of misery and those who know (personal or family) secrets.

One should not be impatient or over-bold; one should not neglect the maintenance of servants; one should not have non-reliance on his own kins man; one should not enjoy alone; one should not have uncomfortable character, conduct, manners and diseases. One should neither rely on everybody nor suspect everybody. One should not be too meticulous at all times." *CS, SS*, VIII: 25-26, pp. 178-179; also *The Sushruta Samhita, Śārira- Sthāna*, Vol. II, X: 2-3, pp. 216-218; see also B. Dash/ L. Kashyap: *Basic Principles of Ayurveda*, New Delhi: Concept, 1980, pp. 287-291, which reproduces parts of the Ayurveda Saukhyam of Todarananda, a compilation of Ayurveda texts composted under the patronage of Todara malla who was appointed Dewan under Emperor Akbar. There ten types of sinful acts are listed: violence, stealing, desire for unnatural things, back-biting, use of strong words while quarrelling with others, speaking, lies, inconsistency in speech and action, desire, to enjoy others's achievement (?) , thinking ill of others, and thinking of taking away of other's wealth. "These sinful acts should be avoided ... According to his capacity,one should serve the unemployed persons, persons suffering from diseases and persons in grief. "*Ibid* ., p. 285. These verses were taken from the Ashtanga hridaya. The translation of "ista" as "desire to enjoy other's achievements" seems to be a bit abstruse. It is hard to understand that this desire is considered to be a sinful act. Instead, I suggest to take the translation of "ista" according to Monier-Williams as "to expect or ask anything from any one". M. Monier-Williams: *Sanskrit-English Dictionary*, New Delhi: Munshiram Manoharlal, 1981, p. 169

288 *CS,SS*, XI: 46, p. 227

289 W. Durant: *The Story of Philosophy, op. cit., P. 383*

290 J.E. Park/K. Park: *Textbook of Prevention and Social Medicine*, Jabalpur: Banarsidas Bhanot, [2]1981, p. 648

291 S.K. Simonds: "Herausforderung an die Gesundheitserziehung "*internationales journal für gesundheit erziehung*, XIX: 4 (1976), p. 245

292 R. Bergler: Mölichkeiten und Grenzen der Gesundeitserziehung durch Massenkommunikation, in: BzgA (ed.): *Bereitschalt und Barrieren in der Gesundheitserziehung*, Köln: BzgA, 1979, pp. 55-77; here: pp.58-64

293 D.A. Read et al: *Health Education: The Search for Value* Englewood Cliffs: Prentice Hall, 1977, p. 16

294 *Ibid.*, p. 16

295 They are, for example, part of the curriculum of the postgradute diploma courses in health education in the country.

296 *CS, SS*, VIII: 18, pp. 171-172

297 *The Sushruta Samhita, Śārīra-Sthāna*, Vol. II, X: 42, p. 232: "The education of a child should be commenced at a suitable age and with subjects proper to the particular social Varna or order it belongs to."

298 J. Ananth: "Is Western Training Relevant to Indian Psychiatry?" *Indian Journal of Psychiatry*, 23:2 (1981), p. 126

299 V.M. Dandekar/N. Rath: *Poverty in India*, Bombay: Economic and Political Weekly, 1971. See also S. Guhan: *Growth Inequalities and Poverty in Tamilnadu*, Madras: Cre-A, 1984, who with regard to Tamilnadu comes to basically similar results according to figures of the 26th Round of the National Sample Survery (1971-72).

300 V.M. Dandekar/N. Rath: *Poverty in India*, op. cit., p. 68

301 B.L. Kalra: "Size and distribution of operational holdings" *Kurukshetra*, XXIX:23 (1981), p. 5. Another, more recent study operated with figures of 1976-77 published by the Ministry of Agricultrure in 1983. Here too there are only marginal changes compared to the figures of Dandekar/Rath - K. Deb: *Rural Development in India Since Independence, op. cit., p. 36; see also C.T. Kurien: Dynamics of Rural Transformation*, New Delhi: Orient Longman, 1981, p. 110, who regarding asset distribution concluded that "the most revealing finding is that in rural Tamil Nadu, the assets of the top 1.0 per cent of the households exceeded those of the lower 90 percent put together both in the early sixties and in the early seventies."

302 In a recent talk, N. Rath has again stressed that more important than to measure poverty is to discuss what has to be done about the poor immediately and that the answer to this would be invariably to give work so that they can earn something. See N. Rath: A Brief Overview of Rural Poverty and Govern-

ment Policies and Programmes, in: Young India Project (ed.): *Tryst with Destiny*, Penukonda: YIP, 1988,pp. 1-7. See also R.C. Panda: "Perception of Poverty and Develoment". *Journal of Rural Develoment*, 9:1 (1990), p. 79: "Employment, to get a decent wage for overcoming the poverty, is the greatest aspiration of a peasant family."

303 V.M. Dandekar/ N. Rath : *Poverty in India,* op. cit., p. 137

304 *Ibid.*, p.138

305 *Ibid.*, p.138

306 N.Ray (ed.): *Papers on Develoment and Rural Poverty,*Penukonda: Young India Project, 1988, pp. 11-12

307 V.E.Reddy: *Generative Sources of Disadvantage*, Hyderabad: State Resource Centre for Adult Education/ Osmania University, 1983, pp. 12-35

308 F.Copleston: *On the History of Philosophy and other essays*, London: Search Press, 1979, p. 71

309 *Ibid.*, p.75

310 *Ibid.*, p.76

311 N.C. Chaudhuri: *Hinduism,* New Delhi: B.I. Publications, 1979

312 *Ibid.*, pp. 9-10

313 *Ibid., p.10*

314 *Ibid.*, p. 297

315 *Ibid.*, p. 303. It is interesting to note that the Siva- Samhita and the Gheranda-Samhita repeatedly emphasize the need of a guru, whereas the Patanjala Yoga-sutra does not impose such a restriction. "As such it would not be unreasonable to infer that a guru is perhaps not a *sine qua non* for purposes of learning Yoga ..." S. Ghosh (ed.):*The Original Yoga*, New Delhi: Munshiram Manoharlal, 1980, p.xx

316 N.Chaudhuri: *Hinduism*, op. cit., p. 304

317 *Ibid.*, pp. 306-307

318 P.V.Sukhatma: "The Meaning and Singnificance of Adhyatma for Education". *Ancient Science of Life*, 8:3-4 (1988-89), pp. 277-278, has taken up this demand again and pleads, amongst other things, for a new syllabus "which gives particular emphasis to aspects of agriculture, health and nutrition and especially moral and communal planning where Adhyatma (= "communication between mind and brain", i.e., the ability to communicate within ourselves, BP) and the belief in individual perfectability form the core of the philosphy. A child cannot possibly develop a feeling of unity with society and

country unless he converse with his own mind on the right and wrong that are involved in moral and social philosophy and is thus able to distinguish between need and greed."

319 H. Schipperges: Geschichte und Gliederung der Gesundheits erziehung, in: *Handbuch der Sozialmedizin,* Vol. II, Stuttgart: Enke, 1976, pp. 550-567; here: pp. 565-566

320 H.Vuori: "Das medizinische Modell und die Ziele der Gesundheitserziehung "*internationales journal für gesundheitserziehung,* XXIII: 1 (1980),p.25

321 L. van Parijs: "Überlegungen zum medizinischen Modell der Gesundheitserziehung und ihren Zielen". *internationales journal für gesundheitserziehung,* XXIII:4 (1980) pp. 224-236

322 *Ibid.*, p. 231

323 G.Schramm et al: *Sechs grundsätzliche Prinzipien der Gesundheitserziehung, in: BzgA (ed.): Bereitschaft und Barrieren in der Gesundheitserziehung,* op. cit., pp. 45-52; here : pp. 46-47

324 R.W. Carlaw: "trends in the organization of health education in three developing countries". *international journal of health education,* Supplement to Vol. XXIII, Issue No. 2, 1980, p. 10

325 ICSSR/ICMR (Indian Council of Social Science Research/ Indian Council of Medical Research) (eds.): *Health for All,* Pune: Indian Institute of Education, 1981, pp. 67-68

326 *Ibid.*, p. 74

327 A. Jha: *The Imprisoned Mind,* New Delhi: Ambika, 1980, who is very critical of it. A more postitive view is found in R.Lannoy: *The Speaking Tree,* London: O.U.P., 1974, who points out that "with the disintegration of traditional social roles and institutions" the guru-shishya relationship "incarnates a specific form of psychological bond". (p.348). See also W. Cenkner: *A Tradition of Teachers,* Delhi: Motilal Banarsidass, 1983, who basically restricts his analysis to the relationship inside the tradition, i.e., the religious domain with which it was originally associated, even in his chapter "The Teacher-Student Relationship Today" (pp. 154-174).

328 C.M.C. Matthews: *Health Education - The Missing Link in Medical Care,* New Delhi : VHAI, n.d.(1974),pp.1-8

329 World Health Forum (ed.) : Target 'Health 2000'". *World Health Forum,* 2:1 (1981), p. 37

330 *HSI 1985,* op. cit., p. 164, 166

331 *HSI 1981,* op. cit., p.58

332 D. Banerji: "Health as a Lever for Another Development", *development dialogue*, 1/1978, pp. 19-25

333 L. Doyal/I. Pennell: *The Political Economy of Health*, London: Pluto, 1981, pp. 12-13

334 D. Banerji: Health as a Lever for Another Development, op. cit., p. 21 and D. Banerji: "Health Behaviour of Rural Populations". *Economic and Political Weekly*, VIII: 51 (1973), p. 2267

335 J.P. Naik (ed.): *An Alternative System of Health Care Services in India*, op. cit.; ICMR (ed.) *Alternative Approaches to Health Care*, op. cit.; ICSSR/ICMR (eds.): *Health for All, op.cit.*

336 J.P. Naik: An Alternative System of Health Care Services in India, in J.P. Naik (ed.):*An Alternative System of Health Care Services in India*, op. cit., pp. 3-27; here: pp. 6-8, 10- 24

337 To this growing problem see W.V. Rane: "Why don't our drugs match our diseases?" *Science Today* , 16:10 (1982), who excellently summarizes the problem of production of luxury drugs. See also the special issue of *Health for the Millions* , VII:2-3 (1981), where the "drug-colonialism" is vehemently criticsed and a list of essential medicines is given. The position of the Inidian drug industry is represented by K. Jayaraman: *Indian Pharmaceutical Industry*, Bomay: Tata Economic Consultancy Services, n.d. (1980), who mainly blames the mechanism of control through the various governments. The international pressure is exemplarily analysed in C. Medawar: *Insult or Injury*? New Delhi: Indian Social Institute, 1981, demonstrating the absence of standards in marketing and advertising British drug and food products, and the apparent lack of concern about this absence.

338 This is a common thought in Ayurveda too as was recently expressed again by T.M. Srinivasan: "Systems Approach in Medical Technologies". *Ancient Science of Life* , 6:1 (1986-87), p.5: the spiritual dimension of all health care programmes would demystify death and dying and would by this provide significance and meaning to life and death.

339 K.G.Rao: Guidelines for Developing Alternative Models for Delivery of Heath Care, in ICMR (ed.): *Alternative Approaches to Health Care*, op. cit., pp. 191-200; here: pp. 195-196. Three programmes were suggested by an ICSSR/ICMR study group in order to achieve health for all by the year 2000 (ICSSSR/ICMR (eds.): *Health for All*, op. cit., pp. vii- xv):

(1) Intergrated development which includes

- rapid economic growth to double the national income per capita,
- full-scale employment,
- improvement in the status of women,
- adult education with emphasis on health education and vocational skills,
- universal elementary education for all children,
- welfare of scheduled castes and tribes,
- creation of a democratic, decentralized and participatory form of government,
- rural electrification,
- improvement in housing ,
- organizing the poor und underprivileged groups, and
- family planning.

(2) Improvement in nutrition, environment and health education:

- Nutrution shall be improved through adequate production of food and through increasing the purchase power of the poor.
- Improved environment shall reduce infection, make programmes of nutrition more effective, and help in reducing mortality. It includes safe drinking water supply, sewage dispersal, proper collection and disposal of solid wastes and their conversion into compost, proper disposal of night soil, town and village planning, housing for the rural poor and clearance of urban slums.
- Health education shall become an intergral part of general eduction.

(3) Provision of adequate health care service for all, espe cially for the poor and underprivileged.

340 It is a well-known fact that women in the country tend (or have to tend) to neglect their diseases. The ratio of men and women seeking medical treatment is reported to be 5:1. N. Murthy: "Reluctant patients - the women of India". *World Health Forum*, 3:3 (1982), p. 315

341 P.R. Warrier: "Problems of Aging", op. cit.

342 *Ibid.*, p.212

343 *Ibid.*, p. 212

344 *Ibid.*, p. 212

345 *Ibid.*, p. 212

346 Some people claim that panchakarma would eradicate diseases permanently and leave "no chance for relapse".

D.Ojah/A.Kumar: *Panchakarma -Therapy in Ayurveda*, Varanasi: Chaukhamba Amarabharati Prakashan, 1978, p.3

347 P.R, Warrier: "Problems of Aging", op. cit., p. 214. Another author says that kutipraveshika should be done for a period of three months to one year. C.K. Ramachandran: "Gerontology in Ayurveda", op. cit., p.7

348 P.R. Warrier: "Problems of Aging", op. cit., p. 215

349 *Ibid.*, p. 215

350 Very recently we have observed a strong trend in Government reports to stress the commitment for the promotion of the Indian systems of medicine as part of the total health delivery, as was done in the Health and Welfare Ministry's annual report for 1989-90, see *Indian Express*, 25.5.1990. We have to see whether this is a serious endeavour or just a joining of a fashionable fundamentalist wave in all what is Indian.

351 J. Laping: "'Traditional Medicine' in India. Decline and Future Perspectives". *Ancient Science of Life*, 7:1 (1987-88), pp. 7-8, comes, therefore, to the conclusion that wherever Ayurveda modernizes it takes place "with quite similar results as in the case of modernized medicine", viz. a "concentration of medical facilities in (big) cities", the "medical training is oriented towards modern diagnostic and therapeutic techniques", and "the therapies are more and more shaped on the drugs which are industrially manufactured, and on their marketing strategies".

352 A. Wiertz: "Psychische Gesundheit als Ziel therapeutischen und pädagoischen Handelns". *Das öffentliche Gesundheitswesen*, 43:6 (1981), p. 283; K.Biener: Gesundheitserziehung der Erwachsenen, in: *Handbuch der Sozialmedizin* (ed.): *Epidemiologie und präventive Medizin*, Vol. II, Stuttgart: Enke, 1976, pp. 568-579; here: p. 569; M.E. Schabacker: Verhalten in Gesundheit und Krankheit - Aufgaben und Probleme der Gesundheitserziehung, in : BFGE (ed.): *Gesundheit für alle bis zum Jahr 2000*, Bonn: BFGE, 1981, pp. 53-56; here: p. 53; J. Simpson: *An Introduction to Preventive Medicine*, London: Heinemann, 1970, p. 7; J.B. Meredith Davies: *Community Health, Preventive Medicine and Social Services*, London: Bailliere Tindall, 1979, p. 160; K.Heller/J. Monahan:*Psychology and Community Change*, Homewood: Dorsey, 1977, p. 116; J.E.Park/K. Park: Textbook of Preventive and Social Medicine, op. cit., pp. 24-31; N. A.

Nath: "Role of Health Education in Health Care". *swasth hind*, XXVI: 9 (1982), pp. 207-208

353 J.A. Muir Gray: *Man Against Disease*, Oxford: O.U.P., 1979, p. 123

354 J. Simpson: *An Introduction to Preventive Medicine*, op. cit., p. 3

355 J.A. Muir Gray: *Man Against Disease*, op. cit., p. 23

356 *Ibid.*, p. 25

357 *Ibid.*, p. 25

358 K. Heller/J. Monahan: *Psychology and Community Change*, op. cit., p. 16 (the authors follow the definitions by G. Caplan in " Principles of preventive psychiatry", 1964, pp. 16-17)

359 J.E.Park/K.Park: *Textbook of Preventive and Social Medicine*, op. cit., p. 24

360. *Ibid.*, p. 28

361 *Ibid.*, p. 28

362 *Ibid.*, p. 30; the decline can, however, also be explained with the disappearance of certain professions, e.g. chimney sweeps due to other forms of heating today.

363 N.Kisnerman: "Social work within the health services". *Adult Education and Development*, No. 19, 1982, pp. 224-225

364 See for example L.W. Greene/K.W. Jonhson: Health Education and Health Promotion, in: D. Mechanic (ed.): *Handbook of Health, Health Care, and the Health Professions*, New York: The Free Press, 1983, pp. 744-765; here: p. 745, and WHO/Europe (ed.): "Health Promotion: A Discussion Document". *Newsletter* (European Bureau of Adult Education), 2-1984, p. 1

365 Despite that it is a common fact that interventions of primary prevention are far less in number than those of secondary and tertiary prevention. Studies in Germany have reported a ratio of about 1:4. E. Seidler: "Gesundheit für alle bis zum Jahre 2000". *Prävention*, 4:3 (1981), p. 70

366 J.E.Park/K.Park: *Textbook of Preventive and Social Medicine*, op. cit., p. 31

367 *Ibid.*, p. 29

368 *Ibid.*, pp. 29-30

369 *Ibid.*, p. 30

370 A young Ayurveda physician in Trivandrum once told me that young Ayurveda physicians today were hardly capable of distinguishing between vitiated doshas, whereas their fathers

were able to do so because they had devoted their entire life to Ayurveda.

371 C.P. Shukla: Principles of Treatment, op. cit., p. 168

372 *Ibid.*, p. 169

373 V.J. Thakkar: "Tridoshas in Relation to Swasthavritta". *Ayurvaidyan*, 2:4 (1989), p. 232

374 *CS, SS CD, XV*, pp. 287-288

375 *CS, SS*, XXVI: 196-216, pp. 528-530

376 *CS, Vimāna Sthāna*, Vol. II, VII: 94, pp. 261-262

377 P.Sabo: "Entwicklung und Stand kommunaler Gesundheitserziehung". *Prävention*, 3:2 (1980), p. 43

378 J.B. Meredith Davies: *Community Health, Preventive Medicine and Social Services*, op. cit., pp. 159-160

379 D.A. Read et al: *Health Education: The Search for Values*, op. cit.

380 *Ibid.*, p. 15

381 *Ibid.*, p. 16

382 *Ibid.*, p. 16

383 *Ibid.*, p. 16

384 M. Nichter/M.Nichter: "Health Education by Appropriate Analogy; Using the Familiar to Explain the New". *Convergence*, XIX:1 (1986), pp. 63-72

385 *CS, Vimāna Sthāna*, Vol. II, VI: 13-18, pp. 191-195

386 *CS, Śārīra Sthāna*, Vol. II, IV: 36, p. 406

387 *CS, SS*, VII:36-37, p. 153

388 K.S. Vakil/S. Natarajan: *Education in India*, Bombay: Allied, 1966, p. 10

389 V.J. Thakkar: "Tridoshas in Relation to Swasthavrita", op. cit.,p. 227

390 P.V. Sharma: "Religion and Health: Their Interdependence". *Ayurvaidyan*, 2:3 (1989), p. 160

391 *Ibid.*, p. 168, 169

392 *CS, SS, CD*, I, pp. 39-40

393 The present Ayurveda colleges are merely training physicians for curative work; see e.g. Ayurveda College Coimbatore (ed.): *Prospectus for 7 years "Ayurvedacharya" (B.A.M.S.) Course*, Coimbatore, n.d. (1982)

394 H.N. Anita: Alternatives to Health Care System, in: ICMR (ed.): *Alternative Approaches to Health Care*, op. cit., pp. 102- 113; here: p. 105

395 W. Schauwecker: Gesundheitserziehung, in: *Handbuch der Sozialmedizin* (ed.), Vol. III, *Sozialmedizin in der Praxis*, Stuttgart: Enke, 1976, pp. 46-65; here: p. 51

396 K.G. Namjoshi: *Health and Population Education*, op. cit., pp. 4-5

397 G. Myrdal: *The Challenge of World Poverty*, London: Allen Lane The Penguin Press, 1970, p. 182

398 D.W. Fisher: "adult education theory necessary in health education practice". *internationales journal für gesundheitserziehung*, XIX:2 (1967), p. 132

399 *Ibid.*, p. 134

400 C. Wulf: "Self-Education: An Essential Element of Education". *Education*, Vol. 26, 1982, p. 13 (emphasis mine)

401 S.C. Bhatia: *Education and Socio-Cultural Disadvantage*, Delhi: Xerxes, 1982, p. 45

402 A.E.Wood: *Knowledge Before Printing and After*, Delhi: O.U.P., 1985, p. 3, who then sums up and says that "traditional culture was organized to be *formal and intensive* in character, where modern culture is *informal and extensive*."

403 *CS, Vimāna Sthāna*, Vol. II, III: 13, p. 223

404 P. Lengrand: *An Introduction to Lifelong Education*, London: Croom Helm, 1975. K.H. Lawson in his essay on "Lifelong Education" finds the roots of lifelong education, which he understands more as a "policy *for* education" than a "concept of education" (p. 44), in European Humanism. In his explanation there is no aspect which could not be applied to classical Ayurveda ideas, e.g.: "'Man' is at the centre, but 'man' is an abstraction, therefore, lifelong education becomes concrete by stressing individual men. The development of knowledge for its own sake, and the development of rationality which are stressed in more traditional views on education, give way to the idea of 'personal development' as a prime objective in lifelong education." (p. 46) K.H. Lawson: *Analysis and Ideology: Conceptional Essays on the Education of Adults*, Nottingham: University of Nottingham, 1982

405 P. Lengrand: *An Introduction to Lifelong Education*, op. cit., p. 21

406 *Ibid.*, p. 150

407 *Ibid.*, p. 22

408 *Ibid.*, pp. 20-21

409 *Ibid.*, pp. 25-37

410 C.T. Kurien: *Poverty and Development*, Madras: C.L.S., 1974, p. 180

411 P. Lengrand: *An Introduction to Lifelong Education*, op. cit., p. 50. See also P.D.Mitchell: Continuing Education, in: D. Unwin/R.McAleese (eds.): *The Encyclopaedia of Educational Mass Media Communications and Technology*, London: Macmillan, 1978, pp. 174-186; here: p. 175, who attributes two aims to lifelong education: "the development of society as a whole and personality development of each citizen".

412 P. Lengrand: *An Introduction to Lifelong Education*, op. cit., p. 111

413 J. White: *The aims of education restated*, London: Routledge & Kegan Paul, 1982, p. 132, 133

414 P. Lengrand: *An Introduction to Lifelong Education*, op. cit., p. 139

415 D.M. Mackay: "Primary health care may be needed but is it wanted?" *World Health Forum*, 3:1 (1982), p. 89

416 Amongst them were the participants of the 1st Conference on the Role of Ayurveda and Traditional Medicine in Primary Health Care conducted at the Institute of Medical Sciences of the Banaras Hindu University in 1980 who tried to take stock of realities, chances and possibilities of how to integrate Ayurveda in the basic health care system. But the papers presented are not impressive according to their summaries published in the conference report; K.N. Udupa (ed.): *1st Conference on Role of Ayurveda & Traditional Medicine in Primary Health Care*, Varanasi: Banaras Hindu University, n.d. (1980). Another get-together of experts was apparently more successful as can be seen from its Proceedings ; Arya Vaidyan Rama Varier Educational Foundation of Ayurveda (ed.): *Proceedings of the workshop on Traditional Systems of Medicine (Ayurveda and Siddha) and Primary Health Care*, Coimbatore, 1984. In its recommendations health is recognised "as a lever for economic stability and progress", its needs should be tackled at individual and community level. The participants took a fresh approach to the health problems of the people taking into account practices and values of Ayurveda without neglecting achievements of modern medicine. They, for example, suggest the introduction of "Community Health Brigades" (Arogya Sena) which "should be constituted with youths and women of the community for specific action in five vital areas, viz. purity of environment

(Des Suddhi), purity of body (Deha Sudhi), purity of food (Ahara Suddhi), purity of water (Jala Suddhi), and purity of mind (Mano Suddhi)" (p. 11).

417 *Health for the Millions*, VIII:4 (1982), p. 33

418 This might be different in future when the research findings of a study on a primary health care model integrating the Indian system of medicine in villages near Coimbatore/Tamilnadu will be available; see to this B. Hyma et al: "Evolving a Rural Community-Based, Participatory Health Care Model Based on Indian Indigenous System of Medicine". *Ancient Science of Life*, 6:3 (1986-87). In a subsequent article by the authors it becomes clear that the people involved in this project are earnestly trying to base their work on popular participation (see e.g. pp. 153, 154-155, 161), on a strong role of health education (see e.g. pp. 147, 149), and on social learning (see e.g. p. 148); B. Hyma et al: "Development of a Rural Community Health Care Model Based on Indian Indigenous System of Medicine". *Ancient Science of Life*, 8:2 (1988-89).

419 Here, it seems appropriate, to refer to S. Kakar, a Western-trained Indian psychoanalyst, who, in his book *Shamams, Mystics and Doctors*, Bombay: O.U.P., 1982 , has described his change of attitude towards Ayurveda: "It seems I could not explore Ayurveda without an a priori idealization or denigration, till a change in the Western theories of healing took place which in a sense accorded me 'permission' to pursue an objective inquiry." (p. 223) Kakar is particularly attracted by the determination of the ancient Indian physicians "to invest the otherwise vague notion of 'wholenness' with concrete content" (p. 229). He also states that today the "latest scientific medical opinion" with regard to nutrition, sleep and healthy behaviour is "squarely in the realm of Ayurveda" (p. 223).

420 N.King (ed.): *Medical Care in Developing Countries*, Nairobi: O.U.P., 1966, p. 14

421 *Health for the Millions*, VIII:4 (1982), p.1

422 *Ibid.*, p.1

423 A.K.N. Reddy: The Technological Roots of Indian Poverty, in: Kamla Bhasin / R. Vimla (eds.): *Readings on Poverty, Politics and Development*, New Delhi: FAO, 1980, pp. 61-62

424 D.R. Pendse (ed.): *Statistical Outline of India, 1982*, Bombay: Tata Services Limited, [15]1982, p. 11. Estimations in a 1984 Planning Commision Reort give 'only' 38% who live below the

hunger and poverty lines; R. Mayur: "The Bhopal tragedy". *Development Forum*, XIII:2 (1985), p. 10. But new calculations come to "about 48.7 and 37.8 per cent, respectively in rural and urban India" for 1987-88 criticising the artificially low estimates of the Planning Commission. B.S.Minhas et al: "Declining Incidence of Poverty in the 1980s". *Economic and Political Weekly*, XXVI (1991) 27 & 28, p. 1673

425 D.R.Pendse (ed.): *Statistical Outline of India, 1982*, op. cit., p. 11

426 M.S. Adiseshiah: *Mid-year review of the Indian Economy (1987- 1988)*, New Delhi: Lancer, 1988, p. 33

427 S.K. Rao The Strategy of Development: The Twin Goals of Reduction in Poverty and Unemployment - A Critique, in: J.M. Reddy et al (ed.): *Seventh Five Year Plan. Performance and Perspectives.* New Delhi: Sterling, 1989, pp. 149-162; here: p.151

428 D.R. Pendse (ed.): *Statistical Outline of India. 1982, op. cit., p. 131; and D.R. Pendse (ed.): Statistical Outline of India 1988-89*, Bombay: Tata Services Limited,[18]1988, p. 142

429 D.R.Pendse (ed.): *Statistical Outline of India, 1982*, op. cit., p. 134

430 D.R. Pendse (ed.): *Statistical Outline of India 1988-89*, op. cit., p. 140; a recent press note published the figure of 32.7 million job seekers being on the registers at the end of 1989 (*Indian Express*, 23.3.1990).

431 A. Ghosh: *Indian Economy*, Calcutta: The World Press, [22]1979, p. 83

432 A.A. Waqif: The Structure of Unemployment and Employment Generating Strategies, in: J.M. Reddy et al (ed.): *Seventh Five Year Plan. Performance and Perspectives*, op. cit., pp. 130-148, here: p. 135

433 J. Dubashi: "Jobs for the Jobless". *India Today*, VIII:16 (1983), p. 83

434 A.Ghosh: *Indian Economy*, op. cit., p. 83

435 J. Dubashi: "The Poverty Syndrome". *India Today*, VI:22, p. 115

436 R. Pennant-Rea: "India. Treadmill or take-off?" *The Economist*, No. 7178, 28.3.1981, p. 44

437 P. Chopra: "The paradox of Kerala". *World Health Forum*, 3:1 (1982), p. 77

438 R. Pennant-Rea: "India. Treadmill or take off?" op. cit., p. 45; and P. Chopra: "The paradox of Kerala", op. cit., p. 77

439 J.P. Grant: "A new way of measuring progress in living standards". *World Health Forum*, 2:3 (1981), p. 375

440 A. Pacey: *The Culture of Technology*, Oxford: Basil Blackwell, 1983, p. 73

441 A. Sen: "How Is India Doing?" *Indian Express* (Express Magazine), 17.6.1990, p. 2

442 See e.g. N.A. Murthy/D.P. Pandey: *Ayurvedic Cure for Common Diseases*, Delhi: Orient, 1982, p.6

443 C.R. Bijoy: "Ayurveda, an Appropriate Strategy for Social Health", op. cit., p. 98

444 P.R. Krishnakumar: "The Alternative for Survival". *Ancient Science of Life*, 4:3 (1984-85), pp. 143-145

445 *Ibid.*, p. 146

446 D. Werner: "The village health worker: lackey or liberator?" *World Health Forum*, 2:1 (1981), p. 47

447 *Ibid.*, p.47

448 J.E. Park/K. Park: *Textbook of Preventive and Social Medicine*, op. cit., pp. 43-44

449 A. Bang: "People's Participation in Health". *Health for the Millions*, VIII:3 (1982), p. 2. In chapter 11 of the recently published *Eighth Plan Perspectives*, ed. by M.S. Adiseshiah, New Delhi: Lancer International, 1990, there is a note by the then Secretary of Health and Family Welfare, R.Srinivasan, which clearly illustrates again this bureaucratic approach in public health: "We have not done enough... to restore the primacy and leadership of the doctor to all issues of publlic health, especially the PHC doctor, easily the most educated on the spot. (...) He has ... to be the leader on all public health issues, and none better than him is available who can be credible to the people who believe anyone, once his curative effectiveness is demonstrated. For this we require both techniques of public health communication and epidemiological skills both in adequate measure given to young PHC doctors." (p. 208)

450 R.H. Cassen: *India: Population, Economy*, Society, London: Macmillan, 1978, p. 205

451 V. Kurien: "The Role of the Elite in Modernizing a Predominantly Rual Society". *ideas and action*, 4/1981, No. 142, p. 10

452 K. Sondi: *Problems of Communication in Developing Countries*, New Delhi: Vision, 1981, p. 131. This was certainly

in tune with the ideas and policies of the eighties and the opinion of many a scientist even today. For example, in M.S. Adiseshiah (ed.): *Seventh Plan Perspectives*, New Delhi: Lancer International, 1985, which contains the papers of 10 panel discussions in 1984 arranged by the International Centre's Economic Affairs Group on the Seventh Plan (1985-90) M.G.K. Menon, in the Section "Education, Science and Technology", stresses the "new biotechnologies" for the production of vaccines of good quality (p. 258) - but the whole document does not contain any other remark by an expert on the development of the health situation in the Seventh Plan! This has changed in M.S. Adiseshiah (ed.): *Eighth Plan Perspectives*, op. cit., which contains a note on issues related to public health (pp. 204-212).

453 H. Volken/A. Kumar/S. Kaithathara: *Learning from the Rural Poor*, New Delhi: Indian Social Institute, 1982, p. 63

454 In Latinamerica this educator is charactistically called "people's educator", "indigenous-organizer educator", "native educator" and "popular educator"; see e.g. L.R. Aspiazu: Ayni Ruway: Indigenous Institutions and Native Development in Bolivia, in: R.Kidd/N. Colletta (eds.): *Tradition for Development*, Bonn: German Foundation for International Development and International Council for Adult Education, 1980, pp. 82-110. F.V. Grossi deffines him as "unusual": "We spend our lives in farming communities, urban shanty towns and tiny settlements. We live close to the oppressed, working with people so that they recognize and mobilize their own skills, overcome the passivity caused by alienation, misery and exploitation. We work to construct power at the base, supporting processes through which people's organizations begin to take control of their own lives. Basically we see ourselves as promoters of a process to deepen democracy and construct a more humane sociiety, one in which there is more justice and solidarity." - J. Marshall et al: *Training for Empowerment*, Toronto: International Council for Adult Education, n.d. (after 1987). How fast the concept of popular education is gaining ground today not only in Latinamerica can be seen, e.g., from the reports and articles in *Voice Rising*, 4:2 (1990), the journal of the Women's Program of the International Council for Adult Education; see, amongst others, the articles "Gender and Popular Education: A Research Project" (pp. 12-14) and "Strategies for Popular Education under Conditions of Repres-

sion" (pp. 25-27). But in strark contrast, people's education (or popular education) in India is understood rather a-political as is proven again by S.R. Mohsini: *People's Education*, New Delhi: Indian Adult Education Association, 1989, who advocates people's education as citizenship and leadership education with a strong functional approach.

455 H. Volken et al: *Learning from the Rural Poor*, op. cit.

456 *Ibid.* pp. 66-67

457 *Ibid.*, p. 70

458 *Ibid.*, p. 77

459 *Ibid.*, p. 81

460 *Ibid.*, p. 87

461 *Ibid.*, p. 87. A similar experience was made by the Gram Vikas Project in Orissa. Once a flood relief project, it later turned to become a basic health project in the tribal area of the Khonds. Today it has achieved the next step: "Gradually the word 'health' was dropped from the name of the village committees, which became focal points to analyze any important development issues." J. Cervinskas: *Organizing for Health*, Toronto: International Council for Adult Education, 1984, p. 12

462 E. Faure (ed.): *Learning to be*, Paris: UNESCO/London: Harrap, 1972, p. 56

463 W. Fernandes (ed.): *People's Participation in Development*, New Delhi: Indian Social Institute, 1981

464 D.A. D' Abreo: Non Formal Education and Awareness Building, in: W. Fernandes (ed.): *People's Participation in Development*, op. cit., pp. 11-26; here: p. 13

465 W. Fernandes: Introduction - People's Development is the Criterion, in: W. Fernandes (ed.): *People's Participation in Development*, op. cit., p. xiii-xxxviii; here: p. xxx

466 D.A. D'Abreo: Non Formal Education and Awareness Building, op. cit., p. 15

467 K. Saint: Development and People's Participation, in: W. Fernandes (ed.): *People's Participation in Development*, op. cit., pp. 3-10; here: p. 7

468 D. Werner/B. Bower: *Helping Health Workers Learn*, New Delhi: VHAI, 1983, pp. 1-24/1-25

469 M. Seshadri: "A people's movement for health" *Indian Express*, 24.2.1990, p. 8

470 In his Convocation address to the Agra University, 1941; Radhakrishnan: *Radhakrishnan Reader,* Bombay: Bharatiya Vidya Bhavan, 1969, p. 511

471 K. Harris: *Education and Knowledge,* London: Routledge & Kegan Paul, 1979, p. 164

472 *Ibid.*, p. 186

473 See to this B. Sen Gupta: "Is India Civilised?" *India Today,* V:24 (1980), who vehemently attacks the various forms of violence in India: ethnic, linguistic, religious, caste, class, urban and rural; or V.S. Naipul's *India: A Wounded Civilization,* Harmondsworth: Penguin, 1981, an attack against the "old equilibrium" and for "first principles", a merciless judgement of the Indian past with its "fantasy of wholeness and purity" which would confuse the present (p.143). But we must not disregard equally powerful and convincing attempts to defend and explain feelings and achievements in the ancient and modern Indian societies which are in the centre of service to society, be it physical, intellectual or spiritual help: e.g. S. Ranganathananda: Philosophy of Social Work - Traditional, in: India, Government of - the Planning Commission (ed.): *Encyclopaedia of Social Work in India*, Vol. III, New Delhi: Ministry of Information and Broadcasting, 1968, pp. 46-51; here: p.52; E.M.Hoch: Bhaya, Shoka, Moha, in: W. Bitter (ed.): *Abendländische Therapie und östliche Weisheit,* Stuttgart: Klett, 1968, pp. 134-160; and I.Y. Wendt: *Japanische Dynamik und indische Stagnation?* Darmstadt: WGB, 1978, who opines that India had never "slept", be it with regard to literacy, population development or religiousness which would stimulate outward activities; she clarifies that none of them would be the prime factor of economic under-development which in turn had been caused by ruthless economic exploitation during the time of colonialism.

474 A. Shourie: "Hinduism: Essence and Consequence". *imprint,* May 1980, p. 98

475 *Ibid.*, p. 43

476 *Ibid.*, p. 44

477 *Ibid.*, p. 44

478 *Ibid.*, p. 44

479 *Ibid.*, p. 45

480 *Ibid.*, p. 45

481 A. Schweitzer calls the Indian world-view "world and life negation" which means "that man regards existence as he experiences it in himself and as it has developed in the world as something of value per se and accordingly strives to let it reach perfection in himself, whilst within his own sphere of influence he endeavours to preserve and to further it."(p. 1) But A. Schweitzer also proves that there was a lot of world and life affirmation in ancient popular ethics (but not in Brahmanism and Buddhism). He cites many verses of the "Kural", a collection of 1330 maxims in Tamil of the 2nd century A.D., attributed to one Tiruvalluvar (p. 200 ff.). A. Schweitzer opines that these thoughts penetrated into Hindu thought through great religious teachers later, e.g. Tagore (p. 205). A. Schweitzer: *Indian Thought and its Dcvelopment*, Bombay: Wilco, 1980. Indeed, the summary of the maxims of the "Kural" of all the three parts by M. Varadarajan: Tiruvalluvar, in: V. Raghavan (ed.): *Cultural Leaders of India- Social Philosophers*, New Delhi: Government of India, 1980, pp. 61-80; here: pp. 63-77, demonstrates that this popular ancient author wanted humankind to be helpful, cheerful and benevolent in this world. The selections and translations from part 1 and 2 by C. Rajagopalachari (see *Kural,* Bombay: Bharatiya Vidya Bhavan, [5]1981) deepen this understanding and show a stupendous similarity in its section "The Art of Healing" with popular Ayurveda knowledge (pp. 98-99).

482 S. Kakar: *The Inner World,* Oxford: O.U.P., 1978 p. 51

483 K.G. Saiyidain: *The Humanist Tradition in Indian Educational Thought,* Bombay: Asia, 1966, p. 35

484 T.M.P. Mahadevan/G.V. Saroja: *Contemporary Indian Philosophy,* New Delhi: Sterling, [2]1983 p. 60

485 S. Gopalan: *Hindu Social Philosophy,* New Delhi: Wiley, 1979, p. 81

486 D. Werner: "The village health worker: lackey or liberator?" op. cit., p.49

487 R.H. Bannermann: "Traditional medicine in modern health care". *World Health Forum,* 3:1 (1982), p. 8

488 D. Werner: "The village health worker: lackey or liberator?" op. cit., p. 48

489 *Ibid.*, p. 49

490 *Ibid.*, p. 50

491 *Ibid.*, p. 50

492 "Popular education is part of a broader process which is the transformation of the social structures in favour of the oppressed. The process takes place within a complexity of activities carried out by the people during the course of their everyday life in order to survive and to meet their needs. The task of popular education is to contribute to the development of people's consciousness concerning the real causes of the problems that they encounter, in order to increase their capacity to mobilize themselves by participating in organizations and supporing them." ideas and action (ed.) "our programme in Latinamerica". *ideas and action,* No. 151, 2/1983, p. 8. In their "Trends in adult education since 1972". *prospects,* XV:1 (1985), p. 19, B. Hall and A. Stock observe that many of the Latinamerican non-governmental organizations have been the "source of much innovation linking social action to educational work."

493 N. Barrow: "Knowledge belongs to Everyone". *Convergence,* XIV:2 (1981), p. 47

494 This is indicated in a series of case studies initiated by the International Council for Adult Education. These case studies examine the relationship between adult education and the abolition or alleviation of poverty, but: "The studies so far fail to prove that it does, or that it is essential to reducing poverty. " C. Duke: Adult Education and Poverty: What are the Connections? in: International Council for Adult Education/Peuple et Culture (eds.) *Towards an authentic development: the role of adult education,* Toronto/Paris: ICAE/Peuple et Culture, n.d. (1982), pp. 103-112; here: p. 104. A similar picture emerges from C.Duke et al: *Grassroots Approaches to Combating Poverty through Adult Education,* Supplement to "Adult Education and Development", No. 34/1990, Bonn: DVV, 1990, which contains descriptions and analyses of eight new case studies. On the other hand could one join those who regard adult education "indispensable for the reduction of poverty" because it "can remove deficiences which are obstacles to development" (Duke, op. cit., 1982, p. 105), and helping empowering people, i.e., from 'I can't' to 'We can '; J. Cervinskas: Organizing for Health, op. cit., p.48.

495 K.L. Shrimali: *A Search for Values in Indian Education,* Delhi: Vikas, 1971, p.4

496 *India Today,* VIII:16 (1983), p.7

497 V.B.Dash:*Fundamentals of Ayurvedic Medicine,* op. cit, p.5

498 *India Today,* VIII:16 (1983), p.7: "We trumpet loudly that we are the world's tenth largest industrial power, that we launch satellites into space and make nuclear reactors, but we blithely allow this to coexist with the most grinding poverty and rapacious exploitation. We have a socialist Constitution but some of the world's most successful capitalists thrive within our borders. Our capitalism is capitve to a 'socialist structure' but our socialism grasps for breath under a suffocating load of controls."

499 R. Fendall: "Ayurvedic medicine and primary health care". *World Health Forum,* 3:1 (1982), p.90

500 M. Racelis Hollnsteiner: "The Participatory Imperative in Primary Health Care".*Convergence,* XV:3 (1982), p.57

501 G. Djurfeldt/ S. Linderg:*Pills Against Poverty,* op. cit., p.216

502 S. Lapping:"The Progressive Potential of Ayurveda and Its Possible Contribution to Health Care Toady".*Ancient Science of Life,* 5:1 (1985-86), p.25

503. D.A. Brundage/D. Mackeracher: *Adult Learning Principles and Their Application to Programme Planning,* Ontario: Ministry of Education, 1980, p.43

504 J. Dubashi: "Industrial Policy: New Wine in Old Bottles". *India Today,* VII:19 (1982), p.117

505 *Ibid.,* p.119

506 *Ibid.,* p. 119

507 A.Jha:*Modernization And The Hindu Socio-Culture,* Delhi:B.R. Publishing Corporation, 1978, p.13

508 N. Ray (ed.): *Papers on Development and Rural Poverty,* op. cit., pp. 20-25

509 *Ibid., pp. 53-56*

510 See e.g. K.A. Majumdar: "Prevention of Common Diseases in India by Ayurvedic Principles". *Ancient Science of Life,* 1:3 (1981-82), p.157, who argues that folk songs, Vedic hymns and mantras recited at different festivals would "keep both the mind and the soul tuned to lead a healthy living". This is exactly the state of mind which A. Shourie regards as the perpetuation of an oppressive society through a particular outlook in religion and philosophy.

511 As is done, e.g., by S. Venkatraghavan: "This way of life, which perhaps is partly medical and partly social and cultural and which laid down definite laws of healthy living, personal clean-

liness, correct dietetic habits, a ban on addiction, promiscuous sex relations, is something which India has to be proud of and make every effort to retain and popularize." "Ayurvedic Approach to Total Health Care". *Ancient Science of Life,* 1:2 (1981-82), p.170

512 C.R. Bijoy: "Ayurveda, an Appropriate Strategy for Social Health", op. cit., p. 100: This consists of "(a) present status of social health and its problems, primarily at local level and secondarily, at the regional level, (b) relationship to socio-economic and cultural environment, and (c) approaches to solving social health problems consistent with the professed strategy."

513 *Ibid.*, p.100

514 G. Joseph et al: *Health Care in India,* Bangalore: Centre for Social Action, 1983,p.132

515 A. Murickan: Non-clinical Apoproach to Community Health, in: K. Arunachalam/K.M. Natarajan (eds.): *Integrated Rural Development,*, Madurai: Koodal, 1977, pp. 185-193; here: p.193

516 H.W. Watts:*Psychotherapy East and West.* Harmondsworth: Penguin, 1973, passim

517 *Ibid.*, p.160

518 E. Fromm: *To Have or To Be?* London: Tape, 1979, p. 24

519 *Ibid.*, pp. 82-85

520 *Ibid.*, pp. 87-88

521 E. Fromm:*The Art of Loving,* New York: Harper & Row, 1974

522 A similar concept, but less elaborated than Fromm's is advocated by S.Akhilananda:*Mental Health and Hindu Psychology,* London: Allen & Unwin, 1952, pp. 129-133, who distinguishes three types of love: the immature and childish which is only for taking's sake, the natural which takes and gives, and the giving which demands nothing in return. Another Indian author who stresses the value of love (for education) is J.Krishnamurti whose opinion centres around some basic truths, e.g.: "There is an efficiency inspired by love which goes far beyond and is much greater than the efficiency of ambition; and without love, which brings an integrated understanding of life, efficiency breeds ruthlessness." J. Krishnamurti:*Education and the Significance of Life,* Bombay: B.I. Publications, 1984, p.13

523 E. Fromm:*The Art of Loving,* op. cit., p. 17

524 *Ibid.*, p. 19
525 *Ibid.*, p. 20
526 *Ibid.*, p. 20
527 *Ibid.* p. 20
528 *Ibid.*, p.22
529 *Ibid.*, p. 23
530 *Ibid.*, p.24
531 Ibid., pp. 24-25. How deeply E. Fromm was most probably influenced by Indian or Eastern perceptions can be seen from the valuations of knowing and knowledge. R.K. Mookerji in his *Ancient Indian Education,* Delhi: Motilal Banarsidass, 1974, says that education in ancient Indian addressed itself "more to the principle of knowing the roots from which knowledge springs and grows, than to the objective content of knowledge." (p.xxiv) E. Fromm also distinguishes between knowledge and knowing: "Knowing means to penetrate through the surface, in order to arrive at the roots, and hence the causes; knowing means to 'see' reality in its nakedness. Knowing does not mean to be in possession of truth: it means to penetrate the surface and to strive critically and actively in order to approach truth ever more close." *The Art of Loving,* op. cit., p. 40. Fromm's concept also resembles much the three ways (margas) recommended in the Bhagavadgita: knowledge, love and action which in the end mingle together. *The Bhagavadgītā,*, ed. by. S. Radhakrishnan, Introductory Essary, op. cit., p. 53 (It has been, however, pointed out, quite a few times in the past two decades, that Fromm's concept of love was quite simplistic against the ancient Indian one.) Or as S. Radhakrishnan puts it: "Knowledge gives us power, life gives us fullness. We should not develop barricades or separateness in the name of social necessity." *Religion and Culture,* Delhi: Orient, 1968, p. 171.
532 E. Fromm: *The Art of Loving,* op. cit., pp. 38-39
533 *Ibid.*, p. 39
534 B. Russell: *On Education,* London: Unwin, 1985, p. 153
535 E. Fromm: *To Have or To Be,?* op. cit., p. 89,90
536 *Ibid.*, p.91
537 *Ibid.*, pp. 91-92
538 E.Fromm: *Man for Himself,* New York: Ballantine, 1984, p. 104. Maybe the best known experiment in education that followed these ideas was A.S. Neill's school Summerhill in England

where love and approval of children was the basis of all work. A.S. Neili: *Summerhill,* Harmondsworth: Penguin, 1982, pp. 114-119, and passim; see also W.A.C. Stewart: *Progressives and Radicals in English Education. 1750-1970,* London: Macmillan, 1972, pp. 415-434; see also S. Datta; *The Place of Love in Education,* New Delhi: Gaurav, 1989, where love is called the "inexhaustible source" for education (p. 103).

539 E. Fromm: *The Art of Loving,* op. cit., p. 91

540 *Ibid.*, pp. 91-92

541 *Ibid.*, p.92

542 *Ibid.*, p. 92

543 *Ibid.*, p. 108

544 *Ibid.*, p. 109

545 *Ibid.*, pp. 110-111

546 *Ibid.*, p.111

547 *Ibid.*, p. 112 (emphasis mine). Here we can see a major difference between love as a social phenomenon and the Hindu concept of bhakti which is understood as a "physico-psychic-spiritual union" which aims at the highest form of salvation. K. Klostermaier:*Hinduismus*, Köln: Bachem, 1965, pp. 212-213. Though the Sanskrit classics use the concept of love also in a secular way as love between parents and children, between the sexes, between masters and servants, emphasis is also laid upon religious love towards a guru, love of God, and the various forms of respect, reverence, devotion and worship. M. Dhavamony: *Love of God According to Śaiva Siddhānta,* Oxford: O.U.P., 1971, pp. 14-19. See also the love of God *and* social duty in the Ramcaritmanas; this thesis was clearly elaborated by E.J. Babineau in *Love of God and Social Duty in the Rāmcaritmānas,*, Delhi: Motilal Banarsidass, 1979, pp. 101-165

548 E. Fromm:*Escape from Freedom,* New York: Avon, 1969, p. 34; here Fromm makes a distinction between the physical and moral aloneness but maintains "that moral aloneness is as intolerable as the physical aloneness, or rather that physical aloneness becomes unbearable only if it implies also moral aloneness."

549 P. Freire: *Pedagogy of the Oppressed,* Harmondsworth: Penguin, 1972, p. 62

550 *Ibid.*, p.65

551 A. Lind/A. Johnston: *Adult Literacy in the Third World,* Stockholm: University of Stockholm/Swedish International Development Authority, 1986, p. 63. See also to Freire's influence the excellent summary of community - based liberation education by J.Carr Campos: "The Politics of Literacy in Latin America". *Convergence.* XXIII:2.
552 P. Freire: *Pedagogy of the Oppressed,* op. cit., p. 12
553 *Ibid.*, p.53
554 *Ibid.*, p. 56
555 *Ibid.*, p. 53
556 *Ibid.*, p. 65
557 *Ibid.*, p. 69
558 *Ibid.*, p. 81
559 P. Freire: *Cultural Action for Freedom,* Harmondsworth: Penguin, 1977, p. 51 (this quote is an editor's note referring to Freire's ideas)
560 *Ibid.*, p. 78
561 P. Freire: *Pedagogy of the Oppressed,* op. cit., pp. 135-146
562 *Ibid.* p. 147
563 C.R. Bijoy: "Integration and Traditional Systems of Medicine in Health Care with the People". *Ancient Science of Life,* 3:4 (1983-84), p. 178
564 K.G. Saiyidain: *The Humanist Tradition in Indian Educational Thought,* op. cit., pp. 203-204
565 *Ibid.*, p. 204. We may here finally point out to this system of thought, humanism, which is yet to be fully explored in relation to our topic. In it V.N. Banerjee, for instance, understands love as the "humanizing principle" (p. vii) and defines this school of thought as "that doctrine which takes its start from the recognition of the fact of the Original Ignorance of man, and reaches its goal in the realization of the all-importance of the principle of love in the conduct of all human affairs." (p. vii) Original Ignorance is explained by him as (1) lack of understanding the world (p.v) due to (2) "man's ignorance of his obligation towards his fellows"(p.vi); V.N. Banerjee: *Buddhism and Marxism,* New Delhi: Orient Longman, 1978

Bibliography

1. Primary Sources

Agniveśa's Caraka Samhitā

Text with English Translation and Critical Exposition
Based on Cakrapāṇi Datta's Āyurveda Dīpika
By Ram Karan Sharma and Vaidya Bhagwan Dash
Varanasi: Chowkhamba Sanskrit Series Office
Vol. I: Sūtra Sthāna, 1976
Vol. II: Nidāna Sthāna, Vimāna Sthāna, Śārīra Sthāna, Indriya Sthāna, 1977
Vol. III: Chikitsa Sthāna, I-XIV, 1988

The Sushruta Samhita

An English Translation Based on Original Sanskrit Text With a Full and Comprehensive Introduction,Additional Texts, Different Reading, Notes, Comparative Views, Index, Glossary and Plates
By Kaviraj Kunjalal Bhishgratna
Varanasi: Chowkhamba Sanskrit Series Office
Vol. I: Sutra-Sthāna, 1963 ([1]1907)
Vol. II: Nidāna-Sthāna, Sārira-Sthāna, Chikitsta-Sthāna and Kalpa-Sthāna, 1981 ([1]1911)
Vol. III: Uttara-Tantra, 1963 ([1]1916)

2. Other References

Adiseshiah, Malcolm S. (ed.): *Seventh Plan Perspectives,* New Delhi: Lancer International, 1985

Adiseshiah , Malcolm S.: *Mid-year review of the Indian economy (1987-1988).* Assessment of the Seventh Plan, New Delhi: Lancer, 1988

Adiseshiah, Malcolm S. (ed.): *Eighth Plan Perspectives,* New Delhi: Lancer International, 1990

Akhilananda, Swami: *Mental Health and Hindu Psychology,* London: Allen & Unwin, 1952

Ananth, J.: "Is Western Training Relevant to Indian Psychiatry?" *Indian Journal of Psychiatry*, 23:2 (1981), pp. 120-127

Aranha, Celine: *Report of The South Kanara District Health Survey,*Mangalore: The South Kanara District Unit of Voluntary Health Association, Karnataka, 1978

Arunachalam, K./Natarajan, K.M. (eds.): *Integrated Rural Development,* Madurai: Koodal, 1977

Arya Vaidyan Rama Varier Educational Foundation of Ayurveda (ed.): *Proceedings of the workshop on Traditional Systems of Medicine (Ayurveda and Siddha) and Primary Health Care,* April 1984, Coimbatore, 1984

Ayurveda College Coimbatore (ed.): *Prospectus for 7 years "Ayurvedacharya" (B.A.M.S.) Course,* Coimbatore, n.d. (1982)

Babineau, Edmour J.: *Love of God and Social Duty in the Rāmcaritmānas,* Delhi: Motilal Banarasidas, 1979

Bala, Poonam: "Ingenous Medicine and the State in Ancient India". *Ancient Science of Life,* 5:1 (1985-86), pp. 1-4

Banerjee, V.N.: *Buddhism and Marxism.* A Study in Humanism, New Delhi: Orient Longman, 1978

Banerji, D.: "Health Behaviour of Rural Populations. Impact of Rural Health Services". *Economic and Political Weekly,* VIII:51 (1973), pp. 2261-2268

Banerji, D.: "Health as a Lever for Another Development". *development dialogue,* 1/1978, pp. 19-25

Banerji, D.: *Health Education and Community Health Behaviour,* New Delhi: Voluntary Health Association of India, n.d. (special print)

Banerji, Debabar: "Primary health care: selective or comparehensive?" *World Health Forum,* 5:4 (1984), pp. 312- 315

Bang, Abhay:. "People's Participation in Health. Some Myths".*Health for the Millions,* VIII:3 (1982), pp. 1-4

Bannermann, R.H.: "Traditional medicine in modern health care". *World Health Forum,* 3:1 (1982), pp. 8-26

Baric, Leo et al: "cancer education in Kancheepuram. a case against transferring health education approaches". *internationales journal für gesundheitserziehung* (international journal of health education), XVII:1 (1974), pp. 32-42

Barrow, Nita: "Knowledge Belongs to Everyone. The Challange for Adult Education and Primary Health Care". *Convergence,* XIV:1, pp. 45-52

Basham, A.L.: *The Wonder that was India,* Calcutta: Rupa, 1971

Bereday, George Z.F.: *Comparative Method in Education,* Calcutta: Oxford & IBH, 1967 (first American edition 1964)

BfGE (Bundesvereinigung für Gesundheitserziehung/National Association of Health Education) (ed.): *Gesundheit für alle biszum Jahr 2000* (Health for all by the year 2000), Bonn: BfGE, 1981

Bhagavadgītā, The. With an Introductory Essay, Sanskrit Text, English Translation and Notes by S. Radhakrishnan, London: Allen & Unwin, 1956 ([1]1948)

Bhasin, Kamla/Vimla, R. (eds.): *Readings on Proverty, Politics and Development*, New Delhi: FAO, 1980

Bhatia, S.C.: *Education and Socio-Cultural Disadvantage*, Delhi: Xerxes, 1982

Bhatia, S.L.: *A History of Medicine with special reference to the orient*, New Delhi: Medical Council of India, 1977

Bhattacharya, Benoytosh: *The Science of Tridosha*. The Three Cosmic Elements in Homoeopathy, Calcutta: Mukhopadhyay, [2]1975 ([1]1956)

Bhave, V.N./Deoshar, N.S./Bhave, S.V. (eds.): *You and Your Health*, New Delhi: National Book Trust, [2]1979

Bijoy, C.R.: "Ayurveda, an Appropriate Strategy for Social Health. An Overview of the Indian Panorama". *Ancient Science of Life*, 1:2 (1981-82), pp. 94-102

Bijoy, C.R : *Health: Emerging trends and Indian reality*. Paper presented at the Third Annual Conference on "Health Manpower Resources for 2000 AD" of the Indian Society of Health Administrators at Goa, Sept. 10-12, 1982 (mimeographed)

Bijoy, C.R: "Integration and Traditional Systems of Medicine in Health Care with the People" (Editorial). *Ancient Science of Life*, 3:4 (1983-84) pp. 177-178

Bitter, W (ed.): *Abendländische Therapie und Östliche Weisheit* (Western Therapy and Eastern Wisdom), Stuttgart: Klett, 1968

Brundage, Donald H./Mackeracher, Dorothy: *Adult Learning Principles and Their Application to Program Planning*, Ontario: The Minister of Education, 1980

BzgA (Bundeszentrale für gesundheitliche Aufklärung/National Centre for Health Education) (ed.): *Bereitschaft und Barrieren in der Gesundheitserziehung* (Chances and Barriers in Health Education), Köln: BzgA, 1979

Campos Carr, Irene W. "The Politics of Literacy in Latin America". *Convergence*, XXIII:2 (1990), pp. 50-67

Carlaw, Raymond W.: "trends in the organization of health education in three developing countries". *international journal of health education*, Supplement to Vol. XXIII, Issue No. 2, 1980, pp. 1-14

Cassen, R.H. : *India: Population, Economy, Society*, London: Macmillan, 1978

Cenkner, William: *A Tradition of Teachers: Saṇkara and the Jagadgurus Today*, Delhi: Motilal Banarsidas, 1983

Cervinskas, Jenny: *Organizing for Health.* A Popular Report of the Study on The Role of Adult Education in Community Involvment in Primary Health Care, Toronto: International Council for Adult Education, 1984

Chaudhuri, Nirad C.: *Hinduism*, A Religion to Live By, Delhi: B.I. Publications, 1979

CHEB (Central Health Education Bureau) (ed.): *Health Education.* Vol. 1 - Syllabus for Ages 6-11, Vol. 2- Syllabus for Ages 11-14, Vol. 3 - Syllabus for Ages 14-17, New Delhi: Directorate General of Health Services, 1972

CHEB (Central Health Education Bureau) (ed.): *Resource Book on Health for Teachers*, New Delhi: CHEB, 1973

Chengappa, Raj.: "Sexually Transmitted Diseases: The Hidden Menace". *India Today*, VIII:14 (1983), pp.52-59

Chengappa, Raj.: "Cancer. A Growing Threat". *India Today*, IX: 19 (1984), pp. 42-47

Chopra, Pran: "The paradox of Kerela". *World Health Forum*, 3:1 (1982), pp. 74-77

Copleston, Frederick: *On the History of Philosophy and other essays*, London: Search Press, 1979

Dandekar, V.M./Rath, Nilakantha: *Poverty in India*, Bombay: Economic and Political Weekly, 1971

Dasgupta, Surendranath: *A History of Indian Philosophy*, Vol. 1, Cambridge: C.U.P., 1973 ([1]1922)

Dash, Vaidya Bhagwan: *Fundamentals of Ayurvedic Medicine*, Delhi: Bansal, [2]1980 ([1]1978)

Dash, Bhagwan/Kashyap, Lalitesh: *Basic Principles of Āyurveda.* Based on Āyurveda Saukhyam of Todarānanda, New Delhi: Concept, 1980

Datta, Shakti: *The Place of Love in Education*, New Delhi: Gaurav, 1989 ([1]1960)

Deb, K.: *Rural Development in India Since Independence*, New Delhi: Sterling, 1986

Dharmalingam, T.: *Health Education in Hospitals.* Developing a Model, Gandhigram: The Gandhigram Institute of Rural Health & Family Planning, 1980

Dhavamony, Mariasusai: *Love of God According to Śaiva Siddhānta.* A Study in the Mysticism and Theology of Śaivaism, Oxford: O.U.P., 1971

Djurfeldt, Göran/Lindberg, Staffan: *Pills Against Poverty.* A Study of the Introduction of Western Medicine in a Tamil Village, New Delhi: Macmillan, 1980

Doyal, Lesley/Pennell, Imogen: *The Political Economy of Health,* London, 1981 ([1]1979)

Dubashi, Jay: "The Poverty Syndrome". *India Today,* VI:22 (1981), pp. 114-115

Dubashi, Jay: "Industrial Policy: New Wine in Old Bottles". *India Today,* VII:19 (1982), pp. 116-119

Dubashi, Jay: "Jobs for the Jobless". *India Today,* VIII:16 (1983), pp. 82-83

Duke, Chris et al: *Grassroots Approaches to Combating Poverty through Adult Education,* Supplement volume to "Adult Education and Development", No. 34/1990, Bonn: German Adult Education Association, 1990

Durant, Will: *The Story of Philosophy,* The Lives and Opinions of the Great Philosophers of the Western World, New York: Simon and Schuster, n.d. (first published in 1926)

Elvin, Lionel: *The Place of Commonsense in Educational Thought,* London: Allen & Unwin, 1977

Emmet, E.R.: *Learning to Philosophize,* Harmondsworth: Penguin, 1968

Faure, Edgar (ed.): *Learning to be.* The world of education today and tomorrow, Paris: Unesco/London: Harrap, 1972

Fendall, Rex: "Ayurvedic medicine and primary health care". *World Health Forum,* 3:1 (1982), pp. 90-94

Fendall, Rex.:"We except too much from community health workers". *World Health Forum,* 5:4 (1984), pp. 300-303

Fernandes, Walter (ed.): *People's Participation in Development.* Approaches to Non-Formal Education, New Delhi: Indian Social Institute, 1981

Filliozat, J.: *The Classical Doctorine of Indian Medicine.* Its Origins and Its Parallels, Delhi: Munshiram Manoharlal, 1964 (French original 1949)

Fisher, Delbert W.: "adult education theory necessary in health education practice". *internationales journal für gesundheitserziehung* (international journal of health education), XIX:2 (1976), pp. 129-135

Freire, Paulo: *Pedagogy of the Oppressed*, Harmondsworth: Penguin, 1972 (Portuguese original 1968)

Freire, Paulo: *Cultural Action for Freedom*, Harmondsworth: Penguin, 1977 (first published in 1970)

Fromm, Erich: *Escape from Freedom*, New York: Avon, 1969 ([1]1941)

Fromm, Erich: *Man for Himself*. An Inquiry into the Psychology of Ethics, New York: Ballantine, 1984 ([1]1947)

Fromm, Erich: *The Art of Loving*, New York: Harper & Row, 1974 ([1]1956)

Fromm, Erich: *To Have or To Be,?* London: Tape, 1979 ([1]1976)

Gandhi, M.K.: *The Nature Cure*, ed. by A.T. Hingorani, Bombay: Pearl, 1965

George, P.O.(ed.): *Health Care Administration Manual - II*. Towards Health For All By 2000 AD, Kalamassery: Kerala Voluntary Health Services, 1986

Ghosh, Alak: *Indian Economy*. Its Nature and Problems, Calcutta: The World Press, [22]1979

Ghosh, Shyam (ed.): *The Original Yoga* as expounded in Śiva-Samhitā, Gheraṇḍa-Samhitā and Patañjala Yoga-sūtra, New Delhi: Munshiram Manoharlal, 1980

Gill, J.G.: "A Morbidity Survey for Chronic Illness by the Household Interview Technique". *Indian Journal of Public Health*, XXVI:1 (1982), pp. 53-56

Goel, Dharmendra (ed.): *Philosophy and Social Change*, Delhi: Ajanta, 1989

Gopalan, S.: *Hindu Social Philosophy*, New Delhi: Wiley, 1979

Grant, James P.: "A new way of measuring progress in living standards". *World Health Forum*, 2:3 (1981), pp. 373-384

Greene, Walter H./Simons-Morton, Bruce G.: *Introduction to Health Education*, New York/London: Macmillan, 1984

Griffiths, Bede: *The Marriage of East and West*, London: Fount, 1983

Guhan, S.: *Growth Inequalities and Poverty in Tamilnadu*, Madras: Cre-A, 1984

Gunaratne, V.T.H.: "health for all by the year 2000. the role of health education". *international journal of health education*, Supplement to Vol. XXIII, Issue No. 1, 1980

Gupta, Satya Pal.: *Psychopathology in Indian Medicine (Āyurveda)*. With special reference to its Philosophical Bases, Aligarh: Ajaya, 1977

Hall, Budd/Stock, Arthur: "Trends in adult education since 1972". *prospects*, XV: 1 (1985), pp. 13-26

Handbuch der Sozialmedizin (Handbook of Social Medicine) (ed.): *Epidemiologie und präventive Medizin* (Epidemiology and Preventive Medicine), Vol. II, Stuttgart: Enke, 1976

Handbuch der Sozialmedizin (Handbook of Social Medicine) (ed.): *Sozialmedizin in der Praxis* (Social Medicine in Practice), Vol. III, Stuttgart: Enke, 1976

Harris, Kevin: *Education and Knowledge*. The Structured Misrepresentation of Reality, London: Routledge & Kegan Paul, 1979

Harris, W.J.A.: *Comparative Adult Education*. Practice, purpose and theory, London: Longman, 1980

Health for thc Millions. A Bimonthly of the Voluntary Health Association of India, VII:2-3 (1981), VII:4 (1981), VIII:4 (1982)

Heller, Kenneth/Monahan, John: *Psychology and Community Change*, Homewood: Dorsey, 1977

Hiriyanna, M.: *Outlines of Indian Philosophy*, London: Allen & Unwin, 1968 ([1]1932)

Hockings, Paul: *Sex and Diseases in a Mountain Community*, Delhi: Vikas, 1980

Hudson, Liam: *The Cult of the Fact*, London: Jonathan Cape, 1972

Hyma, B./Ramesh, A./Subhadra, N.L.: "Evolving a Rural Community-Based, Participatory Health Care Model Based on Indian Indigenous System of Medicine" *Ancient Science of Life*, 6:3 (1986-87), pp. 159-162

Hyma, B./Ramesh, A./Subhadra, N.L.: "Developmcnt of a Rural Community Health Care Model Based on Indian Indigenous System of Medicine" *Ancient Science of Life*, 8:2 (1988-89), pp. 138-166

ICMR (Indian Council of Medical Research) (ed.): *Alternative Approaches to Health Care*. Report of a Symposium Organised Jointly by Indian Council of Medical Research and Indian Council of Social Science Research, New Delhi: ICMR, n.d. (1976/77)

ICSSR/ICMR (Indian Council of Social Science Research/Indian Council of Medical Research) (eds.): *Health for All*. An Alternative Strategy, Pune: Indian Institute of Education, 1981

ideas and action (ed.): "Towards a Rural Health Development Strategy". *ideas and action*, No. 145, 1-2/1982 (special issue on rural health), pp. 44-51

ideas and action (ed.): "our programme in Latin America". *ideas and action*, No. 151, 2/1983, pp. 7-12

Illustrated Weekly of India, The, 27.12.1982

India, Government of (ed.): *Report of the Health Survey and Development Committee*, Vols. I-IV, Calcutta/New Delhi/Simla: Government of India Press, 1946 (= Bhore Report)

India, Government of - Minstry of Health (ed.): *Report of the School Health Committee*, Part I, Faridabad: Government of India Press, 1965

India, Government of - The Planning Commission (ed.): *Encyclopaedia of Social Work in India*, Vols. I-III, New Delhi: Ministry of Information and Broadcasting, 1968

India, Government of - Ministry of Information and Broadcasting (ed.): *India. A Reference Annual*, New Delhi: Ministry of Information and Broadcasting, 1980

India, Government of - Ministry of Law, Justice and Company Affairs (ed.): *The Constitution of India* (as Modified up to the 18th May, 1981), New Delhi: Government of India Press, 1981

India, Government of - Ministry of Health & Family Welfare (ed.): *Health Statistics of India 1981*, Nasik: Government of India Press, 1982 (= *HSI 1981*)

India, Government of - Ministry of Health & Family Welfare (ed.): *Health Statistics of India 1985*, New Delhi: Government of India Press, 1986 (= *HSI 1985*)

India, Government of - Ministry of Information and Broadcasting (ed.): *India 1985. A Reference Annual*, New Delhi: Ministry of Information and Broadcasting,1986

India, Government of - Ministry of Information and Broadcasting (ed.): *India 1987. A Reference Annual,* New Delhi: Ministry of Information and Broadcasting, 1988

India , Government of - Ministry of Health and Family Welfare (ed.): *Health Information India 1988, New Delhi: Ministry of Health and Family Welfare, 1988 (= HII 1988)*

Indian Express, (The), 30.7.1982, 8.6.1983, 22.8.1983, 23.3.1990, 25.9.1990

India Today, VII:13 (1982), VIII:16 (1983)

International Council for Adult Education/Peuple et Culture (eds.): *Towards an authentic development: the role of adult education.* Report on the Paris Conference 1982, Toronto/Paris: ICAE/Peuple et Culture, n.d. (1982)

Iyer, Lakshmi: "Reviving indigenous medicine". *The Times of India*, 5.3.1987, p.17

Jaggi, O.P.: *Indian System of Medicine*, Delhi: Atma Ram, 1973

Jain, L.C.: "The drag". *Seminar*, No. 307, March 1985, pp. 21-24

Jancloes, M.: "Could villages do better without their volunteer health workers?" *World Health Forum*, 5:4 (1984) pp. 296-300

Javalgekar, R.R.: "Utility of Ayurvedic Dietetics in the Modern World". *Ancient Science of Life*, 2:2 (1982-83) pp. 84-87

Jayaraman, K.: *Indian Pharmaceutical Industry.* Present and Future, Bombay: Tata Economic Consultancy Services, n.d. (1980)

Jha, Akhileshwar: *Modernization and The Hindu Socio-Culture*, Delhi: B.R. Publishing Corporation, 1978

Jha, Akhileshwar: *The Imprisoned Mind*, New Delhi: Ambika, 1980

Joseph, George/Desrochers, John/Kalathil, Mariamma: *Health Care in India*, Bangalore: Centre for Social Action, 1983

Joshi, C.B. et al: "An Evaluation of Domiciliary Health Care Rendered by the Trained MPHWs (Multipurpose Health Workers Scheme) in Maharashtra and Andhra Pradesh (1976-1978)". *Bulletin of The Gandhigram Institute of Rural Health and Family Planning*, XV:3 (1980) , pp. 13-37

Joshi, C.B.: "Health Planning Structure in India". *Bulletin of The Gandhigram Institute of Rural Health and Family Welfare Trust*, XVI:2 (1981), pp. 61-88

Kabir, Humayun: *Indian Philosophy of Education*, Bombay: Asia, 1964 ([1]1961)

Kabir, D.N.: "Indigenous and Cosmopolitan Medicine in a North Indian Town". *Bulletin of The Gandhigram Institute of Rural Health and Family Welfare*, XVI:1 (1981), pp. 37-62

Kakar, Sudhir: *The Inner World.* A Psycho-analytic Study of Childhood and Society in India, Oxford: O.U.P., 1978

Kakar, Sudhir: *Shamams, Mystics and Doctors.* A Psychological Inquiry into India and Its Healing Traditions, Bombay: O.U.P., 1982

Kalra, B.R.: "Size and distribution of operational holdings". *Kurukshetra,* XXIX:23 (1981), pp. 4-10

Kidd, Ross/Colletta, Natt (eds.): *Tradition for Development.* indigenous Structures and Folk Media in Non-Formal Education, Bonn: German Foundation for International Development and International Council for Adult Education, 1980

King, Maurice (ed.): *Medical Care in Development Countries.* A Primer on the Medicine of Poverty and A Symosium from Makerere, Nairobi: O.U.P., 1986

Kisnerman, Natalio: "Social work within the health services". *Adult Education and Development,* No. 19, 1982, pp. 219-226

Klostermaier, Klaus: *Hinduismus* (Hinduism), Köln: Bachem, 1965

Kolakowski, Leszek: "Wo sind die Barbaren? Ein Lob des Eurozentrismus oder Die Illusion des kulturellen Universalismus" (Where are the Barbarians? An Appraisal of Eurocentrism or The Illusion of Cultural Universalism). *Der Monat,* 2/1980, No.277, pp. 70-83

Kosambi, D.D.: *The Culture and Civilisation of Ancient India in Historical Outline,* New Delhi: Vikas, 1988 ([1]1964)

Krikorian, Yervaut H./Edel, Abraham (eds.): *Contemporary Philosophic Problems.* Selected Readings, New York: Macmillan, 1959

Krishnakumar, P.R.: "The Alternative for Survival". *Ancient Science of Life,* 4:3 (1984-85), pp. 141-147

Krishnamurti, J.: Education and the Significance of Life, Bombay: B.I. Publications, 1984 ([1]1953)

Kural. The Great Book of Tiru-Valluvar. Selections from Book I & It. With English translation and notes by C. Rajagopalachari, Bombay: Bharatiya Vidya Bhavan, [5]1981 ([1]1965)

Kurien, C.T.: *Poverty and Development,* Madras: Christian Literature Society, 1974

Kurien, C.T.: *Dynamics of Rural Transformation.* A Study of Tamil Nadu: 1950-1975, New Delhi: Orient Longman, 1981

Kurien, V.: "The Role of the Elite in Modernizing a Predominantly Rural Society". *ideas and action*, No. 142, 4/1981, pp. 6-10

Lannoy, Richard: *The Speaking Tree.* A Study of Indian Culture and Society, London: O.U.P., 1974 ([1]1971)

Lapping, Johannes: "The Progressive Potential of Ayurveda and Its Possible Contribution to Health Care Today". *Ancient Science of Life.* 5:1 (1985-86), pp. 21-29

Lap(p)ing, Johannes: 'Traditional Medicine' in India. Decline and Future Perspectives. *Ancient Science of Life*, 7:1 (1987-88), pp. 6-11

Lawson, K.H.: *Analysis and Ideology.* Conceptual Essays on the Education of Adults, Nottingham: University of Nottingham, 1982

Lengrand, Paul: *An Introduction to Lifelong Education*, London. Croom Helm, 1975

Leslie, Charles: "India's Community Health Workers Scheme: A Sociological Analysis". *Ancient Science of Life*, 9:2(1989-90), pp. 40-53

Lind, Agneta/Johnston, Anton: *Adult Literacy in the Third World.* A Review of Objectives and Strategies, Stockholm: University of Stockholm/Swedish International Development Authority, 1986

Mackay, D.M.: "Primary health care may be needed but is it wanted?" *World Health Forum, 3:1 (1982), pp. 88-89*

Madhavankutty, K.: Arōgya Pāthāvali, Trivandrum: KANFED, 1978 (in Malayalam)

Magee, J./Cockburn, W.C.: "The mass media - players or spectators?" *World Health Forum*, 3:2 (1982), pp. 132-139

Mahadevan, T.M.P.: *Invitation to Indian Philosophy*, New Delhi: Arnold-Heinemann, 1974

Mahadevan, T.M.P./Saroja, G.V.: *Contemporary Indian Philosophy*, New Delhi: Sterling, [2]1983 ([1]1981)

Mahler, Halfdan: "The meaning of 'health for all by the year 2000'". *World Health Forum*, 2:1 (1981), pp. 5-20

Majumdar, Kaviraj A.: "Prevention of Common Diseases in India by Ayurvedic Principles". *Ancient Science of Life*, 1:3 (1981-82), pp. 155-185

Majumdar, R.J./Pusalker, A.D. (eds.): "*The Bhāratiya Itihāsa Samiti's History and Culture of the Indian People*, Vol. I: The Vedic Age, London: Allen & Unwin, [3]1957 ([1]1951)

Marshall, Judith et al.: *Training for Empowerment*. A Kit of Materials for Popular Literacy Workers Based on an Exchange among Educators from Mozambique, Nicaragua and Brazil, Toronto: International Council for Adult Education, n.d. (after 1987)

Matthews, C.M.E.: *Health Education - The Missing Link In Medical Care*, New Delhi: Voluntary Health Association of India, n.d. (1974)

Matthews, C.M.E. et al: "education to overcome malnutrition in rural pre-school children". *international journal of health education*, Supplement to Vol. XX, Issue No. 4, 1972

Matthews, C.M.E.: *Health and Culture in a South Indian Village*, New Delhi: Sterling, 1979

Mayur, Rashmi: "The Bhopal Tragedy". *Development Forum*, XIII:2 (1985), p. 1, p.10

Mechanic, Davis (ed.): *Handbook of Health, Health Care, and the Health Professions*, New York: The Free Press, 1983

Medawar, Charles: *Insult or Inquiry*? An Inquiry into the Marketing and Advertising of British Food and Drug Products in India and Malasiya, New Delhi: Indian Social Institute, 1981 (originally published by Social Audit in 1979)

Menon, Krishna T.K. (ed.): *Progress of Cochin*, Ernakulam: Cochin Government Press, 1932

Menon, Sreedhara A.: *A Survey of Kerala History*, Kottayam: Sahitya Pravarthaka Co-operative Society, 1970

Meredith Davies, J.B.: *Community Health, Preventive Medicine and Social Services*, London: Baillière Tindall, 1979

Minhas, B.S./Jain, L.R./Tendulkar, S.D.: "Declining Incidence of Poverty in the 1980s. Evidence versus Artefacts". *Economic and Political Weekly*, XXVI (1991) 27 & 28, pp. 1673-1682

Misra, K.K.: "safe water in rural areas. an experiment in promoting community participation in India". *internationales journal für gesundheitserziehung* (international journal of health education), XVIII:1 (1975), pp. 53-59

Mitra, Jyotir: *History of Indian Medicine from Pre-Mauryan to Kuṣaṇā Period*, Varanasi: Jyotiralok Prakashan, 1974

Mohsini, S.R.: *People's Education*, New Delhi: Indian Adult Education Association, 1989

Monier-Williams, Monier: *Sanskrit-English Dictionary*, New Delhi: Munshiram Manoharlal, 1981 (originally published in 1899)

Monroe, Walter S. (ed.): *Encyclopedia of Educational Research*, New York: Macmillan, 1956

Mookerji, Radha Kumud: *Ancient Indian Education* (Brahmanical and Buddhist), Delhi: Motilal Banarsidass, 1974 ([1]1947, London)

Mooss, Vayaskara N.S.: *Ayurvedic Treatments of Kerala*, Kottayam: Vaidya Sarathy, [2]1946 ([1]1944)

Morris, Ben: *Objectives and Perspectives in Education*. Studies in Educational Theory (1955-1970), London: Routledge & Kegan Paul, 1972

Mouly, George J.: *The Science of Educational Research*, New Delhi: Eurasia, 1964

Muir Gray, J: *Man Against Disease*. Preventive Medicine, Oxford: O.U.P., 1979

Müller, Max: *India. What can it teach us*? Delhi: Munshi Ram Manohar Lal, [2]1961 (originally published in 1883)

Murali, J. et al: "Pattern of Utilities of Health Care Facilities by a Selected Urban Community in Delhi". *Indian Journal of Preventive and Social Medicine*, 12:2 (1981), pp.117-125

Murthy, N. Anjneya/Pandey, D.P.: *Ayurvedic Cure for Common Diseases*, Delhi: Orient, 1982

Murthy, Nirmala: "Reluctant patients - the women of India". *World Health Forum*, 3:3 (1982), pp. 315-316

Myrdal, Gunnar: *The Challenge of World Poverty*. A World Anti-Poverty Program in Outline, London: Allen Lane The Penguin Press, 1970

Nagaraj, S. et al." health education status in teaching hospitals and associated health centres in India". *internationales journal für gesundheitserziehung* (international journal of health education), XVIII:3 (1975), pp. 157-165

Naik, J.P. (ed.): *An Alternative System of Health Care Services in India*. Some Proposals, Bombay: Allied, 1977

Naipul, V.S.: *India*. A Wounded Civilization, Harmondsworth: Penguin, 1981 ([1]1977)

Namjoshi, K.G.: *Health and Population Education*, Ahmedabad: Nandadeep Prakashan, 1979

Natarajan, V.: "Health Education in Policy Formulation". *GIRH & FWT Bulletin* (Gandhigram), XVII & XVIII (1982-83), pp. 78- 82

Nath, Niharika A.: "Role of Health Education in Health Care". *swasth hind*, XXVI:9 (1982), pp. 206-208

Neill, A.S.: *Summerhill*, Harmondsworth: Penguin, 1982 ([1]1962)

Nichter, Mimi/Nichter, Mark: "Health Education By Appropriate Analogy: Using The Familiar to Explain the New. *Convergence*, XIX:1 (1986), pp. 63-72

Ojha, Divakar/Kumar, Ashok: *Panchakarma-Therapy in Ayurveda*, Varanasi: Chaukhamba Amarabharati Prakashan, 1978

Oppolzer, S. (ed.): *Denkformen und Forschungsmethoden der Erziehungswissenschaft* (Ways of Thinking and Methods of Research in the Science of Education), Vol. 1, München: Ehrenwirth, 1966

Oxford English Dictionary, The, London: O.U.P., 1961 ([1]1933)

Pacey, Arnold: *The Culture of Technology*, Oxford: Basil Blackwell, 1983

Panda, R.C.: "Perception of Poverty and Development". *Journal of Rural Development*, 9:1 (1990), pp. 69-89

Pandya, M.M.: "Prakrtivada or Inherent Constitution of an Individual". *Ancient Science of Life*, 1:4 (1981-82), pp. 216-220

Pandya Vaidya Navnitlal B.: "Fundamental Principles of Ayurveda". *Ancient Science of Life*, 2:2 (1982-83), pp. 100-104; 2:3 (1982-83), pp. 160-163; 2:4 (1982-83), pp. 176-180; 3:1 (1983-84),pp. 1-5; 3:2 (1983-84), pp. 53-59

Panikkar, Raimundo: *The Unknown Christ of Hinduism.* Towards an Ecumenical Chirstophany. London: Darton, Longman & Todd, 1981 (revised and enlarged edition; [1]1964)

Parijs, Luc van: "Überlegungen zum medizinischen Modell der Gesundheitserziehung und ihren Zielen" (Reflections on the Medical Model of Health education and its Objectives). *internationales journal für gesundheitserziehung* (international journal of health education), XXIII:4 (1980), pp. 224-236

Park, J.E./Park, K.: *Textbook of Preventive and Social Medicine* (A Treatise on Community Health), Jabalpur: Banarsidas Bhanot, [8]1981 ([1]1970)

Pendse, D.R. (ed.): *Statistical Outline of India 1982*, Bombay: Tata Services Limited, [15]1982

Pendse, D.R. (ed.): *Statistical Outline of India 1988-89*, Bombay: Tata Services Limited, [18]1988

Pennant-Rea, Rupert: "India. Treadmill or take-off: A Survey". *The Economist*, No. 7178, 28.3.1981, pp. 7-48

Pillai, K.Mahadevan/Dutt, P.R.: "Sociology of Medicine and Social Change in India". *Bulletin of the Gandhigram Institute of Rural Health and Family Planning*. X:3 (1976), pp. 69-78

Polanyi, Michael: *Knowing and Being*. Essays edited by Marjorie Green, London: Routledge & Kegan Paul, 1969

Popper, Karl R.: *Objective Knowledge*. An Evolutionary Approach, Oxford: Clarendon, 1973

Prasad, K. Raghava et al: "A Study of Infective Hepatitis Outbreak in Tirupati Town". *Indian Journal of Public Health*, XXVI:1 (1982), pp. 24-33

Racelis Hollnsteiner, Mary: "The Participatory Imperative in Primary Health Care". *Convergence*, XV:3 (1982), pp. 55-66

Radhakrishnan: *Indian Philosophy*, Vols. I and II, London: Allen & Unwin, 1977 ([1]1923)

Radhakrishnan, S./Muirhead, J.H. (eds.): *Contemporary Indian Philosophy*, London: Allen & Unwin, 1958 ([1]1936)

Radhakrishnan, Sarvepalli/Moore, Charles A. (eds.): *A Source Book in Indian Philosophy*, Princeton: Princeton University Press, 1967 ([1]1957)

Radhakrishnan, S.: *Religion and Culture,* Delhi: Orient, 1968

Radhakrishnan Reader. An Anthology, ed. by P. Nagaraja Rao, K.Gopalaswami, S. Ramakrishan, Bombay: Bharatiya Vidya Bhavan, 1969

Raghavan, V. (ed.): *Cultural Leaders of India - Social Philosophers*, New Delhi: Government of India, 1980

Raj, Param Hans: "Image of Some Existing Medical Systems Among Indian Rural Communities". *Ancient Science of Life*, 9:3 (1989-90), pp. 110-115

Raju, P.T.: *The Philosophical Traditions of India*, London: Allen & Unwin, 1971

Ramachandran, C.K.: "Gerontology in Ayurveda". *Ancient Science of Life*, 5:1 (1985-86), pp. 5-8

Ramachandran, L./Dharmalingam, T.: *A Textbook of Health Education*, New Delhi: Vikas, 1983

Ramadasmurthy, V. et al.: "nutrition education and SITE telecasts". *internationales journal für gesundheitserziehung* (international journal of health education), XXI:3 (1978), pp. 168-173

Rane, W.V.: "Why don't our drugs match our diseases?" *Science Today*, 16:10 (1982), pp. 8-10

Ratnaike, R.N./O'Neill, P./Chynoweth, R.: "Village health workers and malnutrition: a project that failed". *World Health Forum*, 5:4 (1984), pp. 316-318

Ray, Nandita (ed.): *Papers on Development and Rural Poverty.* Written by Young India Project Action Groups 1980-86, Penukonda: YIP, 1988

Read, Donald A./Simon, Sidney/Goodman, Joel B.: *Health Education: The Search for Values*, Englewood Cliffs: Prentice Hall, 1977

Read, Stanley/Shepard, S.T. (eds.): *The Indian Year Book 1932-33*, Bombay: The Times of India, n.d.

Reddy, J. Mahender et al (eds.): *Seventh Five Year Plan.* Performance and Perspectives, New Delhi: Sterling, 1989

Reddy, V. Eswara: *Generative Sources of Disadvantage.* The Role of Adult Education, Hyderabad: State Resource Centre for Adult Education/Osmania University, 1983

Reddy, V. Eswara/Sandeep, P.: *Communication for Adult Education and Development In Rural Context*, Hyderabad: Department of Non-Formal Adult Continuing Education/Osmania University, 1983

Ritter, Joachim (ed.): *Historisches Wörterbuch der Philosophie* (Historical Dictionary of Philosophy), Vol. 3, Darmstadt: WGB, 1974

Roşu, Arion: "Medicine and Psychology in Ancient India". *curare* (Journal for Ethnomedicine and transcultural Psychiatry), 4:4 (1981), pp. 205-210

Rusk, Robert R./Scotland, James: *Doctrines of the Great Educators*, n.p., Macmillan, [5]1979 ([1]1918)

Russell, Bertrand: *On Education.* Especially in Childhood, London: Unwin, 1985 ([1]1926)

Russell, Bertrand: *My Philosophical Development*, London: Unwin, 1975 ([1]1959)

Sabo, Peter: "Entwicklung und Stand kormmunaler Gesundheitserziehung" (Development and Status of Community Health Education). *Prävention* (Prevention. Journal of Health Education), 3:2 (1980), pp. 41-45

Safaya, Raghunath: *Indian Psychology*. A Critical and Historical Analysis of the Psychological Speculations in Indian Philosophical Literature, New Delhi: Munshiram Manoharlal, 1976

Saiyidain, K.G.: *The Humanist Tradition in Indian Educational Thought*, Bomaby: Asia, 1966

Salmi, Jamil: "Educational Research on the Third World: a View from the South". *IDS Bulletin* (Sussex), 15:4 (1984), pp. 9-11

Sandhu, S.K. et al: "adoption of modern health and family planning practices in a rural community of India". *internationales journal für gesundheitserziehung* (international journal of health education), XX:4 (1977) pp. 240-247

Sarawasthi, L.S.: "The Content of Adult Education Programme". *Indian Journal of Adult Education*, 39:2 (1979), pp. 28-32

Schweitzer, Albert: *Indian Thought and its Development*. Bombay: Wilco, 1980 (German original published in 1934)

Seal, S.C.: "Present Health Status and Some Suggestions for the Future Action". *Indian Journal of Public Health*, XXVI:4 (1982), pp. 217-228

Seidler, Eduard: "Gesundheit für alle bis zum Jahre 2000" (Health for All by the Year 2000). *Prevention* (Prevention. Journal of Health Education), 4:3 (1981), pp. 67-71

Sen, Amartya: "How Is India Doing?" *Indian Express* (Express Magazine), 17.6.1990, pp. 1-2

Sen Gupta, Bhabani: "Is India Civilised?" *India Today*, V:24 (1980), pp. 149-151

Seshadri, Malini: "A people's movement for health". *Indian Express*, 24.2.1990, p. 8

Sethi, J.D.: "India's Biological Decay". *The Indian Express* (Express Magazine), 5.12.1982, p. 5

Sharma, Keerti et al.: "A Bio-Medical House to House Rural Survey of Village Durgapur (District Patiala)". *The Journal of Research in Indian Medicine*, VIII:3 (1973), pp. 74-78

Sharma, Pandit Shiv: *Ayurvedic Medicine - Past & Present*, Calcutta: Dabur, 1975

Sharma, Pandit Shiv (ed.): *Realms of Ayurveda*. Scientific Excursions by Nineteen Scholsrs, New Delhi: Arnold-Heinemann, 1979

Sharma, P.: "Religion and Health: Their Interdependence". *Āyurvaidyan* (A Quarterly Journal of the Arya Vaidya Sala, Kottakkal), 2:3 (1989), pp. 158-173

Shourie, Arun: "Hinduism: Essence and Consequence". *imprint*, May 1980, pp. 43-118 (condensed from the book "Hinduism: Essence and Consequence", 1979)

Shrimali, K.L.: *A Search for Values in Indian Education*, Delhi: Vikas, 1971

Shukla, K.P.: *Traditional Healers in Community Health*, Varanasi: Gomati Krishna, 1980

Shukla, Vaidya Shiva Sagar: "Conciousness and Its Profound Elevation with Ayurveda and Yoga:. *Ancient Science of Life*, 2:2 (1982-83), pp. 88-92

Sigdell, J.E.: "A Brief Review of Ayurveda". *Ancient Science of Life*, 1:3 (1981-82), pp. 125-134

Silva, de G.V.S./Mehta, Niranjan/Rahman, Md. Anisur/Wignaraja, Ponna: "A Struggle for People's Power". *development dialogue*, 1979:2, pp. 3-70

Simonds, Scott K.: "Herausforderung an die Gesundheitserziehung" (Challenge to Health Education). *internationales journal für gesundheitserziehung* (international journal of health education), XIX:4 91976), pp. 245-259, 280-286

Simpson, John: *Introduction to Preventive Medicine*, London: Heinemann, 1970

Singh, B.P.: *A Dictionary of Modern Politics and Political Sociology*, Delhi: Mittal, 1987

Sivananda, Sri Swami: *Practice of Ayurveda*, Rishikesh: The Yoga-Vedanta Forest University, 1958

Skeet, Muriel: "Community health workers: promoters or inhibitors of primary health care?" *World Health Forum*, 5:4 (1984), pp. 291-295

Sodemann, William A. (ed.): *Pathologic Physiology*. Mechanisms of Disease, Philadelphia/London: Saunders, [3]1966

Sondhi, Krishnan: *Problems of Communication in Developing Countries*, New Delhi: Vision, 1981

Srinivasan, T.M.: "Systems Approach in Medical Technologies". *Ancient Science of Life*, 6:1 (1986-87), pp. 1-5

Stewart, W.A.C.: *Progressives and Radicals in English Education 1750-1970*, London: Macmillan, 1972

Strawson, P.F.: *Individuals*. An Essay in Descriptive Metaphysics, London: Methuen, 1977 ([1]1959)

Sukhatma, P.V.: "The Meaning and Significance of Adhyatma for Education". *Ancient Science of Life*, 8:3-4 (1988-89), pp. 267-278

swasth hind (ed.): "Central Health Education Bureau. Landmarks 1956-1981". *swasth hind*, XXVI: 3-4 (1982), pp. 82-83

Thakkar, V.J.: "Tridoshas in Relation to Swasthavritta". *Aryavaidyan*, 2:4 (1989), pp. 227-233

Thakkur, Chandrasekhar G.:Ayurveda. Die indische Heil-und Lebenskunst (The Indian Art of Healing and Living), Freiburg: Bauer, 1977 (American original first published in 1974)

Thakur, V.J.: "Evolution of Diseases i.e. Samprapti Vignana". *Ancient Science of Life*, 1:1 (1981-82), pp. 13-19

Thompson, Keith: *Education and Philosphy*. A Practical Approach, Oxford: Basil Blackwell, 1972

Tibbi, Bassam: "Development Policy is no Field for Exotic-Romantic Yearnings". *Development and Cooperation*, 3/1982, pp. 22-23

Times of India, The, 9.4.1985

Trivedi, Acharya Raghuvir Prasad: "Function of Vata (Based on Charaka)". *Ancient Science of Life*, 1:4 (1981-82), pp. 184- 191

Tuberculosis Association of India, The (ed.): *Diagnosis, Treatment, and Prevention of Pulmonary Tuberculosis for General Practitioners*, New Delhi: TAI, [2]1981

Udupa, K.N. (ed.): *1st Conference on Role of Ayurveda & Traditional Medicine in Primary Health Care*, March 20-23, 1980, Abstracts, Varanasi: Banaras Hindu University, n.d. (1980)

Unwin, D./Mc Aleese, R. (eds.): *The Encyclopaedia of Educational Media Communications and Technology*, London: Macmillan, 1978

Vakil, K.S./Natarajan, S.: *Education in India*, Bombay: Allied, 1966 ([1]1948)

Venkataratnam, R.: *Medical Sociology in an Indian Setting*, Madras: Macmillan, 1979

Venkatraghavan, S.: "Ayurvedic Approach to Total Health Care". *Ancient Science of Life*, 1:2 (1981-82),pp. 167-171

Verghese, Abraham/Beig, Ahmed: "Neuroses in Vellore Town - An Epidemiological Study". *Indian Journal of Psychiatry*, XVI:1 (1974),pp. 1-7

Voices Rising, 4:2 (1990)

Volken, Henry/Kumar, Ajoy/Kaithathara, Sara: *Learning from the Rural Poor*. Shared Experiences of the Mobile Orientation and Training Team, New Delhi: Indian Social Institute, 1982

Vuori, Hannu: "Das medizinische Modell und die Ziele der Gesundheitserziehung" (The Medical Model and the Objectives of Health Education). *internationales journal für gesundheitserziehung* (international jounal of health education), XXIII:1 (1980), pp. 11-19, p.25

Vyas, Vasudev V. "The Scope and Nature of Ayurveda". *Ancient Science of Life*, 1:3 (1981-82), pp. 135-138

Warrier, P.R.: "Problems of Aging. Jara Chikitsa - The Ayurvedic Treatment for Preventing and Curing Senility". *Ancient Science of Life*, 1:4 (1981-82), pp. 210-215

Watts, Alan W.: *Psychotherapy East and West*, Harmondsworth: Penguin, 1973 ([1]1961)

Weiner, Michael/Goss, Kathleen: *The Complete Book of Homeopathy*, New York: Bantam, 1982

Wendt, Ingeborg Y.: *Japanische Dynamik und indische Stagnation*? Eine Antwort auf theoretische Entwicklungsmodelle (Japanese Dynamism and Indian Stagnation? An Answer to Theoretical Models of Development), Darmstadt: WGB, 1978

Werner, David: *Where There Is No Doctor*. a village health care handbook. Adapted for India by the Voluntary Health Association of India under the supervision of C. Sathyamala, New Delhi: VHAI, [2]1981 (Spanish original 1977)

Werner, David: "The village health worker: lackey or liberator?" *World Health Forum*, 2:1 (1981), pp. 46-54

Werner, David/Bower, Bill: *Helping Health Workers Learn*. A book of methods, aids, and ideas for instruction at the village level, New Delhi: VHAI, 1983

White, John: *The aims of education restated*, London: Routledge & Kegan Paul, 1982

Who/Europe (ed.): "Health Promotion: A Discussion Document". *Newsletter* (European Bureau of Adult Education), 2-1984, pp. 1-2

Wiertz, Anneliese: "Psychische Gesundheit als Ziel therapeutischen und pädagogischen Handelns" (Mental Health as the Aim of Therapeutic and Pedagogical Work). *Das öffentliche Gesundheitswesen* (The Public Health System), 43:6 (1981), pp. 282-285

Wood, Ananda E.: *Knowledge Before and After Printing.* The Indian Tradition in Changing Kerala, Delhi: O.U.P., 1985

World Health Forum (ed.): "Target 'Health 2000'". *World Health Forum*, 2:1 (1981), pp. 36-45

World Health Organization (ed.): *Alma-Ata 1978. Primary Health Care.* Report of the International Conference on Primary Health Care Alma-Ata, USSR, 6-12 September 1978, Geneva: WHO, 1978 (reprinted: 1983)

Wulf, Christoph: "Self-Education. An Essential Element of Education". *Education* (A Bi-annual Collection of Recent German Contributions to the Field of Educational Research), Vol. 26, 1982, pp. 13-19

Young India Project (ed.): *Tryst with Destiny.* Critical Essays on Government, Development Policies and Anti-Poverty Programmes, Penukonda: YIP, 1988

Index

(of select subjects)

Adult (and continuing) education, 14, 46, 100, 101, 102, 103, 112, 114 119, 169, 182, 183
Adult learning and teaching, 80. 104
agni, 27, 28-29, 93
Another Development (in health), 81, 82
artha, 26. 41. 51, 70
ashramas, 14
Ayurveda, 21 22; 38-39, 119, 120, 127
- (adult) learning and teaching principles of A., 96-98
- differences between Allopathy and A., 38-39
- (eight) branches of A., 21-22, 23
- and bureaucracy, 84-85
- fundamental concepts of A., 27-37, 137
- Gandhi on A., 21
- health in A., 27, 30-32
- disease in A., 32-34
- history of A., 22-23
- (means) of knowledge of A., 26, 51, 54-55, 58, 68, 151
- non worldly attitude of A., 54, 55, 63
- and philosophy. 23-27, 57, 116, 150-151
- and philosophy of education, 135
- as a product of (the Indian) society, 75
- and psychology, 26-27
- a re-assessment of A., 75-76
- relationship between teacher and learner in A., 40, 41, 100, 158
- similarity between aims of modern health education and A., 70
- and the structure of the present Indian society, 71-73
- treatment in A., 27, 29, 34-37
- worldly attitude of A., 51, 53, 54, 55, 63, 68, 70, 116, 117
Ayurveda health care, 84, 105
Ayurveda Health Education, 2, 84, 105, 106-108, 115, 119, 122, 123, 124, 127, 129, 130, 132, 134
- a theoretical construct, 105, 134, 135
- definition(s), 107-108, 133
Ayurveda health worker, 118, 119
Ayurveda prevention, 33, 76
- as holistic prevention, 79, 94
- and modern medicine prevention, 91-95
Ayurveda regimens, 35, 53, 55, 59, 65, 66-68, 70, 98, 100, 107, 122, 127, 130, 137, 154-156
Balance (see also Equilibrium), 27, 28, 31, 53, 58, 59, 60, 70, 74, 88, 102, 133
Balance model of, 60-62, 66, 75
Basic desire of life (three), 42, 51, 63, 155
Basic education, 15
Being, 48, 58, 125, 157
Being mode, 124, 125, 128
Bhore report, 7, 8
Caraka Samhita, 22-23, 40-41, 42, 45, 46, 50, 51, 54, 64, 92, 93, 137, 138, 151
Central Health Education Bureau (CHEB), 14, 73
Change, 120, 121, 122, 124, 128, 129, 133, 134
Communication, 13, 14, 17, 65, 62, 80, 95, 101, 102, 113, 130, 143, 147, 167, 177
Community health, 2, 111, 112, 113, 114, 115, 117, 120, 122, 123, 127, 145, 175
Community health education, 113, 114, 115
Community health worker, 81, 84, 113-114
Comparative education, 3
Concept analysis, 1, 6
Congruence between content and form, 2, 50, 56-60, 62, 68, 100, 105, 106, 122, 124, 127, 132, 133
Conscientisation, 87, 123, 130, 131, 144
Content, 2, 56, 57, 58, 59, 60, 62, 100, 107, 132, 136, 160-161
Constitution (of India), 8, 139-140
Culture, 102, 173
Development, 3, 14, 114-115, 121, 122, 169, 179, 183

Developing countries, 3, 120
dharma, 26, 41, 51, 70, 99
dhatus, 27, 28, 30, 33, 53, 54, 93, 94, 160,
Dialogue, 130, 131
diseases, in India, 8-11, 108, 141-142, 145, 169
doshas, 27, 28, 29, 31, 32, 33, 34, 36, 53, 54, 91, 92, 93, 155, 160, 172
Epistemological pedagogy, 134
Equilibrium (see also Balance), 27, 29, 30, 52, 56, 58, 92, 106, 180
Ethnocentrism, 3, 4
Eurocentrism, 4
Form, 2, 56, 57, 58, 59, 60, 62, 100, 102, 107, 132, 160-161
guru-shishya tradition, 80, 85, 166, 167
Happiness, 2, 30, 31, 46, 51, 53, 54, 55, 64, 66, 67, 70, 93, 106, 116, 122, 124, 127, 128, 129, 130, 132, 133, 152, 159, 160
Having mode, 124, 125
Health
- and being, 13, 79-80
- as behaviour, 70
- as an entry point, 113, 122, 124
- and knowing, 79
- as knowledge, 69
- and living, 13, 79
- maintenance of H., 28, 30, 31, 40, 47, 50, 51, 53, 67, 88, 97, 107, 154
- as norm, 69
- and participating, 13, 79
- and poverty, 108, 110, 114
- as value, 69
- variations affecting health (in Ayurveda), 92-94
Health (care) services, 7, 8, 18, 81, 82, 83, 84, 85, 87, 88, 90, 91, 100, 112, 113. 118, 123, 168, 169
Health finances, 11
Health planning, 11-12
Health promotion, 50, 80, 88, 89, 107, 115
Health pyramids, 83-84
- traditional model, 83
- alternative model, 84
Health education, 1, 4, 6-7, 13, 14, 15, 77, 78, 80, 83, 94, 95, 96, 98, 99, 100, 101, 102, 104, 114, 124, 127, 142, 143, 165, 169, 175
- aims, 13, 14, 68, 69, 70
- in Ayurveda, 84-85, 91-92, 96, 98, 99, 100, 101, 102, 103, 104, 105
- by Appropriate Analogy, 96
- content, 78, 80, 88
- and formal education, 14, 15, 17
- and hospitals, 14, 16-27, 145-146
- in India, 77, 78-79, 108
- and non-formal education, 14, 15-16, 99
- and research, 19, 147
- and village health workers, 14, 17, 119, 146-147
Health educators and training, 14, 19, 20
Holistic dependency, cycle of, 61
Holistic disciplines, 37
Holism, 58
Hinduism, its worldly character, 74-75, 116
Humanistic philosophy of education, 135
Humanism, 173, 187
Ideal personality, 62, 62-64, 68, 70, 107
Imperialism, academic, 3
Indian philosophy, 25-26, 29, 55, 63, 73-74, 115, 116, 117, 118, 150
Integration cycle of total, 62, 68
International cooperation, 3
Intervention, strategies of, 95, 131
kama, 26, 41, 51, 70
kapha, 27, 28, 29, 32, 33, 34, 35, 36, 50, 53, 155
Kerala, development in, 109-110
Knowledge and life, 126, 185, 186
Liberation (education), 106, 117, 118, 124, 130, 131, 132, 144, 187
Life, 1, 2, 48-49, 51, 55, 57, 58, 59, 60, 62, 65, 67, 68, 70, 75, 104, 117, 124, 127, 128, 130, 133, 138, 150, 156, 160, 161, 168, 185, 186
Lifelong education, 46, 99, 102, 103-104, 107, 127, 173, 174 Literacy, 15, 17, 110, 180
Love, 124, 125, 125-127, 128, 129, 130, 131, 132, 133, 134, 185, 186, 187-188
malas, 27, 31
manas, 27, 28, 29-30
Matter, 57, 156, 162
- universal preventive utility of M., 50, 59, 60. 106
Modernization, 82, 109, 120-121, 121-122, 122, 127, 170
moksha, 26, 41, 51, 70, 74, 130
National Development Plans, 11
Nihilism, 51
Oneness, 58
Panchakarma, 36, 86, 107, 148, 170

participation, 13, 18, 69, 77, 96, 101, 107, 112, 123, 143, 175
People's education, 119, 124, 127, 132, 179
People's science, 132
Philosophizing, 3, 4-7
Philosophy, 135, 167, 184
pitta, 27, 28, 29, 31, 33, 34, 35, 53, 155
Popular education, 4, 115, 119, 122, 124, 130, 131, 132, 133, 179, 182
Pragmatism, 68
prakriti(s), 27, 29, 63, 94, 97
praxis, 2, 131, 132, 133
prevention (of diseases), 2, 30, 36, 40, 49, 50, 53, 54, 60, 61, 62, 63, 64, 65, 66, 67, 68, 70, 71, 73, 75, 86, 87, 88, 89, 96, 98, 99, 102, 104, 105, 106, 107, 112, 115, 118, 119, 122, 130, 133, 137, 142, 143, 155
Primary health care, 12, 81, 82, 142-143, 174, 175, 177
Primary prevention, 2, 88, 89, 89-90, 91, 92, 94, 99, 107, 136, 171
Productive love, 128
Productiveness, 2, 128, 129, 130, 132, 133
Proto-elements(five), 27, 28, 29, 35, 59, 62, 155
rasayana, 37, 65, 85-87, 107, 162
Reconstruction (philosophical), 105
Responsibility, 62, 66, 68, 69, 70, 71, 99, 101, 102, 107, 113, 115-116, 118, 123, 125, 126
Sanitation (in ancient India), 52
Scienoo, 4-6, 58, 59, 60, 128, 149
Secondary prevention, 2, 88, 89, 90-91, 92, 99, 107, 171
Self-control, 62, 64, 67, 68, 70, 107, 163
Self-determination, 13, 69, 77, 85, 87, 99, 101, 104, 107
Self-education, 99, 102, 104, 107, 108, 133, 138
Self-identity, 70, 77, 85, 87, 99, 104, 107, 133
Self-realization, 106, 107
Self-reliance, 3, 13, 119, 120, 123, 143
Skills, 95-96
- active, 95, 95-96
- affective, 95
- cognitive, 95
- interpersonal, 95, 96
Social action groups, 111
Social health, 111, 112, 123, 184
Social injustice, 108, 111, 114, 115
Strengthening of positive factors, 62, 64-65, 68, 107
Sushruta Samhita, 22-23, 41, 47, 48, 137, 138, 148
- and Biology, 47-48
Sutra Sthana, 40, 41, 137, 138, 154-156
- and interdisciplinary thinking, 45-49
  - in relation to medicine, religion/ philosophy/psychology, and sociology, 43-46
  - structural analysis, 40, 41, 42, 43-46, 49
Tertiary prevention, 2, 88, 89, 91, 92, 99, 107, 171
Third-World-Research, 3, 4
Tridosha, 27, 39
Understanding, hermeneutic, 6
Unemployment, 109, 139, 164
Usefullness, 2, 31, 106, 116, 124, 127, 128, 129, 130, 132, 133
Values clarification, 70, 95
vayu (vata), 27, 28, 29, 31, 33, 34, 35, 42, 47-48, 50, 53, 93, 155
Westernization, 120
World Health Organization (WHO), 12